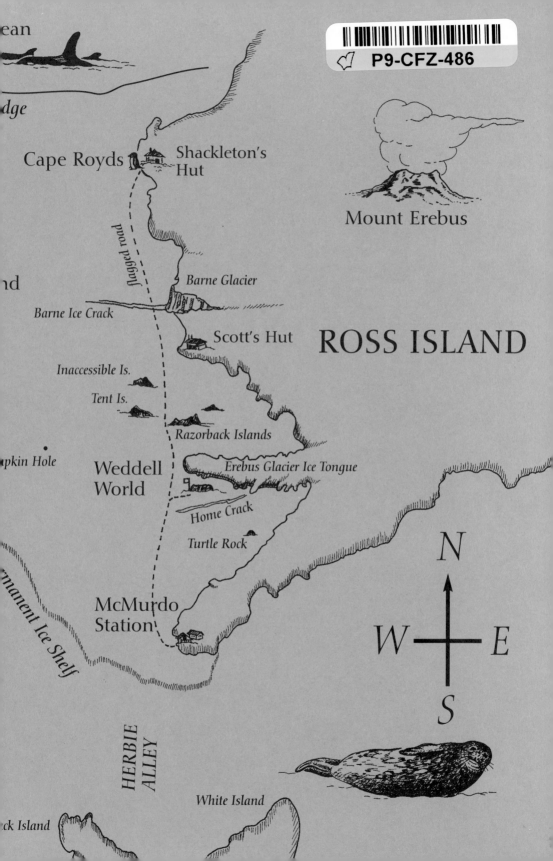

ean

dge

Cape Royds

Shackleton's
Hut

flagged road

Barne Glacier

Barne Ice Crack

nd

Scott's Hut

ROSS ISLAND

Inaccessible Is.

Tent Is.

Razorback Islands

pkin Hole

Weddell
World

Erebus Glacier Ice Tongue

Home Crack

Turtle Rock

Mount Erebus

McMurdo
Station

N

W   E

S

rmanent Ice Shelf

HERBIE
ALLEY

White Island

ck Island

THE HUNTER'S BREATH

THE HUNTER'S BREATH

On Expedition with the Weddell Seals of the Antarctic

TERRIE M. WILLIAMS, Ph.D.

M. Evans and Company
New York

To Mom
Who taught me that girls can grow up to be scientists.
These are the stories I never told you.

M. Evans and Company, Inc.
216 East 49th Street
New York, NY 10017

Library of Congress Cataloging-in-Publication Data

Williams, Terrie M.
  The hunter's breath : on expedition with the Weddell seals of the Antarctic / Terrie M. Williams.
     p. cm.
  ISBN 1-59077-028-5 (hardcover)
  1. Weddell seal--Antarctica. 2. Weddell seal--Research--Antarctica.
I. Title.
  QL737.P64W56 2004
  599.79'6--dc22
                              2003022770

Typesetting by Evan Johnston

9 8 7 6 5 4 3 2 1

Printed in the United States of America

CONTENTS

2001 EXPEDITION MEMBERS:

PRINCIPAL INVESTIGATORS
Terrie M. Williams, Ph.D.
Randall W. Davis, Ph.D.
Lee A. Fuiman, Ph.D.

SCIENTIFIC INSTRUMENTATION
William Hagey
Markus Horning, Ph.D.

FIELD TEAM
Don Calkins
Matthew Rutishauser, M.S.
Jesse E. Purdy, Ph.D.

GLOSSARY OF ICE AND ANTARCTIC TERMS

B-15: largest iceberg ever recorded in Antarctic waters, estimated at over 1,000 feet thick and 170 miles long.

BEAKER: McMurdo Station slang for "scientist."

BLUE ICE: areas of exposed sea ice free of snow. Bluish in color, this solid ice contrasts with the surrounding white snow cover; may be flat and smooth or rippled.

BRADYCARDIA: a decrease in heart rate below resting levels; part of the diving response of Weddell seals.

BRASH ICE: small (less than two meters wide) floating fragments of ice; commonly accumulates in the breathing holes of seals.

CONDITION 1: also termed Weather Condition 1, a classification representing deteriorating weather conditions in McMurdo Station; usually associated with poor visibility due to blowing snow and decreasing air temperatures.

CRACK: break, rupture, or fracture in an ice sheet; length and width may vary from centimeters to kilometers.

CREVASSE: a deep fissure or cleft in the ice.

ECW GEAR: Extreme Cold Weather gear. Clothing deemed essential for survival on the ice in Antarctica; required baggage during travel in the field.

FAST ICE: an area of sea ice that is attached to coastal shorelines; includes first-year and multiple-year-old sea ice ranging in width from meters to kilometers.

HERBIE: McMurdo Station slang for hurricane-force blizzard; a quick-moving storm consisting of high winds and blowing snow.

HYPOTHERMIA: a decrease in core body temperature below resting levels.

ICEBERG: large (greater than five meters in height) pieces of floating ice originating from fresh water sources including the Antarctic ice sheets and glaciers.

JAMESWAY: a soft-sided structure used as temporary housing on the sea ice.

LEAD: a break in the sea ice with open water, often wide enough to allow ships to pass.

McMURDO STATION: the U.S. base for scientific operations on Ross Island once run by the military and now under National Science Foundation management. Also referred to as "the Station," "town," or "Mac Town."

NSF: the National Science Foundation. The Polar Programs Division of NSF provides logistical and financial support for U.S. Antarctic scientific expeditions.

PACK ICE: areas of mixed open ocean and broken sea ice; may include leads, cracks, ridges, and pieces of floating ice ranging in size from one to several meters.

PHOCID SEAL: classification of marine mammals that represents the earless, or "true," seals, in contrast to the eared sea lions. The Weddell seal is one species of phocid seal.

PREWAY: slang for preway stove, a diesel-burning stove used to heat buildings in camp.

SASTRUGI: ridges of snow that have been scoured out by the wind, which create an irregular surface on the sea ice.

SEA ICE: ice that has formed from the freezing of seawater; can take many forms, including slush to solid sheets, single-to multiple-year-old ice.

VDAP: Video Data Acquisition Platform. Custom-designed instrument package worn by Weddell seals containing a video camera and recorder, depth meter and connections for a compass, speed meter, and stroke accelerometer.

WINTER OVER: a man or woman who has spent February through September living in Antarctica; usually involves a total stay of ten to fourteen months for personnel in McMurdo Station.

INTRODUCTION

You can't think what it is like to walk over places
where no man has been before.
–ERNEST SHACKLETON, ANTARCTIC EXPLORER

To survive in the Antarctic, you must be humble to nature. Each day is lived with the possibility of a potentially lethal blizzard, exposure to frostbite, or a fall into a bottomless crevasse. On the coldest, driest, and windiest continent on earth, there is no room for error. Ice shifts quickly and unpredictably, demanding a trained, wary eye to ensure each step. Freezing temperatures coupled with low humidity make your body crave high-caloric foods and water in a continuous battle to stave off hypothermia and dehydration. Constant light in the summer and continuous dark in the winter play games with your mind. It is an inhospitable place for living things, and few creatures can truly call Antarctica home.

Yet in the midst of these seemingly impossible living conditions thrives a mild-mannered species of phocid seal. Large, oblivious to humans, and mysterious in its underwater habits, the Weddell seal is so well adapted for life on and under the ice that it is the only wild mammal able to reside year-round on the permanent ice shelf in Antarctica. For this reason our scientific team sought adventure and Weddell seals in the frozen steps of Antarctic explorers from the previous century.

Our scientific question was a simple one: How do Weddell seals survive in the Antarctic? More specifically, how do they hunt for food in such a hostile environment? As primary predators in the polar ecosystem, Weddell seals have to locate, stalk, chase, capture, kill, and digest prey in order to survive. Although these are the same tasks routinely confronted by any big predator, including African lions or wolves, there is one major difference: the seals have to accomplish all of these behaviors while holding their breath. Imagine an African lion inhaling once and then tearing across the savannah in pursuit of a zebra, and finally tackling, fighting, and killing its prey before taking another breath. Imagine running a 10K race on just a single breath of air. During every foraging trip the Weddell seal accomplishes this and much more. As the seal hunts, it travels to great depths in freezing, dark water where the hydrostatic pressure is so high that it squeezes the animal's lungs to a fraction of their normal size. Water temperatures are so cold that the fish they pursue use cellular antifreeze to keep from turning into ice, and humans would survive only minutes of exposure.

The seals also perform one other envious feat: they explore places beneath the Antarctic ice that are impossible for humans to see. Tortuous ice caves on the underside of glaciers and the bottom of icebergs that are frequented by seals are far too dangerous for human divers or even for remotely operated robotic vehicles.

Frustration born out of our inability to observe what the seals encounter on their dives and ignorance concerning how their bodies withstand the challenge of an Antarctic lifestyle heightened our scientific curiosity. We wanted to join the hunt. Finally, in 1997 miniaturized video technology caught up with our desire to follow the Weddell seal, and our research team began the journey of a lifetime.

For six years we explored the underwater haunts of the Weddell seal. As with any research project, there were successes and failures. Eight of us hunkered down in the face of Antarctic blizzards, cursed the effects of blistering cold on the scientific instruments and our bodies, and worked frantically when the skies cleared. Together my colleagues and I pieced together the remarkable life of the Weddell seal as it traveled beneath the frozen seas. The discoveries were all the sweeter when both survival and science were at stake.

The following is the story of our discoveries and how we learned to live on the ice among the seals and penguins of Antarctica. Rather than a detailed account of our scientific findings, it is the tale of our team's journey towards discovery. All too often the process of science is overshadowed by dry, statistically significant results that smother even the most enthusiastic young mind. The truth is, it is the path of exploration that satisfies our curiosity and the excitement of unraveling nature's mysteries that quickens the heart. The events and dialogue that follow are true. Some names have been changed to protect the privacy of individuals, and the timing of a few events has been altered to enable several years of work to be compressed into one field season.

This is how science happens in Antarctica and how the ideas and energy of eight individuals came together to give the world a glimpse of the underwater life of the Weddell seal.

TERRIE M. WILLIAMS
MCMURDO STATION,
ANTARCTICA
DECEMBER 2002

CHAPTER 1

THE LORDS OF ANTARCTICA

A mong the animals of the land and seas, there is a supreme athlete. Champion swimmer, ultimate diver, and extreme environmental challenger, the Weddell seal has no rival. It is a mammal built of lungs, blood, and muscle like any other, but so remarkable in its design that it can swim twenty lengths of an Olympic-size pool without stopping to take a breath. Paired against a human swimmer in the next lane, the seal's cruising speed of two meters per second would leave gold-medal Olympic sprinters bobbing in its wake, gasping for air; then it would tear away at twice the speed! Beneath the Antarctic sea ice, Weddell seals routinely skim the earth's frozen submerged core in places so deep that only submarines, elephant seals, and sperm whales can reach them. The chests of human divers would be crushed at these depths even if they could withstand the skin-numbing temperatures.

Large and imperturbable, Weddell seals fear no enemy, having little experience with predators. By virtue of their behavior and biology, these large seals are the southernmost residents on earth, with humans serving as mere part-time visitors. They are the Lords of Antarctica, for Weddell seals are the only mammals except human explorers capable of surviving the extreme cold, punishing winds, and depressing darkness of the Antarctic winter.

Inaccessible, mysterious, and renowned—these characteristics make the Weddell seal *the* choice for study by marine biologists.

If you are fortunate enough to encounter a wild Weddell seal, the event will likely be filled with excitement tinged with disappointment. The excitement begins with the rugged, pristine environment. Weddell seals are found only in the most remote southern reaches of the Antarctic and sub-Antarctic seas, as far from human habitation as earthly possible. To find Antarctica, place your thumb on the bottom of a globe and trace a circle with your index finger. The prescribed circumpolar area is home to the Weddell seal. Here air temperatures may plummet to -50°C (-58°F) and the sun sets for months at a time. Only the inland reaches of the Antarctic continent are colder. The surface of the sea is permanently frozen in many places. In other areas the rhythmic, undulating swell of the ocean is dampened by massive icebergs and drifting ice floes, chilling the wild waters of the southern hemisphere into flat calmness.

While standing on sea ice that may be ten feet thick beneath your boots, you spot your first Weddell seal. It is the sole dark object on a solid white plain. The animal has sought relief from the water and sleeps on the snow next to a jagged crack in the sea ice, rounded belly facing up into the Antarctic sun. The naked simplicity of the seal and the landscape adds to the chilled excitement. There is no vegetation or manmade structure to break up the horizon. It is only you and the seal for seemingly endless blue-and-white miles.

The Weddell seal is impressive in size. Over nine feet long, and three and a half feet wide across the middle, the seal is so rotund that rolls of fat fold down its thick neck when it raises its head to look at you. A perpetual grin created by an upturned mouth on a short muzzle, curling thick whiskers, and a head that appears too small for its body give the impression of cat-like contentment. Each hot, humid exhalation by the seal causes another layer of crystalline frost to freeze onto its whiskers. Its pelage (the hairy covering of a mammal) is surprisingly thin for a polar-living mammal, with individual hairs approximately one centimeter (a half inch) in length covering the entire body. Color ranges from bluish black to soft gray with white spots that increase in number on the upturned belly. These spots, as well as the whiskers and grin, undoubtedly contributed to the original name for the Weddell seal, sea leopard. Not to be confused with its leaner, ferocious Antarctic cousin, the leopard seal (*Hydrurga leptonyx*), the Weddell has no interest in attacking you. Instead, it just dozes in the limited warmth of the polar sun.

The first description and illustrations of Weddell seals were less than complimentary, giving full attention to the proportionately small head of the animal. Captain James Weddell's book, *A Voyage Towards the South Pole Performed in the Years, 1822–24: Containing an Examination of the Anarctic Sea,* showed the Weddell seal as a spotted, snarling, snakelike creature reminiscent of extinct plesiosaurs (Mesozoic marine reptiles) and early sea monsters. The head was drawn so small that one had to question whether there was sufficient brain to control the remainder of the enormous body. Several years later, the seal was officially placed in scientific records as *Otaria weddellii* by R. P. Lesson. Reclassification to its present name of *Leptonychotes weddellii* came in 1880 and referred to the unusually small claws on the seal's hind flippers and the captain who first described the animal. In Greek *leptos* indicates "small," and *onux* means "claw." Rhyming with "meddle," the common name for the seal is simply, "Weddell."

Despite the noble name, early treatment of Weddell seals by Antarctic explorers was driven more by the need to survive than scientific curiosity. Fresh seal meat sustained the men and dogs of Captain Robert Falcon Scott's and Sir Ernest Shackleton's polar expeditions in the early 1900s. In *South: The Endurance Expedition*, Shackleton recounted the writings of Frank Worsley, who participated in a Weddell seal hunt on the ice floes surrounding their ship in 1915.

The ship's position on Sunday, May 2, was lat. 75° 23'S., long. 42° 14'W. The temperature at noon was 5° below zero Fahr., and the sky was overcast. A seal was sighted from the masthead at lunch time, and five men, with two dog teams, set off after the prize. . . . The seal was a big Weddell, over 10 ft. long and weighing more than 800 lb. But Soldier, one of the team leaders, went for its throat without a moment's hesitation, and we had to beat off the dogs before we could shoot the seal. We caught five or six gallons of blood in a tin for the dogs, and let the teams have a drink of fresh blood from the seal. . . .This was the first seal we had secured since March 19, and the meat and blubber made a welcome addition to the stores.[1]

Perhaps more important than the meat to these early explorers was the extensive blubber layer of the Weddell seals. Upon butchering, the men discovered a thick sheet of fatty blubber immediately beneath the seal's hide. Since there were no trees or brush for burning, the oil from seal blubber quickly served as a prized fuel for heating stoves when the stores of coal on board the ships and in the camps were depleted. Heat was essential for survival in Antarctica, not only for warming bodies but also for melting snow and ice. It was the only means of obtaining fresh water for drinking, cooking, and washing.

---

[1] Shackleton, Ernest Henry, Frank Hurley (photographer). *South: The Endurance Expedition*. New York: Signet, 1999.

Unlike other fuels, the seal blubber burned dirtily and uncontrollably, causing flames to roar with the dripping oil in coal stoves. Black soot emanating from the hot oil coated every inch of the explorers' clothing, gear, and huts. It permeated their exposed, furrowed skin and was too tenacious to scrub off regularly. In old photographs depicting the dark, grimy, weatherworn faces of these early polar explorers, the oily soot of Weddell blubber is often mistaken for dirt (of which there is very little in Antarctica). One hundred years later, the grime and acrid smell of burned oil from the seal blubber linger in the wind-scoured huts abandoned by the early Antarctic expeditions, reminding visitors of the original association between man and seals.

Dog teams are long gone from Antarctica, having been replaced by powered vehicles, and Weddell seals are no longer used as a source of food or fuel to support expeditions. Instead, the smiling mammals have become an unexpected source of wonder as modern expeditions slowly reveal a biology and natural history unlike that of any other mammal on earth. The change in thinking began with the International Geophysical Year of 1957, which heralded ratification of the Antarctic Treaty four years later. For the first time an entire continent and its natural resources were set aside for one purpose: scientific exploration.

Over the past forty-five years, research expeditions have made their way south to study the ice, atmosphere, oceans, and animals of Antarctica. Some sought out the Weddell seal. The early years of biological science provided meticulous observations of the behavior of Weddell moms, pups, and lone males as they hauled out to sleep on the ice. Many aspects of the internal workings of the seals, from anatomy to physiology, were described. By following seals wearing color-coded flipper tags, scientists revealed their life cycles and distribution patterns. However, these studies literally only scratched the surface of the Weddell seal's biology. With so much of their time spent submerged in deep, icy waters, the seals remained unreachable and unobserved by humans. The biggest piece of the puzzle, the Weddell seal's greatest story, lay hidden beneath a frozen sea.

Herein is the basis for the vague feeling of disappointment during your first Weddell seal encounter. Hauled out on the ice, the seal appears overly large, awkward, and lazy. Ignoring your presence, the seal will yawn, scratch its rump with the longer claws of its front flippers, and then roll over to resume its nap. There is nothing to indicate the underwater athlete that lies within. But don't let the seal's nonchalance fool you. Extrapolating your observations of the hauled-out Weddell seal to its performance underwater would be as absurd as trying to predict the athletic capabilities of Michael Jordon, Lance Armstrong, or Tiger Woods by watching them lounge in the sun next to a pool. There is so much more than meets the naïve eye.

It took the internal workings of a kitchen egg timer and a glass disk coated with fine charcoal for one scientist to finally provide the first rare glimpse of the diving prowess of the Weddell seal. During the 1960s, Gerry Kooyman, a physiologist from Scripps Institution of Oceanography in San Diego, traveled to Antarctica to attach his crude time-depth dive recorders to the hide of Weddell seals. The seals were captured, instrumented, and released back into an ice hole, where they swam off carrying his recorders to depth. Changes in hydrostatic pressure as the seals descended and ascended on their dives forced a stylus to make etches on glass. The timer ticked off the minutes. When the seals eventually hauled out on the ice, Kooyman retrieved the recorders to find that they had traced a remarkable underwater journey. To his astonishment the seals had remained submerged for over an hour—no other mammal had ever come close to this feat. They had traveled to an unbelievable 200 meters (656 feet) in depth, nearly three times the maximum depth of most human scuba divers. How were the seals capable of such extreme underwater exploits? he wondered.

Kooyman continued his research on Weddell seals for the next thirty years in search of the answer. In 1983 he took another risk on the ice by including me—a young, female postdoctoral student—on his expedition to Antarctica. It was my first trip South and my first encounter with Weddell seals. At the time female explorers were still a novelty and could ignite a fight among lonely military personnel at McMurdo Station, Antarctica, by just walking into a room. Out on the sea ice, I learned how to work and live among the seals and to appreciate the powerful beauty of the Weddells' frozen world.

My laboratory assignments included processing film from the submersible cameras used by Kooyman to study the seals' under-ice environment. The pictures revealed an entirely "new" Antarctica: a colorful, frigid ecosystem hidden beneath the sea ice that was home to the Weddell seal. In the darkroom, images of bright orange starfish blanketing black volcanic rock slowly emerged from the chemical pans. Delicate crystalline chandeliers dangled from the underside of the blue-green sea ice, and dive-bombing black-and-white penguins rippled jet-blue contrails from their pink feet as they swam.

With the approach of the winter months, the expedition ended, and I left Antarctica with the empty feeling of having peeked through a keyhole without ever opening the door.

Over the years I became a scientist in my own right and finally headed back to the ice. This time it would be a Weddell seal that would guide me through the door to the underside of Antarctica and reveal its remarkable submerged world.

CHAPTER 2

TO THE ICE

Traveling to the home of the Weddell seal took our research team progressively south: down to southern California, through Los Angeles International Airport (LAX), and south again across the Pacific Ocean. Latitudinal degrees ticked away as we flew over numerous invisible geographic lines: 23°27' north at the Tropic of Cancer, 0° and the division between the northern and southern hemispheres at the equator. Overnight we passed 23°27' south at the Tropic of Capricorn and days later 66°33' south at the Antarctic Circle on our journey towards the earth's bottommost extreme, which lay frozen at 90° south. We passed through temperate and tropical climates before entering the severity of the polar plains. Gray-white jagged ice gradually replaced the familiar dark blue ocean as we crossed into the Ross Sea. We stopped briefly in

McMurdo Station, Ross Island, Antarctica, and then headed out. At 77°48' south, our camp would be built on an isolated stretch of sea ice within 850 miles of the South Pole.

LAX was the rendezvous point for the eight members of our expedition, who were filtering in from Santa Cruz, San Diego, Anchorage, Galveston, and Corpus Christi. Team members had been carefully chosen based on individual skills, the ability to work together in close quarters, and the drive for adventure and scientific exploration. Three of us, Randy Davis, Lee Fuiman, and myself, were biologists with Ph.D.s who had been awarded a research grant by the National Science Foundation (NSF) to support the expedition. Five additional members, some paid and others volunteering their time for the adventure, had been enlisted by word-of-mouth and recommendations from our colleagues. We had promised NSF the nearly impossible—to track one of the deepest-diving predators of the Antarctic as it hunted below the sea ice. Many expeditions to Antarctica had explored its surface. Only the Weddell seals knew what lay below, and it was the purpose of our expedition to follow their path.

Even before our team left the United States, we were on edge. An iceberg the size of Rhode Island had unexpectedly drifted into our lives, which guaranteed that it was going to be an unusual year on the ice. Over 1,000 feet thick and 170 miles long, it was the biggest iceberg ever recorded. For six months before the start of our research expedition, as team members calibrated, packed, and shipped scientific equipment for use in the upcoming field season, we tracked the massive block of floating ice via satellite images from NOAA (National Oceanic and Atmospheric Administration). The fuzzy gray pictures on the computer screen understated the enormous physical events in Antarctica that were forcing the iceberg to come to life. Severe winds and churning seas, hallmarks of relentless midwinter storms in the southern hemisphere, had stressed the permanent ice sheet to the point of splintering. In its wake a giant iceberg had broken free. Large enough to be given its own name by the geologists, B-15 moved so capriciously that they sometimes referred to the iceberg as "her."

Rather than float out to sea as expected, B-15 tumbled across the Ross Sea towards our old campsite on the permanent ice shelf off the western side of Ross Island. Since 1997, for three September-to-December field seasons, our team had called the sea ice of McMurdo Sound our home while we explored the underwater haunts of its most active resident, the Weddell seal. This year, the iceberg was an unanticipated complication. Like a slow-motion movie, the monthly satellite images revealed the step-by-step progression of the iceberg as it rolled closer and then finally ground to a halt on the opposite side of the island. Ross Island, a 45-mile-wide volcanic rock, was now wedged between our field site on the sea ice and B-15. Cape Crozier, located on the eastern shore of the island, bore the brunt of the moving ice. Once jammed onto the rocky coast, the edges of B-15 shattered into a series of dark blue jagged crevasses around the Adelie and Emperor penguin colonies situated on the wind-scoured beaches. The birds were trapped. On the seaward side, pregnant Weddell seals swollen with near-term pups tried unsuccessfully to reach traditional nursery areas, their paths blocked by solid ice.

Local, national, and international news called B-15 a "giant," a "geological curiosity," and a "testament to global warming." The eight members of our research team had other names for B-15. We viewed the iceberg as an immediate and dangerous threat that would have severe ramifications for our expedition.

Our team as well as the penguins and Weddell seals relied on a predictable cycle of ice growth and disappearance to safely move around McMurdo Sound. During October through January, the sea ice slowly blistered and cracked and was eventually shed under the pressure of the winds. Winter blizzards during February and March usually forced the broken ice skirting the northern and western perimeters of Ross Island into the Ross Sea towards the South Pacific Ocean. Refreezing began by late March. By the time we arrived each September, a new smooth layer of sea ice glassed over the frigid water surface. This year the old ice lost the battle with B-15 and was locked in place. Less than four weeks before we were to begin our expedition, it became apparent that B-15 had disrupted the natural cycle, acting as a giant cork preventing the old ice from moving out to the open sea on its annual winter journey. Neither the animals nor our team could anticipate the impact.

As we prepared to travel to the southernmost landmass on earth, there was little time to speculate about the iceberg or its potential threats. With only sixteen days before our departure, preparations reached a new level of urgency. Most of the large instrumentation had already been shipped by freight to the Antarctic. What little time was left was spent testing newly designed instruments, packaging personal gear, stockpiling backup equipment and emergency fix-it supplies, and trying to purchase winter clothing and flu shots during the height of the California summer tourist season. Sleep came fitfully and was filled with anxiety in the final stages of outfitting the expedition:

At times I envisioned a giant wall of ice bearing down on unsuspecting Weddell seals as they hunted, mated, pupped, and nursed. It broke into a million dark blue shards, scattering penguins as the pieces fell onto the gravel beach of Ross Island. Some birds escaped and others fell into deep crevasses, searching the impossibly steep walls with small black eyes, unhurt but doomed to slow starvation. B-15 was heading towards our camp. The iceberg held its ground against the sea ice trying to break into the open ocean by riding the winds and underlying currents. Blocked in, the sea folded into jagged, compressed two-year-old ice that was cemented into place by the winter freeze. Travel on snowmobiles was slower and the view from the underside of the ice darker due to multiple years of accumulated snow. I saw our expedition beginning to move so slowly that we too were in danger of freezing in one spot. But we could only stand by and watch as the animals living around Ross Island suffered the greatest losses to the iceberg.

The first week of September ended with final word from NSF that all of the members of the expedition had PQ'ed—were Physically Qualified to work in the Antarctic. As the responsible agency for United States activities in Antarctica, the Polar Programs Division of the National Science Foundation provided the research funding and logistical support for our expedition. In addition to supplying food, shelter, and clothing, NSF also ensured that each one of us was healthy enough to withstand the rigors of polar living. It had taken months of medical and dental exams to get to this point. Depending on age and gender, we had been subjected to full dental checkups and X-rays, pulmonary function and exercise stress tests. Panels included blood and urine analysis, HIV screenings that allowed you to serve as a "walking" blood bank in the event of an emergency on the ice, eye tests, hearing tests, and tuberculin skin tests. Checks for breast, cervical, and prostate cancer were mandatory.

In the past when McMurdo Station was run as a military operation the physical exams were "standard issue," meaning you went through the same exam whether you were headed for the tropics of Vietnam or the ice fields of Antarctica. In 1983, my first trip South meant typhoid and tetanus inoculations, wisdom tooth extraction, and even consideration of appendix removal for the winter overs. Any organ or tissue that could give an expedition member problems on the ice was simply eliminated. The assumption was no medical intervention on the ice; the flights out were too few and far between. These days the medical and dental scrutiny were no less rigorous under civilian control, just the number of shots and predeployment surgical procedures had decreased. An ironic side benefit of these painstaking physicals was that cancer was often caught in the early stages, a lifesaving measure experienced by two close friends heading to Antarctica on other research projects.

The job of packing scientific gear quickly reached monumental proportions in my lab. All graduate students were enlisted. Crates, duct tape, bubble wrap, and equipment soon littered the bench tops and floors while we tried to puzzle each box together. As the exercise physiologist on our expedition, it was my job to supply the animal monitoring equipment: oxygen and carbon dioxide analyzers, a portable ultrasound machine, blood gas analyzers, heart rate recorders, and body temperature monitors. The same instrumentation that was used to assess the athletic capabilities of Olympic champions and conduct stress tests on cardiac patients was going to evaluate the diving capabilities of Weddell seals. This would be the first time that most of the equipment would leave the safety of my clinical laboratory at the University of California in Santa Cruz and be exposed to the shattering cold of Antarctica. None of it had been built to withstand blizzards, and I seriously doubted that the manufacturers had half-ton seals in mind when the instruments were designed. The potential for damage by freezing and handling during the long, turbulent journey south was high, and my students and I spent long hours packing and repacking with insulating foam sheets.

The same urgent packing was taking place in laboratories and work stations across the United States at Texas A&M University, the University of Texas, Southwestern University, Pisces Designs in San Diego, and the Alaska SeaLife Center in Seward, where the other expedition members tried to squeeze everything they would need to support their part of the expedition into 3' x 3' x 3' crates. I would be making my fifth trip to Antarctica. The rest of the team varied widely in polar experience from two team members who had spent an entire year on the ice to two "newbies" who were experiencing the countdown for the first time. Regardless of experience, the pace was uniformly frantic as the day of departure approached. Each of us had to anticipate our every need for the next three months, from computer disks to toothpaste. Every moment had to count with family and friends.

Federal Express letters containing plane tickets to New Zealand and an Antarctic itinerary from the National Science

Foundation heightened the excitement. Until that point it had all been planning and packing. With a ticket to Christchurch, New Zealand, and orders to show up at the Clothing Distribution Center at the International Antarctic Center, the team's adrenaline level perceptively rose another notch. There was another wave of nervous anticipation when the envelope was opened. With the pieces of paper in our hands—official "hall passes" to the Antarctic—the expedition was suddenly tangible. We had gained admission to a place that few humans would ever experience, to work with a team of explorers who would by necessity have to rely on each other to survive on earth's harshest continent. More than ten years of grant writing, team building and instrument development and testing had already been invested. We could already feel the bite of the cold and hear the crunch of ice underfoot. We were ready to go.

What would we find at the bottom of the world? The scientific goal was to discover the world of a secretive wild seal that hunted in the stillness of the dark waters beneath the polar sea ice. Four species of seal reside below the Antarctic Circle: the Ross seal, Leopard seal, crabeater seal, and Weddell seal. Of the four, the Weddell was the risk taker, the seal that tested the limits. Weddell seals lived colder, traveled deeper, and pushed further south than any other Antarctic seal.

To find them, we would need to do the same.

But first and foremost, we had to survive. Antarctica was one of the most challenging environments imaginable. It distilled personalities and deftly brought explorers to their limits and beyond.

The thrill was in the unknown. And it was impossible to explain to those who would be left behind the inner drive that drew us away from them and towards Antarctica.

In September 2001, as the team's adrenaline was just beginning to peak, all of the intensive packing and rising excitement abruptly ended when the world stopped. The World Trade Center towers in New York were gone, the Pentagon was gutted, and we were told of impending war with a new insidious enemy. The Air National Guard, including the pilots who flew our aircraft from New Zealand to McMurdo Station, Antarctica, was being mobilized to active duty. Suddenly our expedition felt as insignificant and ephemeral as a child's passing daydream as the country turned to the serious business of protecting family and home. There was nowhere to go. In an unprecedented move, the United States government secured airports and halted international travel. With only a handful of days left before we were to fly to the remote reaches of the earth, it seemed as though no one would be allowed in the air again. Nor did our team members want to go. Under the best of circumstances, it is difficult to mentally prepare family and friends for our extended absence. Emotions are heightened when the journey is to an inaccessible part of the globe.

After September 11, family members pleaded, "Please don't go."

While so much around us seemed in chaos, the members of our research expedition experienced an eerie lull. All of our field gear and scientific equipment were packed, scrupulously weighed, and locked in insulated crates. We had no calendar to follow or appointments to keep. We had wiped three months of our home life clean in anticipation of our absence. As far as anyone was concerned, we had already departed. There was little to do except watch current events unfold and pray for the victims with the rest of the world.

As our team anxiously waited for a decision from the National Science Foundation regarding our fate, I gained a greater appreciation of Ernest Shackleton's emotional struggles on August 1, 1914, the eve of his Imperial Trans-Antarctic Expedition. Standing on the polished wooden deck of his ship, the *Endurance,* he must have surveyed his handiwork with dismay. For four years he had creatively pieced together funding from governmental sources and wealthy donors to support his proposed expedition. With those funds he had retrofitted a wooden Norwegian sailing vessel, hand selected his crew, purchased supplies and equipment including sixty-nine barking Canadian sled dogs, and mapped out a polar adventure that was to take the team across Antarctica. Every day was budgeted for in terms of salaries and food for crewmen and animals. The *Endurance* had already left London and was about to leave port in Plymouth. Before the sails had even been raised to begin the journey south, Britain entered the First World War. Shackleton prepared to abandon his dream of being the first to conquer the breadth of the Antarctic continent on foot, and offered his crew and services for military duty for the good of his country. Britain readied for war while the explorer waited for word from the British Admiralty about the fate of his expedition.

I imagined Shackleton on the deck of the *Endurance* feeling a similar sense of confusion as he watched a world in chaos. How could anyone have anticipated the level of madness and destruction? The spirit of adventure tends to extinguish under such foreboding. Eighty-seven years later the conflicting mix of emotions had not changed. Patriotism, the tug of family, and uncertainty at home were countered by the drive to explore and loyalty to the members of the expedition. In 1914 the British Admiralty recognized that the greater contribution would come through Shackleton's discoveries. In a message consisting of a single word, he was ordered to "Proceed." Likewise, in the third week of September 2001, the National Science Foundation decided to proceed with Antarctic science operations as planned. Like Shackleton, our expedition was going South.

With the tenuous opening of airports, our team was issued new tickets to accommodate the few available international flights. This time there was no adrenaline rush—instead, we wondered if we would be stalled, turned back, or denied re-entry into the United States. As eight of us prepared to enter bitter cold, groaning ice, and mind-numbing windstorms, we wondered what kind of world would be waiting for us when we returned.

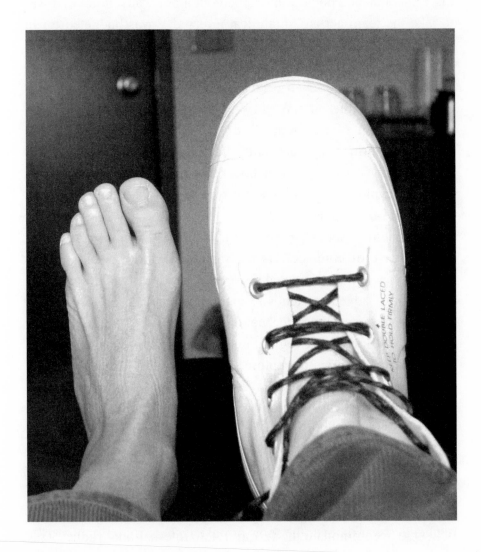

CHAPTER 3

THE TEAM

Randy Davis and I had known each other the longest; it was almost twenty years to the day that we had started our scientific collaboration as post-doctoral students in the same laboratory at Scripps Institution of Oceanography in San Diego. Under Dr. Gerry Kooyman's tutelage, we had learned the facts about Antarctica and about Weddell seals. But it was Kooyman's childlike enthusiasm for polar exploration and the amazing diving seal that had been so infectious. No matter how many times he witnessed a Weddell seal lumber awkwardly over the snow or poke its head up through a layer of slushy ice, he'd laugh and shake his head in wonder.

That laugh had ignited an underlying drive for adventure and discovery that had been smoldering in me. Disregarding the traditions of a Catholic prep school upbringing that rewarded refined behavior and social status, I chose instead the rigors of camping on ice among the wild animals. To me, it bore little difference to growing up in a house filled with brothers, although the decision caused no end of raised eyebrows from my parents and their friends in South Carolina. "Welsh hardheadedness," my dad had sighed, referring to the ancestors who had caused the genetic hiccup. But the desire to be where animals lived was less a calculated rebellion on my part and more natural curiosity.

For Randy, it was the process of polar exploration that had captured his imagination. Despite living in the finer neighborhoods of Texas and serving as a professor of biology at Texas A & M University, he too had chosen the ice. Randy reveled in the details and took charge of the logistics, designing the camp and overseeing the development of the video and instrument package that would eventually have to withstand the abuse of wild, free-ranging Weddell seals. He was the most experienced Antarctic hand on our team, having spent an entire year on the ice immediately after finishing his graduate degree with Kooyman in 1980. Unlike most of us, he had experienced the severity and challenges of an Antarctic winter; for that we were both jealous and respectful of his instincts on ice. Numerous shorter expeditions had followed his winter over, and after twenty years of polar exploration, it was his beard—not his attitude—that had weathered.

Randy and I showed up almost simultaneously at the departure gate in LAX. One by one the other expedition members arrived, uncharacteristically subdued. All of us had found the airports too quiet and the few cotravelers jumpy in the aftermath of September 11. Even the pilots on our connecting flights were nervous.

Our first laugh came when Don Calkins arrived from Seward, Alaska, hidden beneath a massive sea otter–fur hat that he had been given on a trip to Russia. Under the hat it was difficult to tell where his thick lumberjack beard ended and the sea otter began. He was determined not to let his ears get cold on his second trip to the Antarctic. With a hearty handshake he welcomed Matt Rutishauser, my graduate student from the University of California at Santa Cruz, to the team. It was Matt's first trip to the ice and he could only stand by and smile politely as the rest of us hugged with the vigor of camp camaraderie.

Dr. Jesse Purdy of Southwestern University in Austin was the other new wide-eyed, enthusiastic addition to the team. He was a word-of-mouth addition who we knew little about other than his teaching credentials and rabid desire to go to Antarctica. Our first concerns were how he would deal with the cold, the isolation, and the emotional mix of the rest of the team. Along with Don and Matt, he would serve as the backbone of the expedition responsible for the day-to-day scientific and logistical demands that ranged from seal herder to gopher, from snow shoveler to pie maker, and from data processor to video recorder. Regardless of schooling, age, or background, the three of them had to meet one common prerequisite: they had to be willing and able to do it all.

Before we had even finished with the introductions, Dr. Markus Horning walked into our growing circle, sipping his customary cup of coffee. Originally from Germany, raised in Italy, and working in the same marine biology department as Randy Davis at Texas A & M University, Markus could curse fluently in five languages while he tinkered, designed, and "seal-proofed" microprocessors for use on wild marine mammals. He had a wealth of ideas for research and survival that were undoubtedly fueled by his 1980 Antarctic over-wintering experience with Randy and by the strong European coffee that he favored. During the expedition he would add to the creative thinking and technological support that would allow us to track the Weddell seals during their underwater treks.

Over the years I had listened with great envy to Randy and Markus talk about their year on the ice on the edge of White Island in McMurdo Sound. They had witnessed the subtle changes of the Antarctic seasons and the comings and goings of Weddell seals as summer transitioned into the stillness of winter and then back again. The changes in the seals' watery environment below the ice had been dramatic. Three months of total darkness in winter left the ocean crystal clear, for no microorganisms could reproduce in the absence of sunlight. The water, now empty of turbidity-producing plankton, turned so transparent that divers and seals alike were provided with an underwater vista unlike anywhere in the world. Visibility beneath the ice was over 400 feet—forty times the visibility I was used to in the murky waters of Monterey Bay off the coast of California.

In the winter the stars, the moon, and auroras provide the only light for underwater hunting and navigation by the Weddell seals. It is little wonder that the eyes of the Weddell seal are huge in comparison to other animals'—they have to trap what little light penetrates the snow, ice, and seawater in the dead of winter. Human eyes are only an inch in diameter, considerably smaller than a Ping-Pong ball. The eyes of the Weddell are almost two and a half times larger, between the size of a racquetball and a tennis ball. In this regard, Weddell seals follow the pattern of other great marine hunters. Two of the largest eyes ever recorded for an animal belong to marine predators: the giant squid, with an eye diameter of ten inches, and the blue whale, with a diameter of almost six inches.

When underwater, the eyes of the Weddell seal dilate, hiding a soft brown iris and providing a huge surface for absorbing the dim light. I would have expected such enormous eyes placed in the proportionately small skull of the Weddell to result in a buggy appearance. Instead, the eyes, whiskers, and upturned mouth present a disarmingly pleased look both on top and below the ice all year round.

Randy and Markus had found that during winter only a handful of adult Weddell seals remain as the lone underwater resident marine mammal. Crabeater seals, leopard seals, and killer whales beat a hasty retreat with the approach of the winter freeze. Any Weddell pup or yearling trapped after summer is quickly overwhelmed by the severity of the climate and the environs. If they are lucky enough to live until spring, they are severely emaciated.

But the entire process reverses come the following October. With the rising sun, the waters beneath the sea ice churn with activity. Under constant intense sunlight, phytoplankton grow exponentially, creating a murky bloom in the surface waters by mid-December. Fish take advantage of the bounty, with Adelie penguins, crabeater and leopard seals, and killer whales and minke whales following on their tails. Hundreds of adult Weddells and their immature offspring also returned to McMurdo Sound; some sought out mates, others would give birth and nurse young, and still others would hunt for fish.

We, in turn, would follow the hunters, and like the seals found ourselves heading farther and farther South.

With Lee Fuiman already on board, there was only one team member missing. However, heightened airport security left the gate attendant in no mood for delays and despite our protests she shuttled the rest of us onto the plane. As she prepared to shut the door, there was a distant shout of "Waaaaaiiit!" from across the terminal. With jacket and sweater flapping, and papers flying out of a falling wallet, Bill Hagey flashed his passport to the attendant and narrowly made it on board. Frantic, disheveled, and grinning widely, Bill bounded down the aisle and swung into a seat next to Lee, who had already neatly stowed his carry-on bag a half hour earlier. Bill crammed the passport and falling papers into a briefcase and shoved it beneath his feet just as the plane was taxiing down the runway.

Four previous expeditions with Bill had taught Lee that the man often moved according to his own clock. Bill was the creative if sometimes unorganized mind and talent behind the technology for the seal video and tracking instrumentation. With his own business in underwater technology (Pisces Design of San Diego), Bill had the freedom to choose his projects. And this time he was inspired by the challenge of pitting his instrumentation against the rigors of Antarctic waters and the wild seals that could take all of us to places that we had never even imagined.

In Christchurch, before our bodies had even caught up with the time zone and date changes, we were shuttled through customs and the snuffling scrutiny of the drug-detecting dogs. Lee Fuiman watched with bemused detachment as the beagle scratched at his duffel bag. In his buttondown shirt and pressed khaki pants, he was the last person we would expect trafficking drugs. For all of his hard work, the beagle turned up the remnants of a banana. Unscathed by the dog, jet lag, or lack of sleep, Lee began a one-man fire brigade, quickly loading the crates holding our equipment onto a train of luggage carts. "How does he do it?" I wondered through a haze of rumpled sleeplessness.

Lee was the third principal investigator "Doc" on the expedition. His first trip to the ice had been with Randy and me in 1997, which had served as a baptism-by-fire introduction to marine mammal research. To our surprise, Lee immediately revealed his skill at thinking like a marine predator. As an animal behaviorist and software tinkerer, he had spent much of his university research career predicting the behavioral patterns of minuscule larval fish as they navigated the three-dimensional ocean environment.

His usual research subjects were several million times smaller than the seals we studied—not even a decent mouthful for a Weddell. On our expedition, Lee was responsible for synthesizing and coordinating the mountain of data that streamed in from all of the sensors deployed on the seals. He was the virtual seal tracker who was happiest in front of a computer monitor regardless of whether it was in his air-conditioned office on campus at the University of Texas or in a wooden fishing hut in the middle of an Antarctic blizzard. A self-proclaimed "fish biologist," he was more interested in what the fish thought of the hungry Weddell seal than in the reverse.

The expedition was comprised of seven men and one woman, all with one ambition—to follow the Weddell seal beneath the Antarctic sea ice. We completed the first leg of the journey South full of enthusiasm and hope that the next three months would result in a unique portrait of the underwater world of Antarctica. We wanted to provide a foundation of data to ensure the preservation of the polar ecosystem and its animal inhabitants. With that singular goal in mind, the emotional framework of the team slowly began to form.

After collecting the team's mountain of scientific and personal gear, we boarded a bus along with forty Antarctic support personnel for the Clothing Distribution Center (CDC) near the airport. We were divided into two groups: expedition researchers such as ourselves, and the carpenters, cooks, electricians, office managers, janitors, and van drivers who kept McMurdo Station running. Unlike the researchers, many of them would have limited opportunity to leave the proximity of the station, travel out on the sea ice, or ever see a Weddell seal. Regardless, they were as enthusiastic as the rest of us, delighting in each step that brought them closer to Antarctica.

Modeled after the military, the CDC clothing issue was so complete we soon realized that we could have traveled to New Zealand with little more than the clothes on our back and a few sets of underwear, and still be ready for months of Antarctic living. Parkas, wind pants, fleece liners, two types of thermal underwear, ski goggles, three hats, seven different types of gloves and mittens, six pairs of gray wool socks, insulated boots, and even a water bottle were provided by the National Science Foundation. As I tried on the clothing, I noted that the clothing issue for women had definitely improved over the past twenty years. In the 1980s there were so few women headed to the ice that we were just considered "small men." My clothing issue in 1983 consisted of leftover men's sizes. Most of it was too big but could be corrected with layering. The ineffective front hole in the insulated underpants was another matter; I just chalked it up to the Antarctic experience.

In 2001 the Antarctic clothing issue was a blend of old military habits and new high-tech mountaineering designs. One impressive mainstay was the "bunny" boot. Each giant rubber insulated boot weighed over three and a half pounds. That was a combined seven pounds of boot to lug around to keep our feet warm while walking on ice. Even the heaviest leather hiking boots would feel like running shoes after a day of shuffling around in the bunny boots.

One look in the mirror immediately answered the question of why penguins and seals are so rotund. It takes an inordinate amount of insulation to keep a body warm in the face of the blowing snow and subzero temperatures in Antarctica. Because of it, animals and humans alike are uniformly round.

I couldn't imagine adding another layer—as it was I could barely bend my knees and elbows. A minimum of three layers covered most of my body parts: insulated underwear topped by fleece leggings and jackets, and finally wind pants and parkas. In addition to the sweating, the insulation came at a heavy price in terms of sleekness, mobility, and individuality. I could barely walk. Even breathing was more difficult. Dressed in standard-issue red parkas, black pants, and white bunny boots, my team members and I were as indistinguishable and awkward as a colony of Adelie penguins shuffling around the CDC. For us the problem of identification under all of the clothing was solved with nametags Velcroed to the front of our parkas. For the penguins, individual recognition remained a mystery to biologists.

Parka nametags were a big deal in McMurdo. They allowed you to locate your red coat among hundreds of identical red coats, and you could forget names with abandon since everyone was labeled. It was like being back in kindergarten. The tags were also one of the few distinguishable features of your wardrobe. Colored, decorated, and shortened to nicknames, they revealed the wearer's personality. The peak of nametag snobbishness was the revered upside-down tag, indicating that the wearer had once visited the bottom of the world—the South Pole.

After we tried on all of the gear, Mike—the crusty, white-haired CDC instructor—barked out orders above the ruckus of the would-be Antarctic explorers.

"Alright, who has seen the frostbite film?" he yelled over the crowd. Surveying the show of hands, he divided the group with the aid of a wooden pointer and drill sergeant sarcasm. "Newbies" were sent into a room to watch a well-worn video about the dangers of frostbite, dehydration, and hypothermia in Antarctica.

If you learned nothing else from the video, you at least came away with the phrase, "copious and clear." Drink water, and keep drinking until you urinated in huge, straw-colored quantities. The message was, Antarctica was desiccating, and the thirstier you were the colder you would feel. Even Weddell seals seemed to feel the dryness of the air. Most marine mammals do not drink water, relying instead on exceptionally efficient kidneys and the water ingested in their prey. But not Weddell seals. On several occasions we had witnessed the seals chewing on ice and slurping the freshwater surface lens of ice holes. Could it be that the polar air was also challenging for them?

To the rest of us Mike growled with what we had come to recognize as his brand of New Zealand fondness, "Right, you old timers, you know the routine. Get packing."

In the past twenty years the exercise had not changed. We separated our gear into two orange canvas bags—one that was designated as ECW (Extreme Cold Weather) clothing, and another for all of the extra paraphernalia. The ECW bag would never leave our side as we traveled to, from, or across Antarctica. The nondescript orange bag contained the items deemed essential for survival, and we would always know its location until we returned it to the CDC at the end of our expedition—at least according to Mike's orders.

From this point forward our time in Christchurch was dictated by airplane maintenance and weather conditions in McMurdo. We were on constant call for our flight south. Usually we were given twelve to twenty-four hours to mobilize. However, this could be shortened to a handful of hours if the pilots decided it was time to move. They had come on temporary assignment from National Guard units across the United States and from outfits in New Zealand and Australia. With the prospect of being called into a desert war, they could give us no guarantees as to our schedule. All we knew was that when they deemed conditions for flying south were right, we were expected to be on the tarmac dressed in Antarctic gear and ready to go. Our lives were now run in six-hour watches, waiting for their signal.

As we inched closer to Antarctica, the team members mentally began to tally the things they would miss during the next few months. Spring was in full bloom in the southern hemisphere, and the flowers were at their peak in Christchurch's botanical gardens. We would miss the colors, especially the sight and smell of green. Stopping to appreciate the park's foliage, we took time to listen to the songbirds in the trees, something we would rarely be caught doing at home. Just knowing that raucous penguin trumpeting and skua (large, brown polar gulls) mutterings were going to be the only birdcalls that we would experience on the expedition made us pause. Each trip to Starbucks became a memorable experience for Randy, Matt, and Markus. Each passing dog was petted. I was especially going to miss the slobbery silliness of dogs during our time South. Except for a few desiccated skeletons still chained to collars, Shackleton's sled dogs had vanished from the Antarctic.

At 4 A.M. we were awakened in a little downtown bed-and-breakfast, handed a paper sack filled with an assortment of breakfast items, and bused in the cool dark air to the CDC. It was drizzling; through my drowsiness, I added "the last rain I will see until December" to my mental list of to-be-missed items.

Under the harshness of the fluorescent lighting and Mike's caustic humor, we were instructed to put on our ECW clothing and to box up our summer things to be left behind in storage. By 5 A.M. our team members had assembled in a carpeted waiting area with about eighty others, who were similarly bleary-eyed and dressed in parkas, wind pants, fleece sweaters, and bunny boots. It was too early in the morning to recognize that we were sorely overdressed for Christchurch in spring. National Guard personnel in military khaki lined the group up to weigh us individually on a giant platform scale. A petite blond woman who wouldn't crack a smile at the feeble attempts at humor by some of the travelers recorded the weights mechanically. For her and the rest of the flight crew, it was the annual Antarctic cattle drive. Their jobs were to tag us, catalog us, and make sure that we didn't overload the plane.

After weighing we were once again corralled onto buses, this time headed to the airplane hangar. OPERATION DEEP FREEZE, painted in eight-foot-high bold letters over the gaping hangar doors, was another reminder of the military history of Antarctic flights and of the growing Operation Enduring Freedom occurring in deserts on the opposite side of the globe. From the steamy inside of the bus we each craned our necks to see what type of plane we would be flying in. There are no commercial airline flights to Antarctica. Instead large military cargo planes—C-130s, C-141s, C-17s, and C-5s—carry people and equipment to the ice. The flight from Christchurch to the Antarctic took five to eight hours, depending on the type of aircraft going due south. These large, gray planes are the workhorses of the military, and the interiors are spartan by any standard. The seats consist of long rows of metal piping with backs and bottoms of red nylon webbing; life vests and oxygen masks serve as headrests. The guts of the plane exposed on the inside hull, providing hours of mindless entertainment as you track oil and electrical lines during the flight. The only accessible windows are small portholes in the doors, so there is no view.

In the plane, we were usually crammed into the small web seats with a row of people facing knee-to-knee. The bunny boots made it impossible to move our feet once we were seated. Options were few; you could choose to alternate feet positions with the person facing you or select the feet together–feet outside positioning. We tried to maneuver our expedition members into opposing seats. In doing so we felt free to periodically stretch a leg onto one of their laps or alongside their thigh during the flight. It was a luxury permitted by team familiarity that made us look out for one another on the ice.

Before we could move to the front of the plane, we found that the seating arrangement was completely changed. The flight had been designated as a major cargo mission. Our team was quickly directed to a long row of seats down one side of the plane, and we were initially delighted with the prospect of extra legroom. But our good fortune faded when we realized that rather than facing another passenger there was an entire helicopter and a massive bulldozer chained to the floor in front of us.

There are few things more disconcerting than watching large, heavy pieces of machinery strain on metal chains during takeoff and landing, and from where I was sitting I knew there would be no escape should one of the chain's links give out. Randy and Bill pointed and smirked once they realized that one of the cargo straps holding down the helicopter ended directly below my seat. In many ways I would have preferred the hours of boot footsies and knee knocking.

A burley load master was the closest thing to a stewardess on the plane. He checked the integrity of the bolts and chains holding down the helicopter in front of me, handed our group yellow foam earplugs and lunch bags, and then left us to figure out what to do for the duration of the flight. It was too loud to talk, too dark to read.

During the course of the flight, our feet and legs froze while hot air blowing from the machinery above caused our foreheads to develop beads of sweat. Some people attempted to use laptop computers and soon gave up due to the vibrations of the plane. The more experienced passengers just hunkered down in their parkas, periodically chewed on soggy New Zealand cheese-and-butter sandwiches from their lunch sacks, and slept their way through the flight to Antarctica.

As the engines droned on, I stared at the ceiling and went through the mental checklist of scientific equipment for the hundredth time. Each of us had a specific role on the expedition, and I was not going to let the team down by forgetting something.

Figure out how the seals did it. That was my job. Search for the answer in the heart rates, respiration rates, swimming stroke rates, and oxygen consumption rates of the hunting seals. The question was, How were Weddell seals able to exercise so intensely and at such crushing depths while holding their breath in the quest of catching a fish? I had no Einstein- or Darwin-inspired complicated underlying hypotheses; I just wanted to know how Weddell seals swam.

It had begun with a summer job as a gangly college student who life-guarded and taught basic swimming to kids at local community pools. My summers were filled with young boys and girls sputtering and splashing their way in half-drowned efforts to swim across the length of the pool. It seemed so far off, but I could still hear the frantic splashing. Woe to the swimmer who discovered he or she couldn't touch bottom on the other end. A toe left searching in open water initiated such irrational wide-eyed panic and frantic scrambling to the pool's edge that the rest of the swim lesson was spent drying tears. For the most part the parents were not much better. My assessment over the years was that humans are simply not built to swim.

But there is one class of mammals, unlike us, that excel in the water. Marine mammals—the dolphins, whales, sea otters, seals, and sea lions move with such grace that they leave me in awe, awash in their wake. I had spent a scientific lifetime studying how they swim and dive. Weddell seals, like other phocid seals, are perfectly streamlined. The neck that appears so fat on land smooths their body contours to torpedo-shaped perfection when submerged. Water parts for them as they pass through, allowing them to glide on currents in a way that I could never achieve. They dominate the seas without creating a ripple of disturbance.

I was in search of the perfect swimmer, and the Weddell seal was the champion of them all.

Except for snoring, there was little collective activity during the flight save one important event. After four hours, at the halfway point, a noticeable sigh spread throughout the cabin. We had reached the point of no return; there would be no turning back to Christchurch. Like it or not, snowstorm or not, we were destined for McMurdo Station. Until that magic hour had passed, reaching Antarctica had always been a fifty-fifty gamble. Weather patterns change so quickly on the ice that whiteout conditions could easily develop between the time that our C-141 left Christchurch and the time it arrived in McMurdo. Without enough fuel on board to fly to the ice and back without landing, the pilots and crew had to make a critical decision halfway out. Do they proceed to McMurdo Station, or "boomerang" us back to New Zealand? A perceptible groan of disappointment would have arisen if we had felt the plane slip into a wide turning arc as it reversed course for the four-hour journey back to Christchurch. Then the whole exercise would have been repeated the next day and the day after that until we eventually made it to the ice. It all depended on weather conditions in Antarctica, the integrity of the plane, pilot intuition, and luck. The previous year Lee had been especially unlucky and had had the unfortunate honor of experiencing the most boomerangs (seven sequential turnaround flights) for our team. Even he did not have enough ironed shirts to keep from getting rumpled. This year, however, luck was with us. The three-hour, three-and-a-half-hour, and four-hour points came and went with no change in the constant drone of the engines. It was too late to change direction; we were going to be landing on the ice.

Thirty minutes out, we began our descent into McMurdo Station. From the porthole window in the door we could see only white with an occasional interruption created by the shadow of a jagged peak of ice or rock. It was difficult to believe that there was anywhere to land below.

The airport was little more than a scraped section of sea ice and a series of temporary shelters lined up a mile from Ross Island. Incoming planes used either wheels or skis to silently land on an ice runway located out on the frozen sea. Unlike asphalt or cement, the ice was flexible. As a result, airport personnel had to run out and measure the runway after each flight to determine if the ice had compressed during the landing. Too much compression, and the heavy planes would break through the ten-foot-thick ice and sink 500 meters (1,640 feet) down to the bottom of McMurdo Sound.

By now our team had been traveling together for nearly a week. With the crossing of the International Date Line, we had lost an additional day. Our journey south culminated with a thud onto the ice and an emotional mix of excitement, jet lag, and the lonely realization that it would be months before we saw friends or family again. We had dropped out of their lives and would be unable to regularly communicate with them for the duration of the expedition. Staring at a picture of his baby daughter, Bill could only wonder about the milestones in her growth that he would miss. As a new grandfather, Lee looked over his shoulder and understood all too well.

The brief time that it took for the plane to smoothly slide to a stop marked the end of the frantic preparations and the beginning of the demanding work in Antarctica. It was one of the loneliest points of the expedition. Suddenly the distance we had willingly placed between home and ourselves was real. We accepted that as the price of working as field biologists and the desire to be where the animals live. Science was our life. At times it consumed us and cost many personal relationships as the lines between work, play, and home dissolved. The ones left behind always suffered the most.

Reflection abruptly ended and all thoughts of loneliness were quickly erased when the cargo door was opened. Immediately a blast of chilled air froze our sinuses and made our eyes tear. Bright white reflected off of the snow, momentarily blinding us as we left the dark hold of the plane. There was no ground relief as we took in our first Antarctic vista, a view that stretched for over forty miles in all directions across the sea ice to the surrounding islands and the jagged outline of the Royal Society Mountain Range on the continent. Stumbling out of the plane, our team stopped for a moment on the ice to try to take it all in. Mount Erebus, an active volcano on Ross Island, discharged a welcoming cloud of smoke that was blown into a thin platinum wisp by high winds at its peak. To the south, White Island rose magnificently out of the sea ice, its face curtained by a season of snow and wind. Its overpowering presence was rivaled only by the sky, which was such a rich shade of marine blue that we felt submerged. Only the stark white of the ice reminded us that we were standing on a frozen ocean rather than under it.

We had finally arrived in the coldest, driest, windiest, and clearly the most spectacular place on earth—Antarctica.

CHAPTER 4

GATHERINGS

As our team traveled south by air, hundreds of winter-fattened Weddell seals embarked on a similar journey by sea and ice. Living independently around the outer icy coasts and open waters of the Antarctic continent during the brutal winter months, the seals now gathered like vacationing tourists in McMurdo Sound for the summer. For most of the year there was no such thing as a Weddell family. Standoffish, if not downright unsociable, each male and female, adult and youngster, spent its winter feeding and living in isolation, perhaps too hungry to share favorite fishing spots. But the summer months inspired new attitudes. Under the constant sun, Weddell seals congregated to give birth, raise pups, and accomplish all of the necessary reproductive chores associated with propagating the species. Bachelors sought each other's company, at least until the females arrived. Fathers always remained aloof, while Weddell mothers proved so devoted to their pups that they never left their sides, going for weeks on end without food. At best Weddell family ties were loose, with the height of social interaction and warmth occurring from October to December.

Our paths would cross at six small rocky outcroppings huddled in the Sound. Sheltered by the western side of Ross Island, the unlikely rugged sites served as the backdrop for summer romances between the seals. The first to arrive were females heavy with near-term pups. Later in the season nonpregnant females and broad-shouldered males would swim in to set up underwater trysts.

The seals faced a much more onerous trek south than our team. To get to the prime breeding and haul-out sites in McMurdo Sound, they dove cautiously beneath a solid sheet of sea ice. Each foray from the open coast towards the frozen rock outcroppings required precise navigation and a calculated use of each breath of air. Swim too far beneath the sheet or lose direction and a seal could become trapped and drown. As amazing as this journey is for any adult seal, it seemed an impossible course for the pregnant females lumbering along underwater, bloated and unstable with a twenty-five-kilogram (fifty-pound) fetus on board.

Ten miles away, across the ice of McMurdo Sound, our team organized equipment and supplies for the expedition. McMurdo Station, an amalgamation of windblown military structures and metal-sided college campus–styled buildings served as the transition between home and the wild. Resting on the barren volcanic slope of Ross Island and covered in dirty snow and old ice, the Station had the isolated, dusty feel of a decrepit mining town. In outward appearance the Station was deceptively tame. However, this first impression was short-lived, dispelled when I tried to open one of the outside doors to the buildings. With one simple move I recognized how violent Antarctica can become. The reinforced outer doors were like freezer lockers, steel-gray metal sheets latched with heavy-duty bolts instead of doorknobs. The moment you put a mittoned hand on the bulky latch of one of the massive doors and threw your weight into opening it, you realized that nature is not to be taken lightly at the Station. Wind would tear a normal door right off of its hinges.

Our team was one of the first scientific expeditions on the ice for the summer season, so McMurdo was only beginning to shake off the long winter months. From March through August—the Antarctic winter—the population of McMurdo Station averaged 200 support personnel who ran basic operations to keep the place in hibernation through the cold, dark months. The end of September brought the first of the summer visitors, mostly researchers and additional support personnel to move the science forward as quickly as possible until darkness took over six months later. At the height of the summer season, from September to February, the Station swelled to 1,200 adventurers. In addition to scientists such as ourselves, there were the carpenters, electricians, cooks, and janitorial staff who we had met at the CDC in New Zealand. Medical personnel included one doctor, nurses, physician assistants, and a dentist. Machinists, biotechnicians, radio operators, snowmobile mechanics, and search-and-rescue teams also ventured south to help support the NSF-sponsored scientific expeditions.

"Winter overs" were easy to distinguish from the new arrivals. They tended to stare at the crowds of visitors from the incoming flights with bug-eyed excitement, suspicion, and trepidation. Many would be boarding the same planes that we had just vacated for the return flight to Christchurch. In New Zealand they would once again have to enter civilization after spending ten to fourteen months in deep-freeze isolation. Some welcomed the transition, and others resented our presence. Our arrival in McMurdo brought them that much closer to the challenges of the modern, chaotic world that they had been shielded from for nearly a year. We couldn't begin to explain what awaited them back in the States.

Our team didn't waste time thinking about the wind and the cold, or wandering around the makeshift gymnasium, hospital, dormitory structures, and support buildings of McMurdo Station. Our target was the sea ice, along with the Weddell seals that lived below it. From three previous expeditions our team knew that we had only ten weeks of good solid ice to work on. After that the intensity of the Antarctic summer sun would work its way through the sea ice, progressively weakening it. By December, windstorms would cause large fissures to open up in the deteriorating ice. Melt pools would develop, and travel between our camp and McMurdo would become too dangerous to negotiate.

Success of the expedition depended on our ability to quickly establish a camp and find seals that were actively diving and hunting for fish. As simple as that seemed on paper, it was a different matter when our survival was at stake. Early October around Ross Island is notorious for rapidly changing weather systems blowing in whiteout snows and extremely cold temperatures. Moving in unflagged areas on the open ice would have an added element of risk due to the unpredictable weather. Logistical support would also be minimal since we were one of the first science parties to reach the Station for the season. In sum, our first surveys around the rocky outcroppings of McMurdo Sound needed to be like those of the arriving Weddell seals: efficient and cautious.

The command center for our expedition was the laboratory at the Albert P. Crary Science and Engineering Center at McMurdo Station, a low-slung metal building that hugged the gravel hillside leading to the sea ice. All of the crates containing our scientific instrumentation from the United States had been shipped previously to the lab and were waiting on the heated loading dock. On days that we were weathered in town we assembled, calibrated, and tested each piece of equipment. Randy Davis taped cigarette pack–sized satellite tags to railings on the roof of the lab and tried to download satellite "hits." With each satellite pass over Antarctica, he would receive a message through e-mail on his computer giving the latitude and longitude of the tag. Later we would place these tags on Weddell seals and use them to locate the animals as they moved around the sea ice.

My time was spent calibrating the exercise testing equipment, which meant using Matt, Don, and Jesse as test subjects for checking the heart rate monitors, oxygen analyzers, infrared skin temperature detectors, and ultrasound probes. Although good sports about the heart rate and temperature tests, the three were less enthusiastic about the ultrasound images that displayed fat thickness. The portable ultrasound not only measured the blubber layer of seals, it objectively revealed our expanding waistlines. Little exercise combined with overeating in the galley at the Station had already had a measurable effect on the team.

Lee Fuiman hunkered over his computers writing data analysis programs. He politely ignored the acrid haze that hovered in the stagnant air of the laboratory, created by Bill Hagey and Markus Horning as they soldered, glued, and tweaked the miniaturized video equipment and sensors that would eventually be deployed on the seals.

Outside of the lab a fierce wind kicked up snow and road grit that scraped noisily along thick glass windows. The rhythmic rise and fall of the grinding reminded the team of our final destination. There was one last break to be made—the one between the controlled safety of McMurdo Station and the unpredictable wildness of the sea ice.

In addition to the scientific instrumentation, there was a mountain of boxes containing food and supplies for the camp that had to be coordinated and packaged on the loading dock. Designated as the person with the highest metabolism, it was my job to organize the food for the entire team. The task of feeding an entire expedition was daunting. How much food could eight hungry people consume in three months?

Outfitting the camp began with multiple trips to the Berg Field Center, a small Costco-like warehouse where the food and supplies for the field camps were stored. From the open shelves I pulled enough food to last for the first fourteen to forty days in camp. Over thirty cardboard boxes were filled with cereal, rice, cookies, crackers, and pastas, along with cans of vegetables, fruits, jams, and beans. Expiration dates were generally ignored as most of the items had been stored and shipped to Antarctica on an icebreaker more than a year before. Most of the spices had long ago lost their flavor in the dry air. Frozen beef and chicken as well as twenty pounds of butter and one hundred frozen tortillas were added at the last minute, along with fifteen loaves of frozen bread acquired from the galley. To avoid spoilage many items were dehydrated; there were desiccated eggs, beef jerky, dried tomatoes, powdery mashed potato mix that was often confused with the powdered milk and sugar, coffee, and teas. Over 700 pounds of dried goods and 200 pounds of frozen meats, vegetables, and cheeses were pulled from the shelves. Nearly a half-ton of food then had to be moved to camp. And this was just the first cache; several trips would be made during the course of the field season to restock.

There were three prized food items that we bartered amongst ourselves for during the field season:

1. Cadbury chocolate bars
2. Oreo cookies
3. Pringle potato chips

In that order! Part of the mystique of these items was that they were rationed. The cookies and potato chips were issued judiciously by the Berg Field Center, according to their availability. Cadbury bars were issued at one bar per person per day. Although this initially seemed extravagant, especially when multiplied by eight people and several weeks, we used these chocolate bars as part of our survival gear. They went into our ECW bags and the pockets of our parkas, windpants, and shirts as an essential item in the event of hypothermia. Consuming a single chocolate bar could bring your body out of a chill when working on the ice, and the candy bars were as coveted as a warm pair of mittens. We ate them all—bittersweet, milk chocolate, mint, caramel, nut and raisin, and crackle bars—fifty-six bars per week. Only the chocolate bars containing small bits of jellied candies were left untouched due to their tooth-cracking consistency when frozen.

The underlying reason for squirreling away these particular foods, however, was more basic than hunger or cold. We craved them because they contained fat. Just like blubbery seals, our bodies demanded high fat—anything loaded with calories—to keep warm in the Antarctic. Instinctively we were drawn to the fats in foods, butter, and oils, the greasier the item, the better. The sudden transition in our diets amazed even ourselves, knowing full well that if we maintained the same level of fat consumption at home, our bodies would balloon out of control. Yet, on the ice these fats were necessary just to keep warm each day.

Organizing the field supplies was even more complicated than organizing the food. An assortment of tools—from handsaws and chainsaws to hammers, screwdrivers, and screws—was boxed together. There were huge spools of ½-inch and 1-inch rope in 600-foot lengths. Parachute cord on smaller spools, ice coolers, flashlights, camping stoves, cots, sleeping bags, and four large wooden crates of kitchenware, including pots and utensils, were collected and boxed for transport. Dozens of red, green, yellow, and blue nylon flags attached to eight-foot-long bamboo poles would be used to mark roads, dive holes, and dangerous areas around the sea ice camp. These were tied into color-coded bundles and loaded with the rest of the gear. Larger hardware items included gasoline-powered ice augers and ten jerry cans for storing fuel used for the snowmobiles and generators. Snow shovels, breaker bars for chipping ice, dip nets for clearing brash ice from the dive holes, and ice axes for testing the condition of the ground beneath us were indicators of the manual labor that lay ahead. Rather than wasting fuel to heat snow for drinking water, we filled a dozen large, heavy, plastic containers with water from the lab and transported them to our camp. Melted snow could be used in an emergency but had the aftertaste and grit of volcanic dust, a consequence of living downwind of Mount Erebus.

This and more had to be organized, counted, boxed, and secured with all of the scientific equipment at the lab. It took all team members, using the first week in Antarctica as a giant scavenger hunt, to pull together all of the elements for the expedition. Once gathered at the Crary lab, the entire operation had to be transported across the sea ice to the field camp when we decided on its exact location.

Years of planning followed by months of preparation had already gone into the expedition, making our team fidgety and anxious to get out on the ice. But there was one more requirement that had to be met. Before the team members were allowed to set off on our own, we had to complete a series of mandatory survival courses that were collectively called "Happy Camper School." The rule was the same whether you were on your first or your fortieth trip South. Established by the National Science Foundation, the courses were designed to keep the "beakers" (the cynical Station nickname for scientists) from hurting themselves. To our instructors we were liabilities with a college degree—geeky escapees from the laboratory who could find a hundred ways to get into trouble when left on our own in the wild.

Admittedly, this assessment of the scientists was not unjustified. The instructors had seen it all during the forty-two years that NSF had been supporting science in Antarctica. Accidents ranged from amusing to lethal. Countless scientists with egos larger than the tracks of their snowmobiles had tried to "jump" over huge crevasses, sometimes getting stuck, and sometimes sinking the machines and themselves. The walls of the Berg Field Center were adorned with destroyed pieces of machinery that had been inadvertently run over, unoiled, or otherwise abused in the cold by various scientific expeditions. Even our scientific group had added to the walls one year when a well-muscled graduate student managed to shatter a frozen one-inch-diameter iron pole, called a breaker bar, by jamming it with all of his might into the ice. Tents had burned and scientists had nearly asphyxiated themselves by using camp stoves to get warm. Ice axes, shovels, and clothing left lying on the ground were always disappearing in blowing snow—never to be seen again. Despite the apparent lack of common sense in some of these cases, the risky situations had less to do with the naïveté of the scientists and more to do with the compounding dangers of Antarctic conditions, remote locations, and large animal research.

Taking their lead from high school driver education classes, our Happy Camper instructors related sobering stories of lethal mistakes that had occurred on the ice. They began with Captain Robert Falcon Scott who, in March 1912, froze to death with four of his expedition members on the Ross Ice Shelf, only 170 miles from where we were sitting. Sadly, he and his colleagues had died less than eleven miles from One Ton Depot, their supply depot, on their return from the South Pole. Our instructors spoke of the research scuba diver who, in the 1980s, never resurfaced from below the sea ice, a victim of equipment failure and possibly panic in the frigid waters. They told the group about the biologist who had wedged his tracked vehicle into a wide crack on top of the ice near Turtle Rock just six miles from McMurdo. According to the story, his teammates jumped clear and escaped injury, while the biologist decided to retrieve his camera lying on the back seat. The ice gave way, trapping the biologist in the sinking vehicle. He never made it out.

The stories hit their intended mark with the entire team, but were especially poignant for Randy Davis, Bill Hagey, and myself. We had known members from both of the recent fatal expeditions. At the time Randy, Bill, and I had been working in and around Scripps Institution of Oceanography. It seemed as though many polar expeditions were tied to southern California at the time, and we had close personal friends on several different scientific parties in Antarctica. The first messages were cryptic, only relaying that something had gone wrong down South. It was a time before e-mail and satellite phones, when communication from the ice relied on the handwritten word and sporadic delivery by airplanes, ships, or ham radio operators. Following the accidents, details had come slowly and fragmented through gossip and radio. In both cases, we first heard that there had been a casualty on the ice, but no name had been provided. Several tension-filled days passed before we were able to find out whether or not it was one of our colleagues who would not be coming back. On both occasions our close-knit polar fraternity in San Diego had been rocked.

Our specific expedition plans did not make it any easier on the instructors. At one point during a classroom session the ice instructor simply rolled his eyes in despair after our team completed the assigned risk analysis form for our expedition.

"Sheesh, there's no hope for you guys," he concluded while he ran his fingers through hat-knotted hair. We would be working with chainsaws, heavy machinery, and wild seals that were five times larger than ourselves. To make matters worse, we would be in a remote field camp situated near an ice crack over a 500-meter (1,640-foot) deep ocean. The combined potential dangers even made the experienced instructor wince. There was no way to predict what would happen.

Here was the major difference between the historic expeditions of the Old Antarctic Explorers a century before us and our modern attempts. In the past, risk was accepted as a natural part of the adventure. Now every attempt was made to anticipate and prevent it. In the end it still came down to accepting that Antarctic exploration would challenge and could kill.

It took our team five days to organize camp gear and scientific equipment and get through the training. We were in constant motion. There were several sea ice sessions close to the Station that taught us how to identify old and new cracks, safe and unsafe cracks, growing cracks and healed cracks. Survival School was the most comprehensive class and included helicopter etiquette ("Keep your head low below the moving blades"); radio handling ("Keep spare batteries warm in your armpits"); weather predicting ("Find shelter immediately if White Island disappears"); and the basics of dealing with hypothermia, dehydration, and frostbite. The most important message was "Look out for your teammates." Intuition told us that this was critical, but the threat of cold injury added another dimension. Cold was a subtle killer. We learned that the signs of hypothermia and frostbite often went unnoticed and even denied by the victim. It would be up to each of us to monitor others for mood swings, irrational behavior, shivering, and skin discoloration—the early signs of a team member going down. More than one of my team members noted that, as a female, this was my normal emotional state, earning them a long, cold retaliatory stare.

To put our lessons into practice, an overnight polar pajama party followed the classroom sessions. We were given the standard survival gear, including packages of dehydrated food and a handheld radio for emergency calls, and then set outside McMurdo Station on the snow-covered ice. Depending on the team's level of energy, we had to choose between building an igloo (four to eight hours of work) or a snow mound (two to three hours of work). The team wisely went for the easier shelter, which still had an igloo feel to it once the pile of snow had been hollowed out. My opinion was that the more time that could be dedicated to food the better; the cold was already having a mounting effect on my appetite.

Dinner was basic: dehydrated fare warmed with melted snow from a single burner camp stove, followed by hot chocolate. We ate and drank hunkered down in the lee of a snowblock wall watching our shadows grow long in one of the last Antarctic sunsets. After dinner there was little to do except wait until morning for the instructors to return. Before the team had a chance to settle into the evening lull, Bill Hagey was up pacing and routing through his bags with nervous energy.

"I know. Let's play . . .," Bill announced to the group as he reached into his survival bag, ". . . Frisbee!" He proudly displayed the black plastic disk that he had hidden amongst his ECW gear.

Figuring that the exercise would keep us warm, most of the team gave it a try. We trudged in heavy bunny boots out onto a clear area on the ice. The first tenuous throws didn't require much movement other than standing and catching. The fun began when we grew overconfident and the wind started to pick up. Throws got higher and more erratic, causing us to trip over our boots and slide on bare patches of ice. Lee went for a high-flying catch, arching like a cat into the air. He landed on his feet while the rest of us rolled in a bundle on the snow.

Viewing each team member as an essential commodity, Randy warned the group to tone it down for fear of one of us getting injured before the field season had even started. Ignoring him, Bill tried a few diving catches until finally the Frisbee flew out of his reach. Caught on the freezing breeze the Frisbee landed with hard crunch on the ice. The air temperature had dipped so low that just a few minutes of air time was all that was needed to convert the plastic of the Frisbee into the consistency of glass. The fragile plastic shattered on impact, ending the game for the night. We headed back to Randy and the snow mound shaking our heads, incredulous over what the cold had done to our game. At the same time, Bill carefully retrieved the pieces of his Frisbee, confident that he had enough duct tape with his equipment to repair the toy for the rest of the expedition.

Exhausted, we immediately crawled into the claustrophobic interior of the snow mound and our sleeping bags. The team members spent the night lined up like matchsticks on the ice, each cradling a plastic bottle filled with hot water left over from the snowmelt used for preparing dinner. Whether it was the cooling of the hot water bottle, the seeping cold of the ice beneath, or the periodic rush of frigid air from the entryway of the snow mound, sleep occurred in short spurts interrupted by a losing battle over the desire to urinate. "Copious and clear" had revealed its unfortunate side. The official terminology according to the ice instructor was "cold induced dieresis," a condition in which the cooling body responded by contracting blood vessels, thereby altering pressure on the bladder. Shivering in the night, we didn't need medical jargon to recognize that being cold resulted in a crying need to pee. However, in an effort to avoid leaving the limited warmth of our sleeping bags or waking the rest of the team, we each tried to ignore the growing urge. To our dismay as we compared notes in the morning, the team realized that we should have all just gotten up. Each of us had been in the same urgent state throughout the long, long night.

In the morning we were rounded up by cheery, noticeably clean survival school instructors and brought back to the classroom.

"Well, I see you all survived, so I guess you not-so-Happy-Campers pass the course," the lead instructor quipped.

The team was too busy warming up by the preway stove to share in his good humor just yet. Unexpectedly, the tone of the instructor suddenly turned more formal.

"This exercise wasn't about getting a good night's sleep," he said seriously. "The point is now you know that you *can* survive a night on the ice if you ever needed to."

His message stuck. We had learned that a human could use snow and ice for insulation and for shelter from the heat-robbing wind. Our bodies could provide enough heat to remain warm if we kept them well fed and watered. The key to our survival was common sense, teamwork, and always knowing the location of our survival gear.

In the evenings and between classes, the expedition members strategized. The research we were planning had very specific ice requirements. We wanted to be in an area where Weddell seals would be able to hunt for fish. This meant placing the camp over water that was at least 200 to 500 meters (656 to 1,640 feet) in depth. The condition of the ice was another critical factor. It had to contain cracks large enough to allow the seals to breath and haul out, but couldn't be so thin or fractured that it would not support the weight of the camp. Long sessions were spent studying local maps. The permanent ice shelf offered stability but was so thick that we suspected that the under-ice surface was exceptionally dark: How would the hunting seals be able to see their prey? we wondered. Other areas were too thin or too close to traditional seal pupping and nursery areas. We did not want our research activities to interfere with new moms and their young. Instead, we were looking for areas where the bachelor males and single females tended to haul out.

The team selected several potential sites and then decided to split up into two survey parties. One group would conduct aerial surveys of McMurdo Sound via helicopter. The other would take to the sea ice on snowmobiles, crisscrossing the same area looking for cracks and seals and testing the thickness of the ice in several locations using a handheld auger.

We attended our last class, which ironically turned out to be driver's ed. We were taught the basics of cold-weather maintenance and mechanics for pickup trucks, snowmobiles, and bright orange tracked vehicles called Sprytes, which had the blocky shape of a Humvee. Once issued a McMurdo driver's license, we were free to begin our sea ice surveys. During the final lectures on antifreezes, fuels, and oils, I was as twitchy as a first grader watching the wall clock in anticipation of the recess bell. I wanted to *go outside*. I wanted to be in the company of the seals.

CHAPTER 5

WEDDELL
WORLD

October 7–10

A t midday the classes were finally completed. The two survey parties immediately set out on their assigned tasks. Randy, Lee,
Matt, and Jesse comprised the aerial survey group and headed to the
helicopter terminal to begin a general overview of the sea ice conditions from the sky. NSF maintained a fleet of small red-and-white helicopters for sea ice survey work, transporting people and equipment
over moderate distances around the island, and for search-and-rescue
operations. Wearing bowling ball–sized crash helmets equipped with
microphones, there was a definite feeling of impending thrill ride as
you approached the helos. Ascending from the helicopter pad immediately brought you eye to eye with the rumblings of Mount Erebus and
gave you a stunning perspective of Antarctica that Scott and
Shackleton never had the opportunity to appreciate.

Today it was snowmobiles, not helicopters, for me. On the ground the snowmobile team, consisting of Bill, Don, Marcus, and myself, bound down the hill by the Crary lab. We crossed the transition zone between the land and the sea ice and found four shining snowmobiles lined up on the ice fueled and ready to go. The heavy, bright-orange Alpine II Bombardiers were ours for the duration of the expedition, courtesy of the McMurdo Station machine shop. After considerable priming and wrenching on the starter cords to coax the cold machines to life, the four snowmobiles eventually roared in unison. Although we were sweating from the exertion, we bundled clothing even tighter. Every inch of skin had to be covered when we traveled on the snowmobiles for fear of frostbite from the wind chill. In addition to insulated underwear, fleece liners, wind pants, and parkas, we added neoprene face masks, ski goggles, wool hats, and two pairs of gloves—inner wool mittens and furry gauntlets called bear paws that covered our arms up to our elbows. After dressing it was impossible to differentiate who was who, except for Don Calkins. Even with all of the clothing there was no mistaking his build. In stature he resembled the grizzlies that lived in Alaska with him. The extra clothing only made him seem that much larger than the rest of us. As a longtime resident of the snow and ice, it was Don's knowledge of cold engines that helped us get the frozen snowmobiles started. Most of his instructions were conveyed by hand signals, since it was impossible to hear what he was saying through the sputtering machines and muffling face masks and scarves. Instead, we resorted to scuba diver signals and waited for a gloved "thumbs-up" from each team member before taking off across the ice.

Markus Horning, in keeping with his European upbringing, considered the ice an infinite autobahn and was the first out of the transition zone. Roaring off, he quickly disappeared in a cloud of snow. We each followed, forming a train of flying red parkas and kicked-up snow.

The freedom was intoxicating. As we rounded the corner of

the flagged route out of McMurdo Station, we could feel civilization slipping farther behind. We passed Hut Point where a wooden shelter used by Captain Scott to survive the winter of 1902 during his *Discovery* expedition still stood in defiance of the wind. After driving by the historic hut, there was nothing on our horizon that had been created by man. In front of us the sea ice stretched out in an endless white plain, natural and breathtakingly austere in its expansiveness. Only small, dark rocky islands in the far distance periodically broke up the flatness and the lack of color. From maps we knew that we could drive in a straight line north for at least fifty miles before reaching the ice edge and the open ocean, where penguins gathered and killer whales patrolled. In the far distance the Royal Society Range defined our movements to the west and marked the edge of the true Antarctic continent with jagged, wind-sharpened peaks that seemed to rise right out of the ocean. Shadows projected on the peak faces provided subtle changes in color as the sun moved during the course of the day. From the Crary lab windows we had watched the shadows in the early morning and evening when the mountains appeared soft in watercolor shades of pink and purple. In the harshness of midday, the same peaks were hardened into crystal blues contrasted by stark white. Glaciers slipping down between the peaks shimmered in the sunlight. From the sea ice, the range seemed deceivingly close in the clarity of the air; in reality it was over forty miles away and considerably outside our transect line for the day.

Markus led us around Arrival Heights, Hutton Cliffs, and towards the Erebus Glacier Ice Tongue. We skirted around the edge of Ross Island and were soon facing the base of Mount Erebus. Rising over 12,450 feet into the clear Antarctic sky, the volcano was unusually quiet, with only a periodic puff of white smoke rising from the center of the cone to remind us that the peak was scorched and roiling inside.

As we raced along, the character of the sea ice changed, its surface dictated by the prevailing winds. Outside of McMurdo Station we had been able to travel quickly and smoothly over the surface. The only danger was in hitting chunks of sea ice that had been frozen upended in the wake of the ice-breaking supply ships that had visited the station nine months earlier. This was the first time that we had seen the tracks of the icebreakers; in normal years the ice we were traveling on broke out during the winter storms and was replaced by a new, smooth, frozen sea. As we dodged ice blocks that were sometimes three feet high, we realized that the iceberg B-15 had created the obstacle course by preventing the annual winter sea-ice breakout. As we had anticipated from the satellite images viewed at home, we were traveling on the ragged remains of at least two years of frozen seawater accumulation instead of new ice.

Once in the lee of Ross Island, sastrugi dominated. These are ridges of snow scoured out by the wind that were just high enough to catch the front ski of our snowmobiles. There were two methods of trying to move through the sastrugi: either drive as fast as you could in the hopes of skimming across the snow tops, or go painstaking slow, methodically following each upside and downside of the ridges in a seasick rolling motion. We tried them both with only moderate, bone-jarring, stomach-churning success.

As the four of us slowly picked our way along the ice and snow we felt the rumbling of rotors overhead. It was the NSF helicopter with the other half of our team thundering past and whipping a new flurry of snow in its wash. At that moment, as I watched them float effortlessly out of sight, I wondered if they had chosen the wiser mode of travel.

Markus, Don, Bill, and I continued on for another hour and finally called it a day when the sweat generated from controlling the jolting, heavy snowmobiles began to chill our skin. As we turned around the wind that had been at our backs now hit us directly in the face. The wind carried wisps of fine, blowing ground snow, and we reflexively bent down as low as possible behind the windshields of our snowmobiles. To keep our faces from freezing, we pulled the fur-lined hood of our parkas closer to our cheeks. The ruff of fur stuck to our goggles, making it nearly impossible to see the rider in front of us. Worried that we would be separated in the blowing snow, the three of us shadowed Markus's path with the intensity of ducklings tailing their mom. Once out of the sastrugi, we quickly made up time and were able to reach McMurdo Station before the sun sunk as a rosy orange glow behind the Royal Society Mountain Range.

One major concern nagged us as we trudged up the hill back to the Crary lab: we had failed to find even one Weddell seal during the entire time we were on the ice.

That evening our report to the team was minimal—the sea ice was extremely tight, with few cracks observed along the entire transect. We had not encountered one Weddell seal. The news from the helicopter party was equally disappointing. Before they had even left the ground, they had been informed of the unusual ice conditions. When Randy had discussed their flight plan with the pilot, he had laughed out loud, saying, "There isn't a crack in all of McMurdo Sound, but we can certainly go for a ride."

Unfortunately the pilot's evaluation was accurate. The impact of B-15 was becoming more and more obvious to our team. McMurdo Sound was completely choked off with ice that had been trapped around Ross Island by the giant iceberg. Without cracks in the ice, there were no breathing holes. With no breathing holes there was no place for Weddell seals to surface, and with no seals there would be no expedition.

Two-year-old, solid sea ice created a nearly insurmountable obstacle for the seals. They need to follow a dot-to-dot line of breathing holes in the ice during their journey from the open sea to their favorite haul-out and breeding grounds in McMurdo Sound. As they enter the waters of the Sound, they take advantage of any weakness in the ice, thrusting their muzzles into cracks, snow bridges, open leads, and coastal tidal breaks that can provide a welcome breath of air. Calculations based on a Weddell's swimming speed and oxygen reserves had shown that the seals can travel for only four miles in a straight line under the ice before they have to surface to breathe. A cautious seal would travel only two miles under solid ice before turning around for the two-mile swim back to catch a much-needed breath of air. Like the National Guard pilots weighing their options heading to McMurdo, better to boomerang and try the next day than to run out of fuel.

That night our team went back to studying the maps. Our original plan was to work by one of several small crack systems that usually formed in the middle of McMurdo Sound. With B-15 wedged between the ice of the Sound and the open ocean, it was now apparent that the smaller cracks were not going to form this year. We tentatively looked at the historical larger crack systems that eventually grew into wide-open leads. These areas were considerably more dangerous due to the unpredictable nature and size of the gaps in the fracturing ice. They were the types of cracks that could swallow a man, a Spryte, or a snowmobile, and propel them to the bottom of the ocean. Maps could only indicate the general placement of past fracturing and open leads in the ice; it would take several snowmobile transects and aerial surveys to determine their exact location this year.

Shear forces created by ocean currents sweeping around the edges of Ross Island and the small rocky outcroppings in McMurdo Sound were responsible for tearing open leads in the sea ice. The larger leads or crack systems usually occurred near Arrival Heights, Turtle Rock, Cinder Cones, Tent and Inaccessible Islands, and the edges of the Erebus Glacier Ice Tongue. Weddell seals starving for a breath of air as they made their way beneath the ice sheet to the breeding sites sought out the deformities in the ice. For at least a century since man had ventured to this side of Antarctica, the jagged coasts of the outcroppings have been known to provide an escape route for the seals. Early explorers had used this knowledge to their advantage to hunt for Weddells, for meat, hides, and blubber. We decided to use the same strategy to locate the animals for our studies. The best chance for finding seals this year would be in the historically unstable areas. Any seal that succeeded in navigating beneath the ice sheet and into the Sound would have to surface somewhere near one of the major crack systems.

After polling the entire team, a revised plan was agreed upon. Then it was back to the helicopters and snowmobiles. For the next several days our two survey teams systematically mapped the ice cracks and pressure ridges around the western coast of Ross Island. The snowmobile team spent most of its time weaving in and out of sastrugi. Hand-drawn maps indicating areas of unstable ice from the previous year were pulled from the pockets of our parkas and inspected every mile or so. Even the largest gaps were completely drifted over by snow bridges and nearly invisible to us. We were navigating by feel. Often only a slight depression in the snow gave away the position of a sizable crack in the sea ice beneath. Flat white light in the afternoons often made it difficult to detect any ground relief, and there were times when the front snowmobile would cross a snow bridge, shatter it under the weight, and force the next person in line to quickly pull up. When we suspected a frozen lead, ice axes were used to cut away the snow bridges and determine the edges. These were then followed lengthwise for miles. What began as an old break in the ice usually shrunk to hairline fractures that eventually disappeared altogether.

After four more days of backbreaking snowmobiling, Markus, Bill, Don, and I finally came upon an open fissure that meandered towards the edge of a glacier that slid down the side of Mount Erebus. Appropriately named the Erebus Glacier Ice Tongue, it gradually rose to three stories above us as we traveled along its length. The tip of the tongue was marked with an icefall where sections of the glacier shattered and fell onto the sea ice. While gravity forced the glacier down, friction from the sea ice stalled its progression. The sea ice eventually surrendered to the strain of the competing physical forces by breaking into a series of cracks. One of the largest led southwest from the side of the glacier and into McMurdo Sound for several miles.

To Weddell seals, the highly active ice movement meant welcome breathing holes and a chance to haul out of the water. Around the corner of the ice tongue we finally saw what we had spent over a week searching for—Weddell seals. Motionless and snow-drifted, the seals looked like large gray rocks thrown carelessly out into the middle of the sea ice. If it weren't for the fact that the rocks had not been there the first time we passed by, we would not have given them a second glance.

Before we had a chance to get closer, the helicopter team circled above us and landed behind one of the ridges of the glacier. Responding to their hand signals, we raced our snowmobiles towards them.

As the glacier groaned ominously in the background the team discussed its options. After a week of aerial and ground surveys, these were the first seals we had seen. By this time there should have been hundreds of seals scattered around ice cracks all over McMurdo Sound. Instead, only the largest of cracks had begun to form, and the few seals that had made it into the Sound had been forced to haul out before reaching traditional breeding sites. Most of the seals were missing altogether.

The helicopter team reported that B-15 had caused the ice edge to grow and shift nearly thirty miles farther out. This meant thirty more miles of solid ice between the open water and the seals' breeding sites in McMurdo Sound, an impossible distance for the animals to travel underwater. How these few seals had made it to the side of glacier was nothing short of miraculous. Either by inchworming awkwardly over the ice or by finding small pockets of air below, they had made it more than halfway. The movements of the glacier had created the first sizable opening in the ice sheet, allowing the Weddell seals to haul out and rest. Having made it this far, the sleeping seals appeared reluctant to leave. Unexpectedly, this peculiar exposed piece of sea ice, with wind and snow drifting off of Ross Island, was the only site for the returning seals to gather.

The question we faced was whether or not to risk placing our camp in an area of such active ice movement. We could wait to build the camp in a more stable location that historically had larger numbers of Weddell seals, pinning our hopes on a big crack that might open up later in the season. Alternatively, we could change our plans, move to this new location where a few seals had already hauled out, and take our chances with a glacier in the backyard. After much boot shuffling in the snow, the team finally agreed that one more piece of information was needed before we planted our flag. We needed to know the gender of the seals that had hauled out. If they were pregnant females, then we would designate the crack as a nursery area and we would have to find another location. If they were males or nonpregnant females, then we would call the area a seal haulout and build our camp nearby.

Randy and I volunteered to conduct the delicate procedure of determining whether the seals were boys or girls. Taking two of the snowmobiles, we headed back to the crack area. The seals were sleeping so soundly that even the rumble of our snowmobiles did not disturb them. Only when the machines were turned off and we walked close by did the sound of our boots scrunching on the snow vibrate in their pinhole ears as they lay on the ice. The closest seal woke up with a start and rolled over on its back with all four flippers stretched out in total surprise. Snorting at the intrusion and watching us intently with large, wet brown eyes, the seal kept its back away from us. Its breath frosted the air but the animal made no sound. There were no aggressive moves toward us, no sign of fear. Instead the seal just wanted to get on with the business of its nap.

Determining the gender of a Weddell seal is a subtle art. Both sexes are equally rotund and are similar in body length and width. Except for a subjective "maleness" around the muzzle and shoulders, as well as an attitude, there is little way to tell them apart, rather like our team in thick parkas and heavy boots. In contrast to most other mammals, all of the external anatomy that is usually attributed to males—the penis, testes, and scrotal sacs—are internalized in the seal. The advantages for Antarctic living are obvious. Such an anatomical location avoids exposure of these sensitive parts to the sharp ice and freezing water temperatures and enable the seals to maintain a sleek, hydrodynamic profile. The disadvantage is for scientists trying to differentiate between who is male and who is female. However, the belly of the seal presented one clear giveaway.

From the seal's startled position, it was easy to get a good look at its underside.

"Boy?" Randy suggested.

"Definitely boy!" I responded.

There was the distinct indent of the belly button in the middle of the seal's rolling abdomen. And below that, among the splotches of white and black fur, was another indentation. More defined than the belly button, the dent was the opening for the seal's internal penis. There was no mistaking that the nine-foot-long, open-mouthed seal that sprawled in front of us was male, confirmed by the tell-tale location of a yellow spot in the snow. Had the seal been female the urine trail would have started between the two hind flippers, just beneath her stubby tail.

Careful inspection of the bellies of the remaining seals revealed five males and two nonpregnant females. As we turned to leave, a new arrival poked its head through the slush of the ice crack. The fur on the wet seal's petite head was slicked back and dark. On raising its body high out of the water, the seal revealed a beautiful silvery chest covered with delicate white spots. The small muzzle and upturned mouth were so feminine that I instantly decided that the arrival was female. She had two features that distinguished her from all of the other seals. First, her whiskers were extraordinarily long, dark, and straight. I had once been told that marine mammal whiskers were long ago prized in Asia for cleaning opium pipes. The whiskers of this seal would have done a superb job. The second unusual feature was her wink. Rather than glare at us wide-eyed, as did most seals, the wet seal cocked her head, watching me with her right eye while winking with the left. The look was unexpectedly charming and gave the impression of untold secrets.

The report to the rest of the team waiting by the helicopter was all positive. We had found our home on the ice. After digging through the snow and drilling down through the ice with a two-inch-wide auger, we chose a site a quarter of a mile from the active crack and the seals. A bright orange flag tied to a bamboo pole drilled into the ice marked our campsite.

Camp construction began the next day with the drilling of a four-foot-diameter hole through the sea ice. Lumbering slowly across the ice, a giant auger from McMurdo Station was driven to the campsite and used to create the hole. Although the glacier had thinned the ice in the area, it was still over seven feet thick, making the job of digging out a dive hole impossible to do by hand. Amazing as it seemed now, Antarctic scientists were once issued their own dynamite to blast through the ice with a resounding, splashing "bang." These days it was simply a matter of a radio call into McMurdo Station and a somewhat less spectacular process. The immense auger was able to punch through to the water below in less than ten minutes, making a hole just big enough for a Weddell seal to squeeze its body through. Over the next few months, the diving seals would have free access to the hole for resting and breathing during our experiments.

The presence of the dive hole resulted in a new milestone for the expedition; it was the beginning of camp duties. With the extreme cold temperatures of October, the hole was in constant danger of freezing shut. If left overnight, the ice would be so solid that we would have to re-drill the hole and start from the beginning. To prevent that from happening, our team began the endless, muscle-straining job of dip netting. Small crystals called brash ice, which broke off from the underside of the sea ice, created a slurry and continuously seeded the hole made by the auger. We used fine mesh fishnets on long wooden poles to scoop out the ice crystals before they froze together and once again closed the hole. Taking turns, we scooped ice and seawater until our hands blistered and our backs ached, creating an enormous slush pile on the sea ice.

As we worked with the dip nets a team of carpenters and electricians from McMurdo began to build the camp around us. This would be no ordinary camp. Because our experiments relied on the newest miniaturized microprocessors and video technology, as well as satellite tracking capabilities, we needed a secure shelter and the ability to communicate from a remote field site. Instead of traditional expedition tents and wooden fishing huts, we opted for an alternative suggested by NSF, the Jamesway hut. A remnant of the U.S. military period in Antarctica, the soft-sided Jamesway came in four-foot-wide, arched sections made of insulated blankets tacked to wooden ribbing connected to a plywood floor. We linked thirty-two of these sections to create a 128-foot-long structure. Like the C-141 aircraft, Jamesways were the workhorse of the military. The crates containing the sections were marked as vintage 1951 Korean War shelters and proved that the units were as capable in the jungle as they were on the ice.

During construction the wooden ribs of the Jamesway had the skeletal appearance of a beached whale. Military drab-green insulated blankets were laid over the ribbing like sheets of blubber, which added to the leviathan feeling. The interior was as long as a bowling alley until wooden partitions subdivided the structure into a field laboratory, sleeping dormitory, and kitchen. Randy Davis, with the help of his architect father, had designed the interior workings of the structure, and it far exceeded anything ever dreamed of by the early Antarctic explorers. The east end of the building began with an outdoor weighing station connected by a chute to double doors. On the other side was the cold room where we would work with the Weddell seals. The floor in this room was removable and revealed the drilled diving hole beneath. One false step could send a person into seawater that extended over 200 meters (656 feet) below. A wooden partition with a door connected the cold room with the main laboratory, where all of us had separate stations. My physiological instrumentation was placed in one corner, Bill and Markus had an area for electronics, Lee manned the main computer data analysis station, and Randy had an entire corner for the video gear. Several additional computer stations for Matt, Jesse, and Don connected us to GPS tracking satellites and e-mail. Between the eight members of the expedition, we would have twelve desktop computers and laptops running simultaneously in the laboratory.

Additional partitions separated the work areas from the kitchen and sleeping quarters on the west end of the Jamesway. Two other buildings completed the camp: the compass calibration hut and the outhouse. These were modified fish huts made of plywood backed by thick pieces of insulating foam between the walls. Each hut was prefabricated in McMurdo Station and then towed on metal skis out to camp. In comparison to our previous expeditions, we enjoyed the luxury provided by such amenities as an outhouse with a Styrofoam insulated seat and a wooden magazine rack. We had only two magazines: a worn *National Geographic* about travels in Bali and a copy of *Texas Monthly* focusing on George Bush. Given the chilliness of the situation, neither got much reading during the season.

Over the next several days a team of four carpenters and two electricians from McMurdo labored on the camp. A gasoline-powered generator initially provided electricity for all of our instrumentation, computers, and bare overhead lightbulbs. Solar panels and a wind generator would be added later. Preway stoves fueled by diesel provided warmth for the laboratory and kitchen, and, we soon discovered, also made excellent tortilla warmers. With two propane camp stoves, a pantry of dried goods, and several coolers filled with frozen meats buried in the snowdrift next to the Jamesway, the kitchen was well stocked. The only excuse for going back to McMurdo Station would be to resupply food, water, and fuel.

To gain a better vantage point on the location of our camp and to map out the route for a flagged road that would connect our camp to McMurdo Station, we scheduled another helicopter flight. From the air the camp seemed precariously balanced on the edge of the sea ice, Ross Island, an active volcano, and a glacier. Ten miles to the north an Adelie penguin rookery at Cape Royds was beginning to fill with the raucous black-and-white birds. There was an equal distance of rough sea ice and sastrugi between our camp and McMurdo. In our backyard was the Erebus Glacier Ice Tongue—huge, blue, and riddled with crevasses. To our east was Ross Island, with Mount Erebus chuffing gray steam into the sky. Far to the west the Royal Society Range delineated the Antarctic continent and provided a stunning palette of watercolors as the sun drifted across its face. We could not have asked for a more spectacular setting. Yet between the shifting ice of the glacier and the rumblings of the volcano, the team had an uneasy feeling about the long-term prospects of the campsite. Of all of the places in the Sound to establish a camp, this had to be the most unstable. Any one of a number of geological formations had the power to splinter the sea ice and shake the campsite to its foundation.

The perspective provided by the helicopter also added to our feeling of isolation and vulnerability. There was little doubt that our camp was truly adrift on a frozen ocean. Tent Island, Inaccessible Island, and Big and Little Razorback Islands loomed in the distant north as dark, rocky reminders of land versus sea. Our camp was just another dark body floating on the ice.

When the helicopter finally turned past the corner of the glacier, we were reminded of the primary reason we had chosen this site. Five Weddell seals were hauled out on the ice next to a single growing crack that had formed on the south side of the glacier. Representing the only breathing access for miles around, the crack was the only place where Weddell seals could catch their breath as they journeyed beneath the solid sheet of sea ice. These were the only seals to make it into the entire frozen Sound, an area of over

1,000 square miles that should have been home to hundreds of their relatives. By luck and hard work, these intrepid seals were within walking distance of our front door.

With confidence, we christened our new home, "Weddell World."

CHAPTER 6

SEALS AND SCIENTISTS ON ICE

October 11–14

Mid-October unleashed the worst of Antarctica's impulsive temperament. Crystal-clear days pitched temperatures into the minus column, only to be interrupted by dark, fast-moving storms heralded by severe winds that blew snow for hundreds of miles. Through it all our team tried to outrun the storms and shuttle equipment, food, and scientific gear from McMurdo Station to Weddell World. Each morning we called into Mac Weather to get the latest report for conditions on the ice. After hearing the official report, we would then climb to the second story of the Crary lab and use binoculars from the vantage point of the roof to look out across the frozen sea towards our camp. Despite clear conditions in McMurdo, the blurred outline of the Royal Society Range often indicated blowing snow and low visibility on the sea ice next to

Ross Island. Venturing out in snowmobiles was too dangerous under these conditions. We would have quickly been enveloped in the snow and unable to follow our flagged route back to camp. Handheld GPS units served as a guide, but the scarcity of overhead satellite hits in Antarctica and the battery-draining cold often made the units unreliable, especially under whiteout conditions.

The coldest days were often the clearest, calmest, and most hazardous in terms of travel. On those days the stillness of the air was mimicked by the inactivity of machines and people. Nothing moved outdoors, creating the same muffled quiescence that descends with a fresh blanket of snow. It seemed as though everything in McMurdo Station had been frozen in place, including our expedition. As temperatures dipped below –57°C (-70°F), the C-141s in the airport were grounded and the station manager called to inform us, "We have a Condition 1 out there. All travel out of town is denied."

The order was difficult for the team to take because of the deceptively clear conditions. In terms of visibility and the low threat of windblown snow, it was the perfect time to travel across the ice with our equipment. But the gears and lubricating oils of machines strain to work under such extreme temperatures, and human flesh is not built to withstand the exposure. Working with the fuel for the machines was particularly dangerous. A drop of gasoline splattered from the jerry cans as we refueled the snowmobiles caused instant frostbite on the skin. Touching anything metal became a hazard. Cameras froze to our fingers, sunglasses used to protect our eyes from snow blindness froze to the bridge of our noses, and earrings in pierced ears and metal jewelry in other pierced body parts soon turned into a liability as metal touching skin immediately adhered.

Bill Hagey, always the hyperactive engineer, soon grew bored with the delay and decided to test just how cold it was. He poured himself a cup of coffee and then headed outdoors while we watched from behind. Before we knew what he was doing, Bill tossed the contents of the cup high into the air. To both his and our amazement, the drops of coffee froze before they even hit the ground, scattering at Bill's feet. "Now that *is* cold!" Bill concluded, and we wisely followed station orders to stay put.

The chill also had a noticeable effect on the behavior of the Weddell seals. When the sun was high in the sky, the seals hauled out and looked like great sausages lying on the ice, soaking up the warmth. We would pass the sunbathing animals dozing next to the glacier ice crack, jealous of their relaxed state as we shuttled loads of equipment to Weddell World. However, if the sun disappeared behind clouds, if the wind kicked up, or if air temperatures dipped below –50°C (-58°F) then even the blubbery seals could not take the cold. Wind chill, snowstorms, and bitter cold sent the big male, the winking long-whiskered female, and the other seals back into the water. Only their black, leathery slit noses periodically poked out of muzzle-sized holes in the ice to breathe.

The submerged seals were impossible to detect, except for their steamy breath. Each exhalation gave away their position as rising geysers of hot air condensed in loud chuffs. It was the only way to determine if seals were still in the area.

As incongruous as it initially seemed to me, the seals obviously preferred the slushy, still seas below when the weather turned foul above. Once I considered the alternatives, the seals' behavior began to make sense. The coldest seawater only reached -3°C (27°F) in McMurdo Sound; otherwise, it turned into ice. Faced with skin-freezing wind chill and erratic blizzards that made the air feel twenty times colder than the water, the seals sought the predictable temperatures of the calm water below the ice. Egocentric thinking had lulled me into assuming that life was easier out of water. For Weddell seals, nothing could be further from the truth. Food, shelter, and sex were all found below the ice. The water was where they belonged, with only the sun, the rising temperatures of summer, and the chance to lounge peaceably enticing the seals out. It was the need to breathe that connected the seal's submerged world with ours.

The breathing holes that served as that connection were also a mystery to Jesse. He did not understand how the seals' four-inch-wide breathing holes stayed open in the freezing cold. Our entire team had to constantly fend off intruding ice in the four-foot-diameter diving hole that we had drilled in camp, chipping away at its growing edges and dip netting tons of brash ice to prevent the hole from freezing shut. How did the seals keep from being trapped below?

Their secret was revealed one day when Jesse and I took a break from dip netting and stood next to one of the chuffing breathing geysers in the ice. Nostrils appeared, exhaled, inhaled, and then sunk out of sight. As we waited for the seal to return we suddenly felt the ice beneath our boots begin to vibrate. The water in the breathing hole soon churned as the noise grew louder and more frantic. Eventually the muzzle of one of the male seals emerged through the icy slush, swinging from side to side like the head of an angry bull. Stopping to take a quick breath of air, the seal twisted its head back and forth and scraped its front teeth around the perimeter of the tiny breathing hole. By using its huge, protruding front teeth like the prongs of a steel rake, the seal methodically scraped ice from the sides of the hole in a behavior termed reaming. In just a few minutes he had carved the nose-sized hole into an opening big enough to get his entire head through. In time the seal would ream a hole large enough to wedge his body out of the water.

The advantage is provided by the seals' canine teeth. Unlike temperate or tropical species of seals, Weddell seals are exquisitely designed for dealing with ice. Large, reinforced canine teeth stick out and give the skull of the Weddell seal a bucktooth appearance. These unusual teeth represent an important anatomical boost that allows the Weddell seal to be the only marine mammal capable of over wintering in McMurdo Sound. Without these teeth, Weddell seals would eventually drown as Antarctic temperatures entrapped them below the growing ice without a way to breathe. By reaming, the seals can keep a breathing hole open in the ice indefinitely. No other seal or whale is capable of this; unlike the Weddells, they are forced to leave the deep polar regions as winter descends.

A downside tempers the advantage provided by specialized dentition and results in an Achilles' heel for the Weddell seal. Years of tooth scraping on ice, especially during the long winter months, eventually erodes the front teeth. Dental pathologies are common among Weddells. As a result, despite relative freedom from predators, Weddell seals are not especially long-lived. The maximum known age of a Weddell seal is only twenty-two years.

Jesse and I stood on the ice watching the reaming seal with a combination of admiration and envy. Back at camp we had the neverending, muscle-aching job of chipping and dip netting the shrinking dive hole waiting for us. It would take the team hours to accomplish what the reaming seal was able to do in minutes.

CONDITION 1 shouted the message posted in bold letters on the door. It was no use pushing on the metal latch. We were going nowhere.

While the team was in town for supplies, the winds had begun to pick up and the station manager immediately issued the Condition 1. Our expedition was officially grounded. In the Antarctic, weather is classified as Condition 3 when visibility and temperatures permitted work outdoors, Condition 2 when the weather is marginal, and Condition 1 when temperatures or visibility are so low that working outdoors is deemed hazardous. Although it was summer in the southern hemisphere, the high temperature in our corner of Antarctica was -20°C (-4°F) and the low was -27°C (-17°F). With the blowing winds, the wind chill made it feel like -57°C (-70°F) on our skin. Outdoor temperatures were effectively three times colder than the freezers in the lab.

Condition 1 stopped all outdoor activity, including walking between buildings. Severe wind chill, coupled with low visibility from the blowing snow, markedly increased the risk of getting lost even within the perimeter of the Station. The word had gone out in a series of emergency phone calls and hand-scrawled signs posted on all of the exit doors—we were confined to our immediate quarters. Instructors from Happy Camper Survival School strung colorful, braided climbing ropes that strained on bamboo poles between some of the major buildings; these lifelines were the only way to keep from being knocked off your feet or disoriented in the blowing snow if you had to get to another place.

Members from several scientific expeditions including ours were stuck in town, unable to get back out onto the ice. We huddled in a makeshift coffeehouse/pub in McMurdo and used the time to compare notes about the location of major and minor ice cracks, the condition of the seals and penguins, and living arrangements out in the camps. As the wind howled all around us, we knew better than to even open a door. Bill, of course, had to try it at least once and was greeted with a roar of fine snow and frozen eyebrows. In the face of an Antarctic storm, the wiser course was almost always to stay put.

Underestimating the severity of the wind and the speed of the storms as they rumbled across the sea ice was a common mistake for expeditions, especially during their first year on the ice. Often the mistake brought you a little too close to the final edge, and the ensuing adrenaline rush served as a life lesson that was rarely forgotten. These were the stories of Old Antarctic Explorers recounted over pints of beer and mugs of hot coffee, and if you were one of the lucky ones you lived to tell the tale.

As we weathered out the Condition 1 in the warmth of an overheated small hut, the grounded scientists began to tell the tales of past lessons at the hands of nature in Antarctica. Allen, a colleague we had known for over twenty years, offered his tale. In one of his first seasons on the ice he had decided to take a snowmobile out for a "quick," thirty-minute jaunt from McMurdo Station to his field camp on the sea ice. It was a pleasant, calm evening, so he decided to travel light and alone. Traveling alone on the sea ice was dangerous enough, but his other decision was a near fatal error. He left with only the clothes on his back and without his survival gear or a radio. With handheld radios in short supply that year, it had turned out that the few units issued to his expedition party were all back in his field camp.

White Island and Black Island were to his back as Allen sped across the ice, so he had not seen the signs of the impending storm. By the time he realized his mistake, it was too late. The swiftly moving storm hit him from behind. His tracks back to McMurdo Station were already erased in the swirling snow, and his field camp was too far off to see. Without a radio there was no way to call for help or to let his colleagues in camp know where he was. Stuck in a total whiteout, his visibility was cut to zero. Disoriented in the moving snow, there was no up or down, no right or left. He could not detect a horizon, which created a mirage effect that made small nearby mounds of snow appear as giant distant mountains.

"I knew that if I kept moving it would only compound my isolation. I also realized that there was the real danger of driving into a snow-bridged crack in the ice. Honestly, I couldn't see my boots, much less a crack in the ice," Allen told the group as they listened to his story without a sound.

Realizing that his team members would eventually inform the radio operators in McMurdo Station of his disappearance, Allen stopped the snowmobile and did the one thing that would save his life: he stayed put. Without a tent or shovel for building a shelter, Allen used the only materials at hand. Like a cowboy seeking protection from his faithful horse, he huddled beside his snowmobile in the lee of the prevailing wind. Keeping his wits about him, he used the canvas snowmobile cover as a makeshift tent and tried to weather out the storm as best he could.

"It was definitely cold, but the real scare was in the reoccurring thought that I just would not make it out this time," Allen said quietly.

"That was the real trick in surviving—fighting to stay calm."

The wind and blowing snow roared around Allen throughout the night. He fought off hypothermia and his destructive fears by forcing himself to think rationally. As he shivered through the early morning hours, the search-and-rescue (SAR) team in McMurdo mobilized. By morning the storm had subsided, leaving the area coated in new blanket of drifted snow. A SAR helicopter was deployed, and the search for Allen was on. Rumors spread fast through the small, tight community of the station—everyone was on alert with the knowledge that a colleague was missing.

The sea ice was coated in white, providing no visual relief for the rescue team. As far as they could see, there was no trace of the bright orange snowmobile or Allen's red parka; no sign that he was anywhere on the ice. His snowmobile tracks had disappeared in the storm, so they had no idea of the direction he had taken. The only visible life was an emperor penguin that had sidled up against a snow mound for protection from the wind. By SAR intuition, the helicopter team made a pass over the stoic penguin to get a closer look. In an instant they realized that the snow mound was Allen's makeshift shelter under the snowmobile cover. Shaken by the thudding of the helicopter rotor overhead, Allen emerged from his drifted-over shelter—cold, hungry, and surprised to see the emperor penguin next to him.

Years later, with a mug of coffee to his lips, Allen laughed about the day that an emperor penguin saved his life.

"I guess it is only right that I finally do something for them," he mused. True to his word, Allen and his colleagues now spent their time working on the biology and conservation of emperor penguin colonies in the Antarctic. Since the blizzard incident, he had returned to the Antarctic almost annually, a bit older and wiser with each passing year.

Allen's tale was only one of the close calls we heard about that evening. Each scientist in the room had at least one event that had forged a new respect for Antarctica's brutal side. Every expedition had an element of risk associated with it, and often it was only a matter of luck when it came to escaping the fatal edge. Whether it was narcissistic drive, foolhardiness, heroics, or the simple joy of adventure, you had to respect the spirit of the men and women who were willing to risk flirting with nature for the sake of scientific discovery.

While the winds continued to batter the sides of the building, I was coerced into adding my near-miss story to the group. It was our team's first season on the sea ice, and it had been particularly challenging as storm after storm hit our camp. Inadvertently, we had selected a campsite in a location that had been nicknamed "Herbie Alley" by the helicopter pilots. "Herbie" was a term left over from the Navy days in Antarctica and was shorthand for hurricane-force blizzard. Katabatic winds screamed between Black and White Islands to our south and picked up speed as they crossed the open sea ice. Herbies comprised of these wild winds and blowing snow roared through, with our camp acting as the only wind block in their path. It would be another eighty miles before the storms hit the open ocean and slowed. Our poor choice in geographical location combined with another bad decision—we had decided to test out several new types of temporary shelters. Rather than traditional wooden huts, which were cramped for even two people, we tried a small, soft-sided Jamesway for our laboratory and a plastic-and-aluminum temporary building called a Weatherport for the bunkhouse. The kitchen and the outhouse were the only hard-sided, solid standing buildings in camp.

Because it was our first season, no one was exactly sure how to place the insulated blankets of the Jamesway on the wooden ribs. There had also been lively discussions about which way to face the structure on the ice. The final decision had been to face the short end of the Jamesway into the prevailing wind. Although it was not a particularly aerodynamic placement, it meant that only one end would bear the brunt of the storms. The other end would provide a sheltered doorway and theoretically would be scoured out by the winds blowing down the long sides of the building. The benefit was that at least one door would remain snow free.

"The team had just finished moving all of the computers and

scientific instrumentation into the Jamesway when that first Herbie hit," I said. "After setting up a barometer, I didn't believe it when the brass needle indicating barometric pressure dropped in front of my eyes. I've never seen such low pressures, and in all of the years that I've owned the instrument I have never actually seen the needle move!" As I spoke to the close circle of friends, the current storm emphasized my point by banging along the outside of the building.

The needle of the barometer seemed to act like a dial, slowly cranking up the fierceness of the winds hitting our camp as it dropped. Outside the winds began to roar, shaking the blankets of the Jamesway roof and walls. The electrical wires connecting the generators to the camp began to hum in a pitch that was tuned to the intensity of the wind.

"The Herbie gathered strength and the pitch grew higher and higher, causing the hairs to stand up on the backs of our necks," I continued.

For safety we decided to keep the entire team in the Jamesway. We huddled on cold, metal folding chairs, with little to do other than listen to the shivering walls. The pounding of the wind on the building and the banging of the metal stovepipe connected to the preway stove made reading impossible.

To take our mind off of the weather, we took advantage of all of the video equipment required for the seal instruments and used one of the VCRs to play a movie. We tried to sit still, but the sound outdoors was more entertaining and terrifying than anything on the television. The best that we could generate was subdued, nervous laughter. With every gust of wind and snap of the insulated blankets we each looked upward, wide-eyed and wondering if the structure was going to continue to hold up to the abuse. As if to answer the question that was on all of our minds, a blast of wind finally peeled back the edge of one of the blankets, releasing a jet of snow into the room. We noticed small rips in the fabric and realized that the insulated blankets were beginning to tear away from the nails that were holding them to the wooden ribbing. This was the unfortunate consequence of orienting the building into the wind. With each violent gust, larger and larger holes were being opened in the roof as the insulated blankets rolled back. Fine snow began to drift down all around us. Suddenly we were all overcome with a sickening feeling of vulnerability. The Jamesway was not going to make it through the storm if we didn't act fast.

The team quickly considered its options. Safety was paramount, and we had to make sure that each of the team members could reach the other buildings in the camp. Before we could do anything we had to secure the scientific equipment and instruments. If they were destroyed, then the expedition would immediately fail. There were eight expedition members in the Jamesway, so we divided into four groups comprised of two partners each. We quickly shoved the scientific instruments back into wooden packing crates to protect them. One graduate student headed outdoors. Struggling against the blowing snow, he climbed onto the roof of the Jamesway to try to hammer down the blankets from the outside. Meanwhile, inside the building, the rest of us grabbed bags of wood screws and screwdrivers to try to reattach the blankets to the dry, old wood ribbing.

Neither group made much progress against the relentless Herbie. On the roof the graduate student couldn't get a grip on the hammer. Each time he raised the tool over his head to bang down a nail, his hand was thrown backwards by the wind. He hunkered down next to the roof trying to tap in the nails. Without the leverage to swing the hammer, he was unable to pound in even one. Inside the Jamesway the force of the wind was too strong and kept snapping the blankets out of our freezing hands before we could get the screws started in the wood.

The situation rapidly grew desperate as the building began to tear apart at the seams and the Herbie showed no signs of letting up. Looking for another solution, we tore into every box in the building to find anything that could be used. A large cardboard box that had Tools scrawled on the side was filled with C-clamps of assorted sizes. Twenty metal C-clamps lay jumbled in the box. For a moment we couldn't figure out where the clamps had come from. No one could remember ever asking for them; they were just there. But the clamps provided the in-the-nick-of-time miracle that we needed. Grabbing a handful of C-clamps each, the teams acted quickly to secure the blankets. Working in pairs, one person grabbed the wind-whipped edges of the blankets while the other used a C-clamp to secure it onto the wooden beams. Once the blankets were temporarily under control, we could finally work the screws through the material and into the wood. In about forty minutes, we were able to reattach the insulated blankets onto the wooden ribs of the Jamesway. A few tendrils of snow still drifted in by the corners, but the major disaster had been averted.

For the next half-hour the team nervously watched the blankets and the wood screws strain in the groaning wind. After another hour we were confident that the situation was not going to get any worse. The wind was not letting up, but everything was reasonably secure in the Jamesway for the moment.

By the time we finished, it was 2:30 A.M. and we were ready to fall down with exhaustion from the tension. Randy Davis was too nervous to sleep so he volunteered to remain on a cot in the Jamesway to watch over the laboratory. The rest of us headed to our bunks by following a climbing rope that had been strung along the length of the camp.

As we headed out into the stormy night, it was nearly impossible to see. Snow stung our eyes and faces, forcing us to shield ourselves with the hoods of our parkas by looking down at our boots. Bill and I finally reached the Weatherport where our cots were located by feeling our way slowly along the rope trail. We each carried handheld radios and were expected to call into the main radio station with Randy in the Jamesway. By establishing an agreed-upon schedule of checks, we made sure that each team member made it safely into their respective bunkhouses. One radio would be kept on in each building in case there was an emergency anywhere in camp.

That night there would be no breaks to visit the outhouse. Instead, a plastic Nalgene bottle was used discretely to avoid any further risk of exposure to the elements. This was not a night for wandering around the campsite, regardless of the reason.

New problems began after an hour in the Weatherport. Howling wind from the Herbie banged mercilessly on the soft sides of the structure and showed no sign of letting up. The winds seemed to be gaining strength and roared over us with the force of a locomotive. Unlike the insulated blankets of the Jamesway, only a thin plastic sheet separated Bill and me from the violent storm outside. We felt naked and vulnerable lying on our cots and would have much preferred the solid snow mound we had dug out in Survival School.

Wrapping our sleeping bags around our ears, we each tried to shut out the storm but with little success. The pounding resounded off our heads, only adding to the feeling of lying on a train trestle. Aluminum ribbing that provided the skeleton for the Weatherport began to tremble, banging the poles into the metal of the preway stove. Most alarming was the back wall. The driving force of the wind caused the wall to bow severely inwards, pushing our cots back. It was under such tension that we were afraid to touch it for fear that the wall would finally burst open, releasing the storm all around us.

Bill was the first to crack and after another thirty minutes decided that he was going to sleep in the Solar Barn—a small, hard-sided insulated building that was used as our kitchen. Grumbling that "he had taken enough," Bill gathered his sleeping bag and pushed out into the storm. Negotiating the fifteen feet between the buildings, he continued to grumble into the wind and slammed the heavy door of the Solar Barn once he was inside.

I lasted only another fifteen minutes. With the wind pounding the aluminum struts into the preway, the stove was beginning to dance around the floor. In the haze of fatigue I became convinced that the building would either catch on fire or that the preway would backdraft carbon monoxide into the building. Either way, I was not staying one more minute. Like Bill, I gathered up my sleeping bag and its heavy fleece liner, and then made my near-fatal decision.

Rationalizing that I was going only fifteen feet, I didn't bother to shove the sleeping bag into its canvas duffel. With my bunny boots untied, my parka drawn close, and a giant ball of sleeping gear cradled in my arms, I headed to the Solar Barn.

The door of the Weatherport was in the lee of the wind, so getting out was not difficult. Standing in the sheltered spot, I could barely detect the outline of the Solar Barn through the blowing snow. Regardless, I gauged my next move figuring that it would take less than ten steps to reach the other building. I then stepped into the wind whipping between the buildings. Instantly, I realized my mistake.

A blast of wind immediately caught hold of my giant bundle and threw me onto the ice. I rolled in the windstream that funneled between the two buildings, breathing in the fine, blowing snow. Tossed about like a ragdoll, I tumbled around in a jumble of sleeping paraphernalia and boots, not knowing which way I was headed.

"In my mind it seemed as though I was going out to sea and, for a brief moment, in an odd way, it all seemed so funny," I told the group. "I even started to laugh out loud, thinking, If only the rest of the guys could see me now." I took a sip of my hot chocolate and realized that I had never told anyone the details of what had happened out in the storm.

"It still seemed funny as I rolled over and over on the ice," I continued, "Then I realized that I couldn't stand up."

The wind was so strong and the ice so scoured that I kept slipping down and sliding farther away from camp. I rolled away from the buildings and across wind-whipped ice. Each time I tried to stand up, I was thrown down and lost even more ground. My amusement quickly dissolved as the wind pushed me along the flat blue ice.

I saw the buildings disappearing in the blowing snow, and swallowed hard when I added up the situation. Like Allen, it was that pause to figure out a solution that made the difference. Had I continued to fight the wind I would have surely lost the battle, eventually succumbing to the exhaustion and cold. I was exposed and unable to stand. Fine snow was whipping all around me, filling my pockets and coating my hair. I was starting to shiver in the cold. The worst part was that no one knew where I was. The radio check had already taken place and as far as anyone in camp knew I was in the Weatherport in my sleeping bag. Suddenly I was overcome with a feeling of total isolation.

My only chance was to correct my original mistake and present as low a profile to the wind as possible. I slowly began crawling on the ground, using my mittens to grab onto any bit of snow fastened to the ice. Looking for patches of snow I moved off the slick ice and hopscotched on my belly from snowpatch to snowpatch, where I could get purchase. Most importantly, I kept the gray outlines of the buildings in front of me, directly in my sight. If I lost direction, it would all be over.

Time had no bearing, and I had no idea how long it took me to make it to the Solar Barn. Eventually I stood shivering on the steps in the lee of the wind. Pulling open the heavy metal door, I slammed it against the howling wind, waking up Bill. He watched me lazily from the comfort of his sleeping bag trying to figure out why I was breathing so heavily. Without a word, he yawned and turned over, oblivious to what had just taken place outdoors.

By this time I was shaking and only wanted to crawl into my sleeping bag to get warm. After peeling off my parka, I snuggled down into the bag but continued to shake almost uncontrollably.

"I just couldn't find a way to generate any heat," I explained. "Finally, I tried to rub the skin on my back and belly to warm up. Then I realized why I was so cold." I laughed as I revealed the problem to the group. It turned out that a thick layer of snow coated my torso under my shirt and pants. During my tumbling on the ice, fine snow crystals had infiltrated all of my clothing. It was remarkable how the snow had been able to pack into every single layer, from shirt and pants to socks and underwear. It was like sitting on a snowball.

The solution was easy enough, and I was soon warming up after shaking out my clothes.

The rest of the team knew nothing about my adventures in the storm until I sheepishly told them about the snow in my underwear several days later. After a few jokes the response turned serious, and we immediately set new rules regarding moving even to the outhouse at night. The lesson for me was far more personal. It was one of respect for the wind, snow, and cold in Antarctica; I would never underestimate them again.

With the Herbie rattling against the coffeehouse/pub, the rest of the grounded expeditions huddled around their drinks with the sobering knowledge that it was best not to challenge the storm outside.

It took only a day for the Herbie to blow itself out, and our expedition was back to moving supplies to Weddell World. If this had been anywhere but Ross Island, where there are no insects, we would have been likened to an army of ants ferrying all manner of food and housing in well-worn tracks over the eleven miles of sea ice between McMurdo Station and the campsite. Because it had a heated enclosed cab, the Spryte was used for moving sensitive instruments and computers that we did not want to freeze during the transport. The vehicle rumbled slowly across the ice on large metal tracks like a tank, and its pace was so sluggish that if we were not wearing bunny boots we could have easily outrun the Spryte. There was no steering wheel to control its movements. Instead, the driver used two levers to brake either the right or left track. Pulling back on one or the other lever caused the Spryte to spin in circles. If neither lever were pulled then the Spryte would continue rolling steadily in a straight-line trajectory until the motor was turned off. These battered old vehicles had been used by NSF scientific expeditions for over twenty-five years. The orange paint was blistering off the metal in some places, and the exhaust fumes drifting into the cab made you drowsy, but the Sprytes could climb over the worst sastrugi with ease and cross three-foot-wide ice cracks without a worry.

Everything that we didn't mind freezing during transport was piled into large and small sleds that were towed behind the snowmobiles across the sea ice. The most versatile of the sleds was also the oldest in design, the Nansen sled. Originally designed by Norwegian polar explorer Fridjof Nansen in the late 1800s, the sled is constructed of ash and beech slats bound together by rawhide or twine strips. These relatively simple sleds hold up to the cold and travel across the ice better than anything that modern technology has been able to offer. Plastics and other artificial materials lose their flexibility in the cold. In contrast, the rawhide joints of the Nansen sled allow it to bend over ridges on the uneven ice surface even under the coldest conditions. The design is so efficient that a twelve-foot-long sled can be used to pull loads weighing nearly 600 kilograms (over 1,000 pounds). We would have been able to transport a full-grown male Weddell seal on a Nansen sled if we could have figured out a way to keep the animal from slipping off the side. That unique combination of strength and flexibility have made the Nansen sled invaluable for polar exploration for over a hundred years. In Antarctica, the sleds are highly prized and are carefully maintained by hand-waxing with linseed oil.

With the transport of the last of the equipment and field supplies, we added our personal gear to the final sled load and moved into camp. There was a sense of relief as we left McMurdo Station and cut the ties to civilization. In front of us was a world of adventure and scientific discovery. We could not predict what would happen over the next eight to ten weeks. Severe weather could completely shut us down and destroy our camp. The seals might never show up or, worse yet, might swim away with all of our instruments. On the other hand there was the real possibility that we would witness things that had never been seen by human eyes. We placed our faith in a new generation of scientific instrumentation and a remarkable diving marine mammal, and trusted that we would find an extraordinary hidden life beneath the Antarctic sea ice.

CHAPTER 7

HOT BODIES

A lone female seal, weighed down in pregnancy, wriggled her sleek head out of the slush and water of the ice crack. Breathless, she let her chin rest on the icy sloping walls while her swollen body floated in the slush behind. She was on the verge of having her pup, immensely fat with this year's fetus and carrying enough blubber to feed herself and her offspring for the next two months. Her arduous underwater journey was complete, and she took the moment to gulp in cold, fresh air in long, deep inhalations. Snow crystals blew into the crack and melted on her forehead and eyes as soon as they settled.

Despite her condition, she had accomplished what few other seals had been able to do. In a series of dives she had swum over eighty miles beneath solid sea ice, making her way from the open waters of the Ross Sea into ice-choked McMurdo Sound. She had taken advantage of every trapped air pocket, hole, and pressure ridge along the way. At each breathing spot she had inhaled deeply and then dove towards her next opportunity to catch a breath of air, zigzagging but always moving in a southerly direction. When the holes were too small to fit her muzzle through she tore at their edges, reaming the stubborn ice with her front teeth until she reached air.

Instinct had driven her from the open-water feeding grounds to the dark depths beneath the ice. Every summer of her adulthood had been the same, drawing her back to the rocky breeding sites in McMurdo Sound. Each summer season was spent giving birth and nursing while lying on the ice at the foot of Mount Erebus. Under platinum clouds formed by the puffing volcano and stretched thin by the winds, she cared for her new pup. A one-year-old and two-year-old from her previous summers were in the vicinity, but she paid them no heed. Her focus was only on the newborn.

This year she had proceeded slowly, farther and farther beneath the ice sheet until there was no turning back. In the chill of early October storms, old breathing holes had frozen shut behind her. The journey was difficult enough in normal ice years—a thirty-mile southerly swim under the ice. B-15 had nearly tripled her effort this year. Despite the obstacles, she had shown up on schedule, the first pregnant seal to arrive in the Sound.

With a loud "Chuuuufff," the pregnant seal announced that she had gone as far as she could, ending up at the glacier ice crack in front of our camp.

A row of red flags waving on bamboo poles led off into the horizon from Weddell World. The flags were planted every seventy-five feet and meandered in more or less a straight line across eleven miles of unbroken sea ice back to McMurdo Station. This was our umbilical cord, a lifeline that allowed the research team to move between camp and the Station even in blinding, blowing snow.

Finally isolated in Weddell World, our team began to fall into a routine that took advantage of the unique skills of each member. There were no "girl" jobs or "boy" jobs. Instead, the tasks were assigned solely on practical abilities. Our priorities were simple compared to the complexities of modern living at home. First, we needed to survive. Second, we needed to conduct the science. With these simple objectives at hand, all expedition members were expected to participate in the everyday tasks of maintaining a remote field camp as well as helping with each of the research projects. By practical necessity, egos and political correctness soon took a back seat. Laziness was not tolerated by the group any more than overestimating your ability to the point of getting hurt. We could not afford to have an injury sideline anyone on the team. Randy was particularly adamant about avoiding injuries, often chastising those of us participating in spontaneous games of ice soccer and ice Frisbee. As tempting as it was for Bill, Markus, Matt, and me to grab a rope and be towed on skis behind a snowmobile, for the most part we chose the safer path.

Daily life consisted of the immediate duties of tending to the diving hole, setting up the laboratory instrumentation, and organizing the living quarters. If you weren't working in the lab, then you were preparing a meal in the kitchen, fueling generators, or shoveling snow. When ice encrusted the diving hole, it did not matter whether you held a doctorate degree or whether you were male or female. You just started chipping and dip netting until the hole was once again clear for the seals. No one told you what to do—you just saw what was needed and did it. Life in camp was dictated by necessity and how mentally and physically competent you were for the task.

We quickly discovered that living under the constant cold, extended polar sunlight and extreme dryness of Antarctica was having a marked effect on our bodies. The most obvious response was to the cold. When we first arrived on the ice, medical personnel at the McMurdo General Hospital had told us that it would take approximately two weeks for our thyroid glands to respond to the chilly conditions. As the body's hormonal thermostat, the thyroid gland is responsible for secreting several hormones that regulate metabolism. Acute exposure to the Antarctic cold sent our thyroids into natural overdrive.

Our metabolic rates shifted into high gear, with the side benefit that we began to feel warmer. We no longer had to meet each trip outdoors with a jaw-chattering shiver. Our core body temperatures dropped several degrees from the normal 98.6°F to about 96°F. Had we been living at the South Pole, where air temperatures were more than thirty degrees chillier than on Ross Island, we could have expected even lower body temperatures. The human body resets its internal thermostat appropriately when suddenly faced with prolonged cold exposure. In its most extreme form the mammalian body would enter hibernation, letting core body temperatures plummet and activity levels sag—a strategy used by wintering bears.

As biologists we watched with great curiosity as each of us adapted to the Antarctic. Rather than a single response, individuality ruled. Genetics rather than experience seemed to determine how adaptable our thyroid glands were. Eventually we found that the expedition party could be divided into two groups: the "high metabs" and the "low metabs." Exposure to the cold stoked the internal fires of the high metabs. Matt, Lee, Bill, and I fell into that category. At the dinner table we downed extraordinary quantities of food, surprising even ourselves with the amount of butter and fatty items that we could consume in one sitting. Sometimes it was only the size of the plates and politeness that limited how much we ate. Despite it all we remained fairly lean, give or take a few extra pounds.

Our metabolic fires burned particularly hot, and with plenty of calories to fuel us we tended to feel warm all of the time. We could get away with wearing only the basic parka and wind pants even on the coldest days, never having to break out the thick thermal underwear issued in our ECW gear. Given our ravenous appetites, the four of us noted that we would not want to be adrift together in a lifeboat with food supplies running low. The joke was that we would be the first to start eyeing each other as a potential main course for the next meal.

By comparison, the low metabs were prone to go into a hibernation-like state in response to the cold, resembling bears. Randy, Don, and Jesse maintained reasonably normal diets and would complain of gaining weight as they tried to keep up with the dietary pace of the rest of us. We noticed that Jesse would take any opportunity to wear every possible piece of ECW clothing, up to five insulating layers in all, to try to keep warm.

The one outlier was Markus, who fueled his body with thick coffees that he conjured up on a portable espresso machine he had shipped to the ice. With a cheery *"ciao,"* he kickstarted each morning with a double espresso on an empty stomach. Caffeine kept him hyper-hot and most days he beat us all in terms of internal heat, wearing only the lightest windbreakers and sweaters regardless of weather conditions.

The downside of all of these hormonal changes was a detrimental effect on our ability to remember things. According to the doctors the same thyroid hormones that made us feel warm came with the loss of our short-term memory. They couldn't explain the connection, and we tended to pass it off as medical mythology. On the other hand, we soon found ourselves carrying small pads of paper and pens next to the survival chocolate bars in our parkas. Even simple instructions for errands and people's names seemed to drift in one ear and out the other. Whether it was the cold, hormones, or the fact that we had a million things on our minds to keep the camp going didn't matter. We relied on those pads of paper to keep it all straight for the duration of the expedition.

Polar sunlight was another environmental phenomenon that clearly affected us emotionally and physically. On October 18, we experienced our last sunset for the season. The sun dipped slowly behind the Royal Society Mountain Range one final time, producing a twilight glow that persisted for several hours late into the evening. Drifting clouds skirting towards the continent blushed purple and then pink, punctuated by long golden ribbons of sunlight that seemed in proper celebration of the celestial milestone. In McMurdo, the residents gathered with tequila sunrises in gloved hands along the western-facing roads to witness the event. They watched silently as plumes of crystals from snowblowers cleaning the airport runaway provided a shimmering polar fireworks display.

For a brief moment, our team also stopped the ruckus of camp activities to appreciate the quiet splendor of Antarctica. The intensity of our schedule and self-imposed pressures momentarily melted under the soft glow of the sunset. Looking to the west, the red marker flags lining our icy road appeared to be on fire with the brilliant backlighting while the sky filled with expansive, luminous colors. The glacial ice ridges behind our camp lost their edginess in the soft-pink and baby-blue shadows. It was remarkable how nature in Antarctica could wear such exhilarating and treacherous faces.

For the rest of the summer season the sun monotonously circled the horizon, never getting any higher or lower in the sky during twenty-four-hour cycles. On the sea ice 2 A.M. looked identical to 2 P.M. The only difference was in the direction of the shadows.

As would be expected, the constant sunlight played havoc with sleeping cycles, particularly those of the high metabs. Low metabs like Randy and Don were more likely to maintain a rigid daily clock: up at 7 A.M. and asleep by 10 P.M. Conversely, the biological clock of the high metabs seemed to drift more freely, and left to our own schedules we would wake and work an hour later each day. Because of this, the high metabs were the ones who didn't mind going onto the night shift when it became apparent that the camp and the research needed twenty-four-hour attention. Night was relative, anyway. The only conflict was the chaotic "breakfasts," when the rising low metabs tried to prepare oatmeal and pancakes while the high metabs were fixing spaghetti or steak before going to bed.

Clearly each member of the team had a unique response to living on the ice, and one of the wisest things we did was recognize these differences to our advantage. Biology had dictated the way in which each of our bodies responded to Antarctic conditions. Rather than fight an individual's natural patterns, we let people choose their general schedule of eating and sleeping and then used the diversity to keep the science going throughout the long days and nights. In the end it was biology that elected me the best person to monitor food stores, Jesse the best driver of the slow-moving (but well-heated) Spryte, and Bill and Matt the ideal night shift personnel. Randy, Lee, and Don were the wisest choices for bright-eyed morning patrol, while Markus could straddle the shifts with coffeemug in hand.

With twenty-four hours of sunlight now at our disposal, Weddell World was in constant motion. There were three major scientific tasks that were divided among the team members: instrument calibration, environmental mapping, and seal surveying. Randy Davis, Bill Hagey, and Markus Horning spent their time calibrating the miniaturized scientific instruments that would be carried by the Weddell seals during the diving experiments. The laboratory section of the Jamesway soon took on the dusty, noisy, cluttered characteristics of a machine shop and Swiss watchmaker's benchtop as they soldered, drilled, and tinkered with camera heads, depth gauges, and speed meters. At the same time, Lee Fuiman, Jesse Purdy, and Don Calkins mapped out the local ice and sea conditions to provide a profile of the seals' underwater environment near our camp. From the dive hole in the laboratory floor they lowered oceanographic instruments on weighted ropes to measure the ocean currents that drifted below us and monitor the daily fluctuations in light levels and seawater temperatures. With GPS units and ice axes in hand, they would take off on snowmobiles to map the location of the ice cracks and favorite breathing holes of the seals around Weddell World.

While the others worked in and around the laboratory, Matt Rutishauser and I conducted local surveys of the Weddell seals. Each day we hiked or rode snowmobiles from Weddell World to the nearby crack beside the Erebus Glacier Ice Tongue to record the numbers, approximate ages, and gender of the seals that had hauled out during the night. We named the local crack "Home Crack," to distinguish it from the other areas of McMurdo Sound. And we soon got to know the personalities and habits of the individual seals in our front yard.

Walking within a few feet of the Weddell seals resting on the ice elicited surprisingly little response for such a large wild mammal and allowed us to easily conduct our surveys. It didn't take long for Matt and me to confirm via an up-close belly inspection that the winking, long-whiskered seal was indeed female.

The reason for the calm attitude of the long-whiskered female and the other Weddell seals was the absence of natural threats in Antarctica. Simply put, there are no polar bears at the South Pole. In the northern Arctic regions, lumbering white bears routinely prey on seals. The difference is easily detected in the behavior of Arctic seals. In the Arctic, ringed seals and harp seals are skittish and nearly impossible to approach even if you could find them lying in the open on the surface of the ice. They tend to hide in the water under the cover of ice in an effort to stay out of sight of their hungry nemesis.

In contrast, without the continued threat of harm on the ice surface, Weddell seals of the Antarctic often lie out in the sun and view approaching humans with complete indifference. Only killer whales and the occasional leopard seal are threats to the Weddell seals in open water; neither venture under the solid sea ice, making McMurdo Sound the perfect area for raising a naïve young pup.

Home Crack proved to be a welcome rest stop for the diving Weddells as they tried to reach the nearby rocky outcroppings that served as their traditional gathering spots. Some seals visited briefly for a day or two, resting on the ice, and then disappeared back into the crack—never to be seen again. Others showed up one day and stayed for the summer.

On any calm, sunny day Matt and I would usually find five to sixteen adult Weddell seals lounging on the ice next to the crack and several others trying to climb out of the water. The immense effort that the glossy seals put into squeezing their wet bodies through the cracks made us grateful for being able to live on top of the ice rather than under it. It didn't take long for me to find the humor in the seals' behavior, as they wedged and wiggled their hind ends with the same twisted-face determination that my fellow Antarctic travelers displayed when trying on their spandex thermal underwear for the first time at the CDC in Christchurch: eyes squinted, lips pursed, and necks strained.

During an initial attempt at hauling out, one large-shouldered, scar-faced male swam up from beneath to poke a wet, curious nose through the brash ice of the crack. He had a broad black muzzle that had been bitten in a recent fight. Exposed white flesh in rakes along his cheek and nose gave him a pugnacious look. After testing the width of the ice walls with his dripping whiskers, the seal began the grueling task of reaming and wedging. Furious tooth scraping on the walls was followed by grunting efforts to stuff his muzzle, head, and neck through the small opening.

He began with his chin, straining with every upper body muscle to gain purchase and inch his way up the slippery slope. Eventually gravity prevailed, causing the seal to slide backwards with an uncontrolled splash into the water. When the chin-hold technique failed the seal, who we uncreatively named Scarface, he reamed the hole larger so that he could begin bobbing higher and higher up in the water until his front flippers were clear. Using the small claws on his flippers as crampons, Scarface gained a little more traction. But with most of his mass still in the submerged tail, he once more slipped back below the water surface.

Finally, the seal disappeared altogether. Several minutes passed, and Matt and I realized that he was preparing for a "running start." Ascending as quickly as possible, the slippery seal flew out of the hole in an explosion of water and ice to land with a blubbery thud along the side of the hole. Bouncing and inchworming forward with his front flippers and body, Scarface slid quickly away from the crack as if afraid that someone would grab him by the hind flipper and drag him backwards again.

The seal's comical behavior continued once he was a safe distance from the water. With his dark gray spotted pelt saturated with seawater, Scarface immediately tried to dry himself before the water froze to his fur and skin. Without the benefit of legs and too round to shake out like a wet dog, the saturated seal began to rock lengthwise from side to side. Using the dry snow as a towel, he rolled his giant body in twisting circles. Digging his whiskered, scarred muzzle deep into the powdery snow, he came up snorting with his eyebrows outlined in white.

Scarface rolled and tumbled in the snow until it compressed beneath his weight, and then moved on to fresh dry patches to repeat the process. For nearly twenty minutes the 425-kilogram (935-pound) giant that outweighed me seven times vigorously rubbed himself until his delicate gray-black fur puffed out clean and dry. Rubbing his back along the snow, Scarface soon developed the continence of relaxed satisfaction that I associated with having scratched a difficult itch. It didn't take long for the Weddell seal to fall into a deep sleep, dozing belly-up in the sun.

As amusing as the seals were, I began to wonder just how cold the skin of the Weddell seals got while they slept on the ice. If I had stretched out next to the ice crack, even with heavy parka, thermals, and boots on, I would have quickly succumbed to a fit of shivering. Yet, the seals slept exposed on the ice for days at a time.

Their frantic rolling reminded me of the time that I was a tender for an Antarctic scuba dive team in 1983. My assignment was to sit outside next to a hole in the ice while the divers took photographs of the sea life below. When the divers surfaced, I grabbed onto their air tanks to help them climb out of the slippery ice hole. They had little use of their hands due to the thick three-fingered neoprene mitts that they wore. As they sat on the ice edge, I would loosen the straps of their large, heavy fins so they could be removed.

The coldest that I have ever been in Antarctica was during those dives. Because my own gloves were too bulky to maneuver the fins, I had to work the freezing wet straps off with bare hands. To this day I can recall the ache in my fingers after just two minutes of exposure to the freezing water and cold polar air. Human flesh is not made to contact the -3°C (27°F) seawater of McMurdo Sound. To get the circulation going and stop the ache, I hopped around shaking and rubbing my hands—looking every bit as foolish as Scarface rolling in the snow.

How Weddell seals were able to wallow in the slushy water and then pop up soaking wet after a dive without freezing was a complete mystery to me. It seemed impossible that the wet floppy flippers of the seals didn't automatically stick to the ice and then fall off with frostbite.

The next day I decided to bring along an infrared thermal camera on the seal survey. About the size of a handheld video camera, the unit provided a color picture of the surface temperature of a subject. Typically used to detect heat loss from buildings and pipes, the infrared images would indicate how much heat the Weddell seals lost through their skin. If the seals appeared blue or black in the picture, then they were as cold as the snow and ice that surrounded them. Conversely, a red or yellow seal meant that their skin was toasty hot.

I wagered my next post-dinner kitchen duty with Matt that the seals would appear as blue as ice. All of the textbooks said that seals were insulated with a thick layer of blubber. This meant that their body heat would remain on the inside while their skin temperature would drop to that of the surrounding air. I was particularly confident in the bet since I had conducted previous tests on the skin temperatures of dolphins, dogs, and sea otters. The research had proved that well-insulated animals kept the skin or fur covering within one degree of the surrounding temperatures. Whoever lost the bet would be cleaning a lot of dirty pots.

We turned the camera on and waited for it to detect the seals lying on the snow next to the crack. At first we saw nothing in the viewfinder, and I figured that the seals were so cold that the camera couldn't distinguish them from their surroundings. I started to smirk, thinking that I had easily won the bet. As the batteries of the infrared camera finally warmed up, both Matt and I made our first major discovery of the expedition. Weddell seals weren't cold—they were hot! Scarface, the long-whiskered female, the pregnant seal, and the others were so hot that they glowed red and yellow in the infrared pictures. To make sure that the camera was working properly, I had Matt stand next to one of the seals. In his insulated parka, gloves, wind pants, and boots, Matt looked like a tall cold, blue ghost standing over the seal. Only his exposed face was as red as the Weddell seal lying near his feet.

From this one simple experiment I suddenly knew why Weddell seals don't freeze to the ice. By precisely controlling the blood flow to the skin on their torsos and their flippers, the seals can bypass their blubber and warm body parts whenever they need. Shifting the warm blood around allows them to use their flippers and skin as radiators if they get too hot. Alternatively, they can turn off the flushing. It is just like the hot blush we experience on our cheeks when we are overheated. However, the Weddell seal can flush blood over its entire body with elegant control.

"Now I understand the seal tubs!" I told Matt excitedly.

On several occasions during our seal surveys, Matt and I had slipped in large, smooth depressions in the ice. When we backed away we had noticed that the depressions were the size and shape of Weddell seals. A long, football-shaped body and floppy hind flippers were clearly outlined in the ice. The middle of the depression was several inches deep, giving the impression of a large seal bathtub. At the time we thought that water on the fur of wet seals had caused the ice to momentarily melt and then freeze over, creating the outlines. Now we knew that the seal tubs were actually the result of heat coming from the skin of the hot animals as they slept and then melted down into the ice. The area around Home Crack was littered with the imprints of hot, lounging seals that had come and gone.

The infrared images of the seals also explained why, in a blowing snowstorm, some seals are dusted in snow and others are not. It all depends on the internal thermostat of the seal. By precisely controlling the blood flow to its skin, the Weddell seal can clear the snow off of its body with the efficiency of an automobile windshield defroster—or, it can conserve its heat and let the snow build up until the storm is over.

With each new infrared image we learned more about the hidden lives of Weddell seals. The most impressive hot areas on the seals were their eyes. In the infrared pictures the eyes of the seals glowed in a ghostly manner, two large hot coals floating on a cool blue skeletal head. The surface of the eyeball and the entire brow area framing each eye were ten degrees warmer than the rest of the head. It seemed curious that the seals would waste so much precious heat to warm their eyes until we thought about how they live. The seal's eyes are essential for hunting and have to function properly in the -3°C (27°F) icy waters of Antarctica. Bare skin would freeze within minutes at such temperatures. Curiously, the eyes and the face of the seals remain soft and pliable even in slushy ice water. As we studied the infrared images we realized that either the blood flow or underlying muscles must be responsible for keeping the eyes of the Weddell seal exceptionally warm. In many ways the seal eye is analogous to the footpad of an Arctic wolf. By pulsing just enough blood into the pads of its feet, the wolf is able to keep the tissue temperatures just above freezing. In that way they are able to walk on snow and ice with little fear of losing a toe to frostbite. It would take a lot more data to determine if Weddell seals use a similar physiological mechanism, but I found the idea intriguing.

This was not the first time that nature had surprised me with a better solution to an animal's problem than I could have imagined. However, my price for doubting its perfection on this occasion, as Matt quickly reminded me, was several days of kitchen duty back at camp.

CHAPTER 8

LIFE AND
DEATH IN
ANTARCTICA

OCTOBER 21–25

In the laboratory at Weddell World, the rest of the team labored over the instrumentation that would be used with the diving seals. The success of the entire project hinged on a custom-designed unit called the VDAP (Video Data Acquisition Platform). Created by Randy Davis and Bill Hagey, the guts of the VDAP were a Sony 8mm video camera connected to a sophisticated microcomputer. These, in turn, were connected to a wide variety of sensors that would record every movement of the seal. Dive depth, swimming speed, and compass bearing would be measured second by second, allowing us to trace the three-dimensional track of the diving seals. For the first time we would dive with the Weddell seal as the animal maneuvered below the Antarctic ice.

Simultaneously, a tiny accelerometer designed by Markus Horning and mounted near the tail of the seal would measure the swing of every flipper stroke, providing us with a profile of the swimming abilities of the seals. A miniaturized heart rate monitor modified from the same wristwatch units used by joggers and triathletes would also record every heartbeat of the seal as it descended and ascended. On the audio channel of the videotape, we would record the underwater sounds emitted and heard by the seals from a tiny hydrophone. Lastly, the seal would carry a small thermometer wire that would record the water temperatures it encountered during its underwater travels. Completely outfitted, the seals would have enough technological gear to act as oceanographer, athlete, and cameraman in one self-contained package.

It had taken over ten years to develop the instrumentation to make it small enough and robust enough to be carried safely by a wild marine mammal. Our first attempts to deploy submersible cameras on swimming seals had occurred in behind-the-scenes pools at Sea World in San Diego. The trainers and animal care personnel had been incredulous at first, but were excited about the idea of obtaining a "seal's-eye view." With their assistance several harbor seals had been the test pilots for "seal cam." Wearing the cameras on a neoprene blanket, the seals inchwormed around the perimeters of their pools and then finally went for a dip. The resulting videotape provided a seasick bounce across the concrete and an uninspired view of fish debris near the drain on the bottom of their pools. But the concept had been proven; it was possible for marine mammals to videotape their own behavior and record the sights and sounds of their environment.

The VDAP was also field-tested on trained bottlenose dolphins from the U. S. Navy marine mammal program and wild elephant seals through my lab, off the coast of California. Each test had shown us exciting, although short-lived, glimpses of the marine mammals' underwater world and we were hooked. As one of the premiere diving mammals, Weddell seals would allow our team to take an even larger step. Through the combined instruments and the camera we would witness what the seal encountered as it dove, hear what it heard on its travels, monitor how the animal swam and navigated under the ice, and even record the pounding of the seal's heart when it chased a fish. The VDAP was going to take us through the door that I had left unopened nearly twenty years earlier, and into the mysterious deep-sea world of Weddell seals.

All of the instrumentation was packaged in a reinforced metal canister that looked like a small scuba tank. Because the seals would be diving to depths twenty times deeper than those experienced by human scuba divers, the canister had to withstand crushing hydrostatic pressures. Neoprene rubber and Styrofoam taken to similar depths were compressed to a fraction of their original size. To ensure that the closures remained watertight as the VDAP contracted and expanded during descent and ascent, each hand-milled canister was pressure tested to over 1,000 meters before use. As the rubber o-rings and aluminum strained during the tests, and I stood back for fear of a pressure line bursting, I had to question why Weddell seals felt no ill effects when exposed to similar squeezing pressures when diving.

Snaking from the front of the VDAP canister was the camera head, a heavy-duty unit the size and shape of a baseball that was originally designed for plumbers to drop down clogged pipes. A set of blue LED (light-emitting diode) lights encircling the lens provided enough light at the darkest depths for us to see three feet into the black water ahead of the cruising seal. By using LEDs that shined in the near-infrared range, Bill made sure that only humans were able to see the light. It was invisible to the Weddell seals and the fish that they hunted so neither would be disturbed by an unexpected spotlight.

Each sensor, underwater connector, and battery was calibrated on the laboratory bench before the VDAP was packaged and closed tight. In the final test, Randy and Bill slowly lowered the entire VDAP on a rope into the dive hole beneath the Jamesway. The simulated test gradually exposed the sensors and VDAP electronics to the temperatures and pressures of the Antarctic sub-ice environment. If the instruments didn't operate properly while tied to a rope, there was little chance they would work on the back of a hunting seal.

As the instrument calibration neared completion, Matt and I started to whittle down the list of possible candidate seals for our research. We had over a week's worth of survey data and recognized many of the seals by their favorite sunbathing spots and scar patterns on their pelts. On the tenth survey of Home Crack we found that the neighborhood had unexpectedly changed. B-15, the giant iceberg that had haunted our expedition from the beginning, had added yet another hurdle. Pregnant Weddell seals were giving birth at Home Crack. Unable to reach their traditional pupping sites several miles to the south, the females had just given up. Suddenly, our camp was in the middle of a Weddell seal nursery.

One pup with a fleshy pink, rubbery umbilical cord still dangling from its belly crawled about on the bloody snow next to its mom. Matt and I stayed on to watch as another Weddell seal pup made one of the most difficult entrances into the world imaginable—born at temperatures near -17°C (1.4°F) in blowing snow on the Antarctic sea ice. It seemed a cruel trick to play on such a brand-new animal. However, the seal pups instinctively acted like any other newborn and quickly sought out mom for food and shelter.

The infrared camera showed us just how difficult it was to be a little seal in the Antarctic. Although the moms appeared red-hot in the pictures, their tiny pups were chilly blue. Because they were so young the pups did not have the robust blubber layer of the adults. Instead, the pups relied on their fuzzy pelts to keep warm. With all of their heat retained on the inside, the outsides of the pups were as cold as the Antarctic air surrounding them, appearing as ghostly as Matt in his parka in the infrared images.

Charmed by the antics of the new pups, we took a little time during the surveys to observe their behavior. We kept our distance so as not to disturb the new moms, knowing that if we accidentally got too close the moms would admonish us with an ineffective snap in the air as if to say, "Can't you see I'm busy with a youngster here?" The moms would then nudge their pups forward on the ice out of our way. No other large, wild mammalian mother is so tolerant. The seals' maternal behavior is in stark contrast to that of terrestrial mammals such as grizzly bears or tigers in which an inadvertent stroll between a mother and her cub or kitten could well be your last. With Weddell seals it is not unusual to be able to walk within a few feet of a nursing mom without eliciting a reaction.

At Home Crack the newborn pups squirmed next to their moms wearing what looked like soft, oversized, gray fur pajamas. Their front and hind flippers were much too large for their bodies as they flopped awkwardly about trying to keep in close contact with the small teats on their mom's abdomen. Just like puppy dogs, the seal pups were going to have to grow into their huge feet. The newborn pups already weighed as much as an adult golden retriever and, despite their size, displayed the mild temperament of their parents.

When Matt and I passed by, the pups looked up at us with large brown eyes and issued a low throaty, "Mmmaaawwww." There was only one way to interpret the call—"What's for dinner?" From the pup's perspective, we were just another potential source of food.

The pups had a lot of eating and growing to do in six short weeks, while their mothers would barely eat—if at all. Reclining in the sun nursing and protecting their pups, the moms relinquished any chance to dive below the ice to feed themselves. But the focused attention was short-lived. After six weeks the pups would be weaned, abruptly left on their own to hunt for fish and grow into adulthood. Weaning day would be as harsh as their birth day, with their moms silently slipping below the ice never to return.

Before that day in December the moms dedicate everything to give their pups a head start in life. In less than one and half months the moms deliver an entire childhood's worth of nutrients to their pups. By the time weaning occurs the seal mom is a skeleton of her former plump self, while her pup rivals her size. There could be no sister or brother for Weddell seal pups—just trying to feed one youngster is taxing enough for the moms. Each pup will double its weight in the first eleven days. Moms see their pups balloon from 30 kilograms (nearly 70 pounds) at birth to 140 kilograms (over 300 pounds) at weaning. It is as if this golden retriever–sized pup had grown to the size of two Saint Bernards in less than two months.

To accomplish this amazing growth spurt, the Weddell pups spend much of their time nursing on one of the richest milks produced by any mammal. They ingest eight to nine quarts of mom's milk per day. In addition to quantity, Weddell seal moms produce a blue-ribbon, high-quality milk for their offspring. Packed with over 60 percent fat, the milk of the Weddell seal is twelve times richer in fat than cow's milk, at 5 percent fat, or human milk, at 4 percent fat. Even the milk of cats and dogs can't compare, at only 3 to 10 percent fat.

Watching the two pups flopping around on the ice after their moms it was difficult to imagine that they would be nearly three times my weight by the time we parted in December. Each day they nursed until their bellies were the size of soccer balls. Then they would roll over on their backs to fall contentedly asleep on the ice, miniature versions of their snoozing moms.

Just three days after we first encountered the pups, Randy took time to accompany Matt and me on the seal survey. We took snowmobiles on a bright sunny day in order to survey all of the seals along the entire two-and-a-half-mile length of Home Crack, up to the edge of the glacier. We were finishing our counts when I looked up to find a strange dark cloud obscuring the base of the Royal Society Mountain Range in the distance. The cloud was particularly out of place with the sunshine and the intense bright-blue sky above. Only an occasional white puff from Mount Erebus broke up the color, making the sky overhead exceptionally clear. It had been calm all morning with so little breeze that the red flags leading from camp had barely twitched when we left. The tops of White Island and Black Island were also clearly visible, so there was no reason to suspect the onset of a Herbie. Feeling uneasy, I could see that there was something dark and ominous in the color of the horizon.

Randy noticed it, too. He looked around, tested the wind, and sternly told us, "We've got to get out of here. Now!" He didn't have to repeat the order.

We were several miles from camp on the open sea ice with no flagged route to follow. Usually this was not a problem since the dark outline of the Jamesway building at Weddell World could easily be seen in the distance. We were within a fifteen-minute snowmobile ride to camp. On days that we felt energetic we could even walk between Weddell World and Home Crack within forty minutes.

With no local landmarks, the route could become tenuous and slow-going in poor visibility. Our biggest concern, should the snow start blowing, was the meandering Home Crack. Negotiating the crack was a matter of locating a narrow section and a sturdy snow bridge, both of which required us to be able to see the ground in front of our snowmobiles.

While we yanked on the starter cords of the Alpine II Bombardiers, the wind began to shift direction. The sun was still visible above, but blowing snow began to swirl around our feet. Increasing in intensity, the wind shifted again and began blowing from the east. From this direction the wind climbed over Ross Island, down the side of Mount Erebus, skidded across the glacier, and slammed into us on the sea ice. Snow carried from the island streamed across the ice, creating instantaneous drifts beside any object—flagpoles, humans, and seals—that blocked its path. The snow had the consistency of fine salt that was being sifted into higher and higher piles as we urged the snowmobiles to life.

I turned around and saw that most of the adult seals had already abandoned the surface of the ice to seek shelter from the storm by diving. Below the ice the ocean was calm, and much safer than trying to weather the cutting wind and stinging snow on the surface. Only one adult seal remained; it was the first pregnant seal we had seen arrive at Home Crack the week before, now a new mother attempting to shelter her pup. She stoically faced into the wind using her body to form a barrier from the biting gusts for her newborn pup. Both the dedicated mom and her calling pup were already coated with a fine layer of snow. It drifted around the two bodies, nearly burying them as we watched.

Although it would have been much easier for the mom to dive below with the rest of the adults, her pup could never follow. His puppy fur was too fine and would have saturated to the skin if he entered the water. As it was, he didn't know how to swim. So the mom closed her eyes against the blowing wind and huddled next to her newborn out in the open on the ice. Together they endured the brunt of the unexpected storm.

Strangely, the blue sky above gave a false sense of security as the blowing snow swirled around us. How bad could it really be when the sky above looked so inviting? Conditions on the ground, however, told an entirely different story. Although I could see the sky, I could barely make out a gloved hand in front of my face. Almost immediately the wind reached over thirty knots and cut us to the bone. The -23°C (-10°F) now felt like -51°C (-60°F). As we rode on the snowmobiles, the wind-chilled air temperatures reaching our skin were even lower.

Randy led the way from the crack, checking back every now and again to make sure that Matt and I were still behind. Rather than try to hop Home Crack, we followed along its edge heading due west to try to intersect the flagged route where the crack petered out into a pencil line. It was a longer course that added another mile, but was considerably safer. Fortunately, the sun provided enough light in the blowing snow to allow us to follow each other's snowmobile tracks. After riding with the wind at our backs for twenty minutes we finally saw two distant red flags through the blur of white. They marked the middle of the flagged road leading to Weddell World. Never was I so grateful to the see those flapping pieces of red cloth.

Stopping to make sure that the group was still together, I noticed Randy slightly bent over and rubbing his cheek. By this time fine snow caked his mustache and beard and his breath frosted the tips of the hairs with each breath. Matt, on the other hand, was unrecognizable with his black neoprene face mask, dark ski goggles, and parka hood drawn around his head. Like mine, every inch of Matt's skin was covered. Only the black-and-white nametags Velcroed to the breast pockets of our parkas gave away our identities. We continued on, still over two miles from camp, only to have the storm overwhelm us in milky white, severely reducing our visibility. Once on the flagged route we slowly made our way in the seventy-five-foot increments between each flag, knowing that we would eventually end up at Weddell World with the last one.

Although the snowmobiles could top out at over thirty-five miles per hour, we crawled along with the speedometer needle not even registering on the dial. We carefully rumbled up to each flag, spotted the next one down the road, drove on, stopped, looked around to locate the next flag ahead of us, and then moved onward. Using these slow, staggering steps, we picked our way back to camp.

The wind refused to give an inch the entire time we traveled, relentlessly hitting us from the side. Our arms and legs on the right exposed side began to ache as the wind cut through our parkas and wind pants. I tried to hunch below the windshield of the snowmobile to keep the freezing wind from creeping up through the bottom of my coat. Despite the wool hat, parka hood, and scarf, I felt the tip of my right ear start to freeze. With one hand on the steering and the other held against my head, I tried to keep up with Randy while watching for Matt behind me. Low visibility caused us to hit hard into the snowdrifts created by the bamboo poles holding the flags. Driving the snowmobile with one hand was impossible on the uneven road, so I gave up trying to warm my ear and focused on simply staying on the vehicle through the windstorm.

Within an hour we made it back safely to Weddell World, but were chilled to the toes. Standing with our backs to the preway stove in the kitchen, the three of us peeled off our snow-covered clothing onto the floor as we related our frigid adventure to the rest of the team. It occurred to me that we would have appeared as blue as glacial ice if someone had thought to turn the infrared thermal camera on us. Slowly the feeling began to return to the tips of my fingers, toes, and right ear. They ached with cold and then with heat as the circulation tried to make amends for shutting down. Randy had not gotten away as cheaply. In the blowing wind, his clothing had shifted, leaving small

patches of skin exposed on his wrist and cheek. During our snowmobile ride he had felt his cheek getting frostbitten and had tried to rub
the circulation back when we stopped at the flagged road. Now a small
triangle-shaped area above his beard and another on his wrist were red
and swollen. Over the ensuing weeks both exposed spots blistered and
the surface of the skin flaked off. The marks left on his skin were one
more reminder of how poorly humans are adapted for Antarctic conditions compared to an adult Weddell seal. In less than ninety minutes of
exposure to the windstorm, we had experienced frostbite and the
beginnings of hypothermia even in insulated clothing.

By the next morning the windstorm had blown itself out and
the sun once again shone above Mount Erebus as if nothing unusual had happened the day before. Matt and I headed out on our daily
survey of the seals of Home Crack to find that the cold temperatures and snow had taken their toll on at least one of the seals.
Alone in a small snowdrift we discovered one of the young pups
that we had been watching for the past week. He lay curled with
his large eyes shut and his fine gray fur packed with snow. Matt
placed a gloved hand on the little seal's body to find it as cold and
unyielding as the surrounding ice. It was obvious from his location
that the pup had wandered several yards away from Home Crack
and his mom. Whether his mother had tried to find him or had just
abandoned him to the storm was difficult to say. She may have
tried to call to the pup, but in the roar of the wind been unable to
hear her newborn call back. The little pup may have been a bit too
rambunctious and then, like ourselves, got caught in the unexpected weather. The end result for the pup was the same. Without a
mom to protect and feed him, the little pup grew weaker and colder in the blowing snow. Finally, he lay down next to a small ridge
in the ice and froze to death as the snow continued to drift all
around his body for the remainder of the night.

The frozen body of the pup would remain on the ice for years.
No insects or bacteria exist in Antarctica to initiate the decay of its
flesh. Only the wind and dry air would slowly desiccate the tissues

and organs, leaving a leathery pelt draped across bones. The skeleton of the pup would be added to the bones of Weddell seals that had died on the ice centuries before, until they melted through to the bottom of the Sound.

As Matt and I stood over the dead pup, we looked across to the other side of Home Crack and noticed a small snow mound huddled next to a large snow mound. I caught my breath when I realized that the mounds were exactly where we had left the other pup and his mom in the storm the night before. We hopped the ice crack expecting the worst. Matt once again placed his gloved hand on the small snow mound only to be greeted by the loud yelp of a pup.

Both Matt and the pup jumped back in surprise, awakening the larger snow mound, the dedicated mom. The pup's mom shook off the dusting of snow, called to her still yelping pup, and led the youngster away from us by humping across the ice. From their speed of travel, it was clear that the two of them had weathered the storm with no ill effects. Once the mom had put enough distance between her pup and us, she rolled over on her side to let him nurse. The pup, who we now called Lucky Pup, readily accepted the offer.

For the next five weeks we periodically visited Lucky Pup at Home Crack. On most occasions he lazily nursed on his mom's rich, fatty milk as she stretched out in twenty-four hours of summer Antarctic sun. During that time he grew larger, fatter, and healthier with the dedicated care and the watchful eye of his mom.

The events of the previous weeks—from our discoveries of hot Weddell seals on ice to the human and seal misadventures in an unexpected windstorm—served as constant reminders for the members of our research expedition. We realized more than ever that the line between life and death is often drawn quite thin in the Antarctic.

CHAPTER 9

LIVING WITH
NEIGHBORS

October 26–31

Back in McMurdo, fall was in full swing with cardboard cutouts of red and yellow autumn leaves decorating the galley hallways. Excitement over the annual Halloween party resulted in bits and pieces from around the Crary lab being absconded with for costume construction. Penguin costumes made of white lab coats, black-plastic-bag bow ties, diving fins, and a paper-cup beak tied to the forehead were a favorite but had been done so many times before that they were now considered cliché. Instead, the multiperson ice worm, an exact replica of an A-Star helicopter rendered in plywood, and Elvis impersonations won crowd approval on the dance floor in the gymnasium.

Out on the ice, Halloween came and went with barely a nod. We were so focused on preparing for the experiments that the days began to meld into one another. Often we lost track of the day of the week as well as the date. We didn't remember that it was October 31, much less recognize it as Halloween. Weekends, weekdays, nighttime, and daytime were all the same. There was only one objective now—get the instruments calibrated for the seals.

Each morning began with a cool rinse of water on the face to wipe away the sleep, dressing in wrinkled field clothes, a groggy walk through the kitchen to grab a cup of Markus's coffee, a juice box, or a bowl of cereal, and then through to the laboratory section of the Jamesway. The days were filled with working on computers, chipping out ice in the diving hole, conducting seal surveys at Home Crack, and soldering by Bill's workbench. In the evenings, the team's seventyfoot path would be reversed from the lab through the kitchen for dinner and to our cots for sleep.

Lee finally remarked, "I can spend entire days walking less than a hundred feet from cot to computer and back." Although he considered this the height of efficiency, I would have been overcome with cabin fever if I had not been outside working on the surveys or shoveling snow for at least part of the day.

In many ways it was like being shipwrecked or imprisoned.

After five weeks of living together, the honeymoon period that kept expedition members on their best behavior was over. Now we had to learn to live with each other's habits, good and bad. Thoughts of home and the people left behind began to drift in and out, depending on our moods.

Bill and Markus started to feel the strain as days of confinement and intense work dragged on. Bill was an underwater hockey player and Markus an avid downhill skier. Under the claustrophobic conditions of camp and the high level of concentration needed for the detailed electronics, computers, and micro-tweaking of instruments, their mental and physical outlooks were strained. Bill kept it all in perspective by taping the picture of his smiling baby daughter on a shelf over his computer. Markus had a picture of the new Mini Cooper that would be waiting for him when he got home.

McMurdo Station, Ross Island, Antarctica has the look and feel of a dusty mining town. The brown barn-like, metal buildings on the left serve as dormitories. The Crary Science and Engineering Lab is the large, tan building on the right.

B-15, an iceberg the size of Rhode Island, smashes into the eastern shore of Ross Island. Emperor penguins and Adelie penguins became trapped in the jumble of ice as the iceberg shattered.

The wooden skeleton of the Jamesway had the look of whale ribs. Insulated blankets (lying in the background) were nailed to the ribs and provided a remarkably sturdy structure in blowing winds.

The author helps to calibrate the VDAP compass according the to the measured bearings.

Weddell seals haul out of the water to catch a few summer rays while lying on top of the ice. Each day our team surveyed the area to determine the ideal seals for our project.

Randy Davis (left) checks the calibration of a depth gauge to be used in the VDAP. The calibration table was just one of eight workstations set up in the laboratory section of the Jamesway.

Pressure ridges formed in the sea ice from underlying ocean currents flowing around Tent Island. Weddell seals took advantage of these deformities in the ice to create breathing holes. Mount Erebus, an active volcano puffs in the background.

A newborn Weddell seal pup announces his arrival in the frozen world of the Antarctic. Note the fresh pink umbilicus still attached to the pup's belly.

Locating the instrumented seals took a lot of patience and snowmobile driving across miles of rough ice. In the top picture the search team waits for Markus to pick up the radio tag signal by using a hand-held antenna. One of the seals wearing our camera poses on the ice before we remove all of the instrumentation to retrieve our data. The antenna from the radio tag can be seen sticking straight up.

The underwater world of the Weddell Seal. These pictures were taken by diving Weddell seals wearing the VDAP instrumentation while diving from 15 meters to 500 meters. The lower part of each picture shows the muzzle and whiskers of the instrumented seal. Encounters with other seals ranged from friendly to confrontational if a breathing hole was at stake.

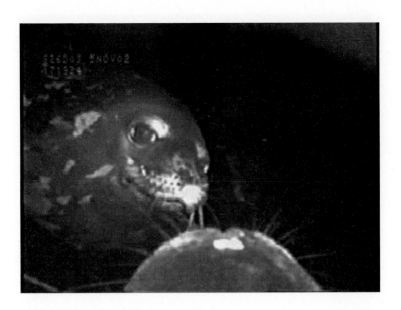

At one point Seal 27 caught seal 26 on camera (upper photo). The lower right picture shows an octopus that was encountered (and eventually eaten) at 300 meters depth.

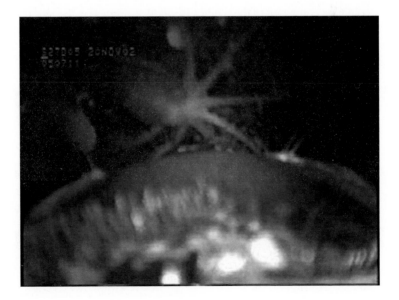

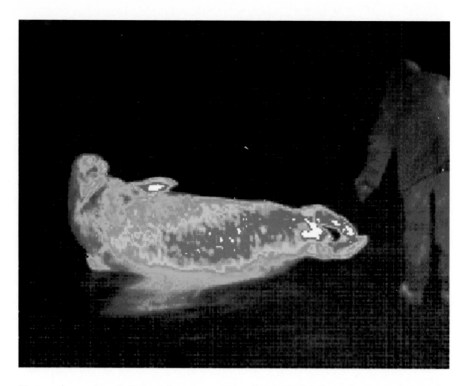

Hot seals on ice. Infrared thermographs of the Weddell seals showed that the animals were surprisingly warm when they hauled out on the ice. In the infrared pictures yellow and red denote hot surface temperatures while blue denotes cold. In the upper photograph a researcher in an insulated parka and wind pants looks ghostly cold blue compared to the red hot Weddell seal lying on the ice. The lower pictures compare a seal's face photographed by a conventional camera (left) and by the infrared thermal camera (right). Note the blue cold whiskers and the hot areas around the eyes.

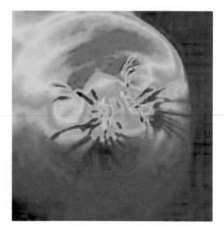

Marker balls were used to determine where the seals came up to breathe. Matt places the orange marker balls into the Weddell seals' breathing holes. Some went into tidal cracks.

In the end, the Weddell seals kicked many of the marked balls back onto the ice. Here one of the culprits is caught in the act of checking out R ball.

Ally McSeal (Seal 19) was the first to show us the remarkable underwater world of the free ranging Weddell seal.

Godzilla (Seal 20), our long, deep diver, takes a cold snooze on the ice.

Ms. Apnea (Seal 21) took us on an amazing tour of the underside of the Erebus Glacier Ice Tongue.

Ms. Zodiac (Seal 22) unfortunately lived up to her name and spent most of her days in "dry-dock" asleep on the ice

Mayflower (Seal 23) was our big girl that liked to hunt for fish.

Sunday (Seal 24) took the day off and spent most of her time sleeping on the ice.

The Hunter's Breath. Breathing is accomplished quickly and forcibly when a Weddell seal emerges from a dive. Often salt water and ice are sprayed for several feet on the first exhalation.

Scarface was easily identified from the open bite wounds around his muzzle. He made things difficult for Ally McSeal by blocking access to one of the breathing holes. In the end Ally won out with a swift nip to his flippers.

Lucky Pup and the swimming lesson. Calling from a diving hole Lucky Pup's
mom tries to coax him into the water for the first time. Refusing to get wet the
small pup remains on the ice and eventually goes back to sunbathing with his
mother beside him—delaying the swim lesson for another day.

Mr. Pink weathers an unexpected snowstorm while sitting in his dive hole on the sea ice before we constructed the Jamesway around him.

Mr. Pink faced off with unidentified male intruders in his private dive hole at Weddell World. Female intruders on the other hand were invited to stay.

Scott's Hut (left) and Shackleton's Hut (right) still frozen in the Antarctic nearly 100 years later.

The Barne Glacier dwarfs a Weddell seal and our snowmobile party (seen as small dots on the horizon). The wall of ice has been a source of wonder since the early Antarctic explorers.

The Weddell World team on top of White Island. From the left Lee Fuiman, Bill Hagey, Randy Davis, Markus Horning, and Matt Rutishauser. The author is in the front row middle. Missing are Don Calkins and Jesse Purdy.

Walking in the footsteps of the great Antarctic explorers that came before us.

Eventually the pressure was relieved by going outside to shovel snow. On the occasions that Bill and Markus found themselves outdoors at the same time, their shoveling usually ended in a snowball fight that escalated into a wresting match in a snowdrift. Covered in snow with faces steaming and red they would return laughing, ready for another serious sixteen-hour bout at the workbench among the electrical wires, Dremel drills, and soldering irons.

For me, each day was kept exciting by meeting up with the Weddell seals at Home Crack. There was always something new to discover about the animals and their surroundings, although I can't say that the seals returned the curiosity. In general, the Weddell seals were indifferent to my presence as well as to the other seals that had hauled out nearby. Except for the moms and pups, no sleeping seal lounged closer than ten feet to its neighbor. This appeared to be more a polite understanding between Weddell seals than an aggressively defended boundary.

Squawking skuas were another matter for the seals, pushing the animals to the brink of their tolerance. For nearly a month it had been only our team and Weddell seals living in peaceful co-existence on the sea ice. At the end of October a new raucous neighbor flew in, skuas. The scavenging birds have the noisy, gang-war temperament of seagulls, and look much like a brown version of the gray-and-white sea birds. They survive on any discarded waste they can find on the ice, and had flown in specifically to take advantage of the afterbirth of the Weddell seals. Wings raised and calling to dozens of their group, the skuas mucked around the blood-covered ice, placentas, and withered umbilical cords near Home Crack.

Adult seals nipped at the flocking birds as if swatting gnats, and pups cried at the disturbance. If a pup slept too soundly the birds would test the animal with a quick peck until protective moms snapped back in warning. Skuas are the hyenas of the Antarctic, and I had to at least admire their ability to survive. In retrospect, if it were not for the scavenging habits of the skua, the debris of life would be left to accumulate in frozen perpetuity on the ice.

Accommodations in the camp were plush when compared to a Scott tent and spartan if compared to home. Three diesel-burning preway stoves along the length of the 128-foot-long Jamesway usually kept the air temperatures comfortable. The only real complaint was the floor; situated on the sea ice, there was little that could be done about the constant chill that crept up through our boots. Solar panels and generators provided power for overhead lights, scientific equipment, and our computers. With twenty-four hours of sun we were able to supplement the heat and light with natural yellow warmth through several small Plexiglas windows sewn into the insulated blankets of the Jamesway walls.

Three features made our camp unique: the sinks, the kitchen, and the shower, all of which relied on one innovation—the ice sump. Using the four-foot-wide auger that had punched out the diving hole, large basins were created by drilling only halfway through the seven-foot-thick ice. The outhouse had been placed over one of these cutouts about twenty-five feet from camp. The novel feature was the creation of a series of these sub-ice sumps below the Jamesway floors for the gray wastewater that resulted from washing hands and dishes. In the past we had washed in basins, collected the dirty water in large plastic buckets, and then carried the heavy buckets outdoors. A considerable amount of the brash water spilled onto pants legs and boots on the trip to the designated dump spot on the ice. It was especially messy in the wind, and eventually opportunistic skuas would invade the dumpsite picking at any bit of food before it froze solid. The joke in McMurdo was that the cleanliness of a camp could always be determined from the number of hungry skuas that hung around.

Another problem was trying to wash hands under the press-button spigot of a water cooler. We could not afford to waste precious water with an open faucet, and in the past space had been so limited that only a single container was used for holding the water for drinking and washing. Weeks of use resulted in an accumulation of soap and grime on the spigot of the cooler, to the point that we were in danger of contaminating our only drinking supply. Disgusted with the arrangement, a graduate student on a previous expedition had rigged up the "handless" wash station. From string and several bamboo flagpoles, he fashioned a ladder-like device that pressed into the spigot button of the plastic cooler when a foot pedal was depressed. The bamboo device had a Swiss Family Robinson feel to it and worked well until someone tried to wash their hands while wearing heavy bunny boots, ultimately crushing the foot mechanism.

With the under-ice sumps we were able to plumb in separate sinks in the kitchen and bathing area. The sumps collected and froze the wastewater, which eventually broke out with the sea ice during the winter storms. The indoor sumps of Weddell World also provided the most sought-after luxury on the sea ice—a shower.

Bathing in a field camp was usually limited to the occasional sponge bath, if bothered with at all. To avoid the risk of a sudden chill, expedition members often did without for days on end, relying on the low humidity of the Antarctic air to keep odors at bay. Over time, sweat would combine with the acrid smell of gasoline and diesel from filling snowmobiles and preway stoves, and the pungent fish oil odor characteristic of seals. Eventually the aroma of camp life numbed the noses of the team members. It was only when heads turned in quizzical disgust on the occasional trip to McMurdo for supplies that we noticed the smell.

The Weddell World shower changed all that and was the envy of the other sea ice camps. We used snow melted and warmed on the preway stove to fill an overhead plastic bag with a hose connected to the bottom. A plastic curtain and basin with a pipe drain in the center directed water to the sub-ice sump. The results were luxurious. A hot shower of melted Antarctic snow softened the darkest of temperaments and the most tangled hat hair better than any conditioner known to man.

Days and nights continued to drift into one another, accentuated by the constant sunlight and the slow, painstaking process of preparing the camera and sensors. In addition to ensuring that the instruments would withstand the sub-zero water temperatures and the high hydrostatic pressures encountered when the seals swam to depth, there was the problem of calibrating the compass. By simultaneously measuring dive depth and compass bearing, Lee Fuiman planned to recreate the three-dimensional dive path of the hunting seals on his computers. It would be a virtual ride with the seal under the ice.

There was one major problem, however. Magnetic compasses do not work well near the poles of the earth. To this day skeptics argue over which of the early explorers were the first to reach the North and South Poles; it all depended on the accuracy of their compass readings. In Antarctica the magnetic South Pole was shifted hundreds of miles away from the geographical South Pole, rendering compasses questionable on the continent. This left our team with the problem of correcting for the troublesome shift.

For travelers on top of the ice, navigation was less of a concern these days due to the availability of satellites and handheld GPS units. However, GPS units didn't work on diving seals; satellites could not communicate through ice and seawater.

The answer lay in celestial navigational theories that predated even Columbus. Sailors often relied on the position of the North Star for navigation on the high seas. Due to the constant light, we had no such navigational aid; however, Randy reasoned that we did have the sun. Even in Antarctica, the sun followed a predictable path in the sky throughout the day and night. Its compass position was known, as long as you knew the exact time of day and your exact location. From that single bearing, north, south, east, and west could be established according to a standard compass rose.

The process of establishing our first compass point was a little easier for us than in the days of Columbus and the early Antarctic explorers. With the availability of a handheld GPS unit, we could determine our exact position on top of the ice. A celestial calculator purchased at a marine supply shop provided a precise compass position of the sun in our area by entering our GPS coordinates and time. Now it was just a matter of facing the VDAP's compass into the sun on our horizon and entering the calculated compass position into its microprocessor.

On a chilly evening under the pale-pink glow of a midnight sun, Randy, Bill, and I headed from the Jamesway to the compass calibration hut. The ten foot by ten foot wooden hut was part of the Weddell World complex and served only one purpose—calibration of the VDAP compass. Constructed of wood, brass screws, and aluminum fixtures, the building contained no ferrous (iron) parts that could distort the magnet in the VDAP compass. Large Plexiglas windows provided a 360° view of the Antarctic horizon and warmed the small room without the need for a preway stove. Bill held onto the VDAP while Randy and I positioned the compass table. On top of the table, a large compass rose had been etched onto a brass plate in degree increments. The tabletop spun on a single central bolt, which allowed it to be set to true north. At exactly midnight Randy "shot the sun" through a brass polaris that consisted of a viewfinder and sighting rod mounted on top of the compass rose. The sun glowed orange as it skirted the top of the Royal Society Mountain Range while casting shadows on Mount Erebus behind us. Wearing a pair of polarized sunglasses covered with ski goggles to protect his eyes, Randy looked directly into the sun and aligned the sighting rod with its position. We already knew the predicted compass bearing of the sun from the celestial calculator, so it was a matter of swiveling the compass rose drawn on the tabletop to coincide with the alignment of the sun. From the one known position provided by the sun, the compass rose now showed us true north, south, east, and west for our part of Antarctica.

The rest of the calibration was up to Bill. He positioned the VDAP compass on the tabletop and tweaked the electronic readout until it gave the proper compass bearing. Once calibrated, the instrument would automatically make the correction for the polar magnetic shift when it was on the diving seal. We now had an accurate compass that would work underwater.

From a technological and logistical standpoint, our expedition ranged from crude, make-do innovation to state-of-the-art scientific instrumentation. The research we had planned was particularly challenging. We were working with instruments that had never been intended for use in the Antarctic environment or for deployment on a wild free-ranging animal. I would be using nearly $100,000 worth of specialized scientific instrumentation to measure the health and athletic capabilities of the seals before and after a dive. As they hunted for fish below the sea ice, the seals would carry custom-designed, miniaturized computer and video equipment. Although placing instruments on wild animals was not a new idea, the amount of instrumentation involved, both on and off the animal, was unprecedented. There had been many studies in which wild animals had been radio-collared or had carried small instruments. Our study would be the first to try to match video images with physiological and behavioral data of an undersea predator. It was going to take a lot of creativity on our part and an extremely cooperative wild animal.

Fortunately, Weddell seals are uniquely qualified. They are large, carnivorous, and exceptionally docile. Weddell seals are two times larger than a male African lion and can efficiently kill prey that is easily half its body length. Unlike lions, the Weddell seal show no aggressive tendencies and no fear of humans. Lying on the ice, they viewed our research team with a chilly air of nonchalance. On our approach, they rolled over on their backs and waved a front flipper at us in response to our rudeness for awakening them from their naps. Once we moved away the seals would roll back into their original sleeping positions with a yawn.

At long last, after weeks of preparation, we heard the announcement that we had all been waiting for.

"I think we're finally ready," Randy declared.

With everyone in agreement, we quickly pulled on parkas, boots, and gloves for the drive out to Home Crack to select the first seal of our expedition. The VDAP camera and sensors sat on the laboratory table, shining in their black-and-silver anodized cases. Everything was calibrated, packaged, and ready to journey below the Antarctic sea ice. One of the Antarctic's most pervasive predators would be our guide, and we were finally going to decide which seal would take us on the underwater adventure.

CHAPTER 10

THE BIG PLUNGE

Selecting a Weddell seal for our study was akin to taking the family to pick out a Christmas tree. The entire team piled into the Spryte and snowmobiles to head to Home Crack. As we surveyed the seals, each member of the research team had a different opinion about the ideal animal. Some seals were obviously too large, others too small; others were not full enough, and some were chewed up on the edges from skirmishes with other seals. We wanted to work with a calm, confident, healthy adult Weddell seal. To avoid disturbing a pregnant animal or a mom with a pup, we searched among the resting seals to find a relatively lean-looking animal. Choosing between a male or female seal depended on what we were willing to risk. Females tended to be more obstinate while the males were more territorial and lazy.

Scarface was immediately rejected; we did not want an animal prone to fighting that could destroy the instruments. The Dedicated Mom was also ineligible due to her obligations with Lucky Pup. After surveying sixteen seals on the ice by Home Crack, the team agreed to take a chance on a skinny, nonpregnant female. It was the long-whiskered, winking female that Matt and I had been watching for weeks.

On approach she was especially mild-mannered, and we found her easy to herd into our seal sled with the aid of an open mesh net. The sled had the look of a railroad boxcar, painted bright orange so that it was easily detected in the middle of a snowstorm. Even the largest Weddell seal could stretch out in comfort along its ten-foot length. Metal runners and a sturdy metal hitch allowed the box to be pulled easily across the ice by our little Spryte. Because there was no top, we could look in on the seal as she traveled to camp. One member of the team could also ride along in the sled to guarantee a safe trip for the seal across the ice.

The female seal gave a quick look around the box sled and then lay belly-down on the bed. She appeared quite content to be out of the wind, but could have done without the occasional bump from the pressure ridges on the ice. A short ten minutes later, we arrived at Weddell World with our precious cargo. Slowly Jesse backed the sled up to the wooden chute leading to the back door of the Jamesway.

Now we had to make our first, and perhaps most difficult, measurement on the seal. We needed to know how much she weighed. Despite being lean for a Weddell, the long-whiskered seal is at least four times heavier than any of the team members. There is no bathroom scale large enough for weighing an animal as heavy as an adult Weddell seal, and just trying to maneuver the seal into weighing position relied on our patience and the animal's cooperation. We used a soft sling made of finely woven nylon netting and a large electronic hanging scale that would weigh the seal in the same manner as a basket of fruit at the market. The scale had been mounted on a robust overhead wooden beam and the entire contraption connected to a heavy duty winch with a steel cable and a set of carabineers, the same releasable metal rings used for safety lines in mountaineering.

Sliding the door open on the end of the sled, the female seal was given a clear path down the chute. She surveyed the situation, yawned, and went back to sleeping on her side in the sled. We huddled, shivering in the cold wind beside the chute trying to stay out of sight so that the seal would not be intimidated by our presence. She could have cared less and continued to sleep in the windless comfort of the box sled until we knocked on the wooden side to awaken her. Opening her large, wet eyes, the seal finally looked down the chute, snorted, and slowly inchwormed her way forward. After four great humps of her body she positioned herself on the sling that we had spread out on the chute. Lee started to lift her and the sling up by using all of his weight to pull down on the handle of the winch. Gradually, the sling snugged around her massive body. She cleared the ground by barely an inch but it allowed us to get her weight. Our "lean" seal weighed over 316 kilograms (695 pounds). That made her a lightweight among Weddell seals, but equivalent to lifting two grand pianos. In fact, with her hind flippers poking out of the end of the sling we realized that she was also the length of two grand pianos placed end to end. This was a big animal to try to maneuver indoors.

Following her less-than-demure weigh-in, the seal was guided into the Jamesway though the wooden chute. She appeared more curious than concerned about her new surroundings, but the team agreed that we should give her a light tranquilizer. This would prevent her from possibly injuring herself indoors, and keep her calm while we assessed her health and outfitted her with the VDAP camera and sensors. A light dose of ketamine and Valium injected into her massive thigh muscle caused no reaction as the seal snuffled around the floor of the Jamesway and poked her head at the Plexiglas window. She seemed especially fascinated by the window, which must have looked like a layer of ice to her. If it were not for the tranquilizer starting to take effect, she was ready to start reaming. Instead the seal rolled onto her side to snooze.

The entire team of eight people worked efficiently to complete the body measurements and custom-fit the VDAP for the seal as she slept. Don continuously monitored her breathing rate and behavior while she was in the Jamesway. Knowing that the tranquilizer would wear off within twenty minutes, he counted down our time with a stopwatch.

Matt and I measured the length of the seal from nose to flipper tip with a tape measure; she was exactly nine feet long. We checked her for scars and bites from other seals as well as examined her eyes and listened to her heart. With a portable ultrasound machine used for monitoring pregnancy in humans, we discovered that the seal had a two-and-a-half-inch-thick layer of fatty blubber encasing her entire torso. This blubber layer equaled the width and consistency of two sticks of warm butter stacked on top of one another, and provided the seal with enough insulation to keep her warm during her dives.

As I filled out the data sheets with the seal's vital statistics, I realized that we needed to give her a name. Her official scientific title for the project was Seal 19, representing the nineteenth Weddell seal that our team had studied in the past five years. Seal 19 was how she would be referred to in our research papers. However, we would be working with this seal for the next five days, and calling her Seal 19 would be an awkward mouthful, if we even remembered the right number. Despite our best efforts to remain scientifically distant and objective, each Weddell seal we worked with had a unique personality deserving of a unique name.

"Sleepy?" suggested Don who was watching the seal snore. The team groaned in disapproval.

Markus chimed in with "Ouzo!" a Greek liquor that had inspired much dancing in a Christchurch restaurant back in September.

Whiskers, Spot, and Winky were also proposed and immediately rejected.

Names were spontaneously shouted out the entire time that we measured and outfitted the seal. Finally, the team considered the seal's most obvious features. Seal 19 had a veneer of confidence, big eyes, and a thin body (at least among Weddell seals), the same qualities as the television character Ally McBeal. Accordingly, we decided to name our long-whiskered, winking seal Ally McSeal.

Matt and I finished our measurements, vacating a space for Randy, Bill, Lee, Jesse, and Markus to arrange the calibrated VDAP and sensors on Ally. The streamlined shape of the seal presented a major obstacle in terms of securing the instruments on the animal. Collars are typically used for putting tags and sensors on terrestrial mammals, but these would have quickly slipped off of the narrow head of the seal. Harnesses were possible, but were bulky and created turbulence around a swimmer. In the past, researchers working on marine mammals had used everything from epoxy and cable ties to suction cups, and even surgical implantation to attach scientific equipment to seals, sea lions, dolphins, and whales. We wanted something more versatile, flexible, and noninvasive for the Weddell seals.

The team chose a special neoprene pad made of wetsuit material that adhered like a Band-Aid onto the skin and fur. The pad was tailored to cover part of the seal's back, looking very much like a blanket on a horse. Various sensors were then attached to the pad and kept in place with a light coating of neoprene glue.

The main instrument to be attached to the neoprene pad was the VDAP containing the video recorder and the computer brains for all of the other sensors. Many of the sensors were identical to those used by recreational scuba divers: clocks to monitor how long the seal was diving, swimming speed meters, a compass, a heart-rate monitor, and a depth gauge. The lens of a camera connected to the VDAP was positioned up front to give us a "seal's-eye view" over Ally's muzzle.

There were two special tags attached to the pad that would enable us to relocate Ally after her dives. One was a radio tag that continuously signaled us through a radio receiver if she hauled out on top of the ice. This was the same old-fashioned tag that had been used by wildlife biologists for decades to follow the tracks of large and small mammals such as wild cheetahs in Africa, wolves in North America, and pandas in China. The second was a satellite tag that provided a broader location of the seal. Like a small handheld GPS unit, the satellite tag produced a signal from the seal to an over-flying satellite. The signal was subsequently downloaded through e-mail to our computers in the Jamesway and translated into the latitude and longitude position of the seal when she hauled out.

As technologically advanced as the tags were, there was one major limitation shared by both—neither tag was able to transmit through water. Thus, the instrumented seal had to haul out on the ice for them to work and for us to find her.

Ally intermittently looked about and dozed through the fitting while the research team worked intensely all around her. It took less than two hours from start to finish. We had successfully recorded the seal's health and body condition, and with one last cinch of the water-tight cables, Bill put the final touches on the VDAP and sensors. Then the entire package was smoothed with syntactic foam to make it hydrodynamic in profile and neutrally buoyant in water.

The small size of the instruments belied their powerful technology and was a testament to electronic miniaturization. In the end, the massive seal dwarfed the instrument package, and we feared that she would crush the sensors and the camera under her weight when she rolled over during her nap.

Rather than disturb the sleeping seal, the team chose to let Ally determine when she would leave the Jamesway. Initially, she took advantage of the warmth and quiet to sleep for several hours. After her nap Ally McSeal was bright-eyed and curious. She inchwormed over to the end of the Jamesway and peered outside through one of the Plexiglas windows. Raising the front end of her body, she pushed at the window with her muzzle in the same behavior she used to test the thickness of a skin of ice on the water surface. While she was preoccupied, the team moved the floorboards of the Jamesway to reveal the 4-foot diameter diving hole beneath. The water was crystal clear, turning from deep blue near the surface to black at 200 meters (656 feet) below our camp. To a Weddell seal it could not have been more inviting. Ally was free to take a dip.

Instead of rushing into the water, the seal inspected the new hole by sticking her muzzle underwater. Ally looked right and then left, and then lifted her head and dripping whiskers to look at us as we stood shuffling in nervous anticipation. Again she dipped her head and scanned right and left. We could only presume that she was trying to determine if there was another seal in this unusual hole, but the wait was agonizing for us. For fifteen minutes the seal sipped, dipped, and blew bubbles at the edge of the diving hole as if deciding whether a post-nap swim was worth the effort of getting wet.

Finally, Ally "delicately" rolled off of the floorboards sideways, hitting the water with a resounding splash and causing a seawater tidal wave that soaked the legs of Randy's pants. Only three big strokes of her hind flippers were needed to propel her through the seven feet of ice and into the open water below. We felt as if we had launched a high-tech submarine as the seal disappeared with all of our equipment. The team cheered, cutting congratulations short as we rushed to a video monitor in the laboratory. From an underwater camera mounted next to the diving hole, we watched as Ally patrolled the underside of the ice beneath our camp. She floated in typical Weddell seal fashion, paying no attention to the instrumentation or neoprene blanket. In the distance other Weddell seals calling to one another gave Ally the bearings she needed. Home Crack was a mere half-mile swim away, an easy jaunt for a Weddell seal. Ally finally pointed her nose straight down and slowly swam to depth, disappearing from our sight.

Within an hour she was back. She arrived with an explosive breath, so we heard her before we saw her. Ally bobbed at the surface of our diving hole as she breathed and sprayed water with each exhalation. Her nostrils pumped open on exhalations that were so forceful we could feel them across the room. After a quick inhalation her muscular nostrils snapped shut. She held her breath for a few seconds and then began the cycle again.

Bill rushed to the edge of the dive hole to inspect the equipment on the seal. His first concern was damage due to scraping. The sensors and the camera were vulnerable to sharp ice and could peel off if Ally swam too close to the edge of the dive hole or along the underside of the surface ice. One awkward turn by the seal could have destroyed years of his work.

Ally calmly floated on the water of the dive hole as Bill twisted every cable connection and checked the glue of each patch. Everything appeared to be in working order. No damage had been done on Ally's first dive, and she was oblivious to her new attire. Our confidence in the seal and our experiment soared.

Barely acknowledging our presence, Ally stayed on the water surface resting for several minutes. All of the sudden her breathing quickened like a swimmer preparing to go the length of a pool. She took several enormous breaths, exhaled, and then sank forward, drifting headfirst through the bottom of the dive hole. Ally was gone.

We sat with stopwatches counting: twenty minutes—the duration of a typical Weddell seal dive; forty minutes—the length of an exploratory dive; sixty minutes; seventy minutes; and eighty-two minutes—the longest dive ever recorded for a Weddell seal. After ninety minutes, we knew that Ally had finally returned to the wild.

This was an exciting, open-ended moment filled with infinite scientific possibilities conjured up by my imagination. There was no predicting where the seal would go, what she would do, or what she would find. Ally McSeal had just swum off to the deep-blue depths with over $50,000 of our scientific instrumentation and much more in terms of our hard work. On her journey she would record the ocean temperature as she swam and the sounds of other Weddell seals calling in the area. During her travels the instruments would monitor *her swimming speed and the whoosh of every stroke she took on ascent and descent. I hoped that she would hunt for giant Antarctic cod and enter schools of flittering little Antarctic silverfish. Through the video camera I wanted to experience everything that a seal experienced when it dove to the bottom of McMurdo Sound. I wanted to know what it would be like to swim effortlessly through the water.*

At that moment, as I stood in the Jamesway looking down into the empty diving hole, I realized that Ally McSeal was in charge of our hopes and our science. We were merely collaborating lab assistants who would interpret the data she collected for us. The potential for new discoveries was endless.

The success of the entire study revolved around radio and satellite tags that would enable us to find Ally McSeal after she completed her foraging dives. Because all of the data was contained on the videotape and microcomputer cards tucked inside of the VDAP, we would lose everything if we couldn't relocate the seal. We were gambling on the proclivity of Weddell seals to sunbathe in the radiant heat of the Antarctic summer sun. Our plan was to wait for Ally to haul out somewhere on the surface of the ice to sunbathe, locate her using the tags as beacons, and then remove all of our scientific gear.

We were well aware that Ally McSeal could swim away from McMurdo Sound, taking all of our instruments and hopes with her. If she chose that dark path, then the neoprene patch would peel off as she swam along or when she molted her fur coat in the next month. In either case, the instruments with all of our data would be lost to the bottom of the ocean.

Conflicting thoughts raced through our minds as we continued to stand over the diving hole, staring blankly into the depths and Ally's diminishing wake. In what appeared to be a foolish move, we had just let a wild seal swim away with it all.

CHAPTER 11

LOST IN
THE STORM

NOVEMBER 3–7

Suddenly our expedition faced an unexpected setback. For six days blowing snow and high winds rolled across the sea ice as one Herbie hit our camp, followed by another and another. Each time, the needle on the barometric pressure gauge in the laboratory dropped in anticipation of the approaching storm. Soon afterwards a dark gray cloud loomed in the distance, first obscuring Black Island, then White Island, then McMurdo Station, and finally us.

We knew that something was up the moment that we awakened on the first day. Rather than the usual light breezes that caused the red flags on our road to flap noisily on clear days, the flags fell limp and silent in the hours before the storm. We took advantage of the lull to prepare for the incoming blow.

Snowmobiles had to be covered and faced into the wind away from the buildings. Their position was critical as large drifts developed behind any object on the ice that obstructed the steadfast path of the blowing snow. Ice axes, loose bamboo flagpoles—anything that could blow away or get lost in a drift—were secured in an upright position next to the Jamesway walls. The location of all fuel barrels, outdoor equipment, and frozen food boxes were each marked with a red flag on an eight-foot-long bamboo pole so that we could find them in the snow afterwards.

Shovels were placed in the vestibules of the doorways in case we had to dig ourselves out. An unfortunate shortcoming of a Jamesway, which had been designed for use in the Korean War, was that all of the doors opened outward. This may have worked well in jungles, but it was a major disadvantage in snow-covered terrain. Even a foot of new snow or drifting made it impossible for us to open the doors. During stormy nights we had to periodically dig out at least one door, only to return to recurring nightmares about snow drifting so high that we would be forced to break out the Plexiglas windows to free ourselves. This never happened, but with snow climbing three feet per day it was not outside the realm of possibility with the nine-foot-high Jamesway. The wooden huts around camp were built with escape hatches in their roofs for just such an emergency. There were no escape hatches in the Jamesway, but its soft-sided insulated blankets made getting out only a matter of cutting through them with a knife.

When the first storm bore down on Weddell World, the wind reversed direction, swinging 180 degrees from a southerly blow to due north, straight down Herbie Alley. The serious wind arrived with a slam directly into the side of the camp. With it, fine snow that had been scraped across hundreds of miles of the Antarctic continent covered us in a thick cloud. The sky, ground, and horizon disappeared, leaving us holed up and isolated in the Jamesway. In one day, the drifts grew to over five feet in camp. Soon we were standing on tiptoes peering out of the last few inches of the top edge of the windows to catch a glimpse of the outdoors. It felt like we were drowning in snow.

We occupied the long hours by working individually on small projects. Each of us had manuscripts, letters, and paperwork from home that we attempted to complete during the storms. At times all of us were silently hunched over computers in the laboratory as the snow drifted higher and higher over the windows of the building. Under such claustrophobic quarters it was necessary to have these quiet times to avoid getting on each other's nerves. The clinking of a spoon on the side of a coffee mug, the repetitive nervous clearing of a throat, the tapping of a pencil on a table, or even the furious clicking of keyboard keys could grow to irritating proportions. Eight of us were confined together twenty-four hours a day in a 128-foot-long drafty cave of a building for several days at a time with each storm; there was no escape other than a trip to the outhouse. Even then we had to announce to the group our intentions to go out-side, and we had to carry a radio in anticipation of getting knocked off our feet or lost in the storm.

Despite all of the free time, it was impossible to concentrate. Friends, relatives, and coworkers wanted news from "down South," but we found that we were unable to focus our thoughts long enough to put them on paper or display them on a computer monitor. We were preoccupied as the howling wind and the sound of snow scraping along the insulated blankets constantly remind-ed us that we were far removed from the events of the rest of the world. Ensuring our survival on the ice was paramount, leaving little emotional reserve for anything else.

When we spoke to radio operators in McMurdo Station during our daily check-ins, they mentioned something called anthrax scares that had tossed the United States into turmoil on the heals of September 11. Taken out of context while a storm raged outdoors, it was difficult to understand what was happen-ing or to grasp the significance of the events at home. It was better to know nothing.

Moving between the buildings in camp was a test of nerves and attempted only if absolutely necessary. In the face of the howling wind, we could lean forward in a 45-degree ski jumper's angle without falling down. We learned that a person can stand upright in winds blowing at forty miles per hour, trudge slowly through snow with head down pushing against the wind at fifty miles per hour, lean with a shoulder forward to struggle slowly against a sixty-mile-per-hour gale, and be buffeted to the ground in anything much higher. At Weddell World the Herbies began with sustained winds of forty to fifty miles per hour and often gusted to over seventy-five miles per hour. Each storm could last for days.

The team was grounded. And, worst of all, there was no chance of finding Ally McSeal. Doing nothing was agony. So as futile as it was, the team began an hourly vigil with binoculars, searching for our seal on the snowy horizon.

Dusty-dry, fine snow began to seep into every crack of Weddell World and completely drifted over the windows. Before the snow built up, convective cooling from the blowing wind chilled the Jamesway down, overpowering the little preway stoves. The wooden floors hardened, sending the chill straight up through our boots. Soon we could see our breath rising in frosty puffs as we spoke to each other in the laboratory.

We each began to add layers of clothing in an effort to keep warm. Blue jeans and knit turtlenecks were replaced with insulated wind pants with fleece liners and thermal vests. I stuffed thick wool socks into my vest to warm them up before slipping several pairs onto my white-cold toes. Jesse bundled up in three layers of insulated underwear, flannel liners, wind pants, and several fleece jackets. Matt resorted to wearing fingerless hunting gloves when working on his computer. With the keyboard in his lap, he would tap away while resting his feet on the edge of the table to keep them from freezing to the floor. He had quickly learned to take advantage of the thermocline created by the limited rising heat of the preway stoves. Near the floor, temperatures were freezing and snow piled in scattered drifts through small openings in the insulated blankets. Near the roof, temperatures hovered in the fifties immediately above the stoves. The entire range of temperatures occurred between the two.

We kept careful watch over those with the lowest metabolic rates as they sank into hibernation mode, sometimes seeking the shelter of their sleeping bags to shiver, sleep, and warm up. Afternoon naps and ten-hour bouts of sleep during the night were not unusual. The high metabs drifted in the opposite direction and seemed to eat continuously. Throughout the storms Lee, Matt, and I grazed on Oreos, Cadbury bars, and trail mix, finding instant heat in every bit of chocolate consumed. Markus manned a mini-Starbucks in the kitchen, first grinding fresh aromatic coffee beans he had brought from Christchurch and then resorting to desiccated Folger's Instant as supplies ran out. For everyone, the fattier the food the better. The team ate five pounds of butter during the three days of one storm and still craved more. When the butter ran out we turned to oils, cheeses, and chocolate to help our bodies generate heat and insulation.

Winds continued to howl through the nights at over sixty miles per hour, sounding like roaring oncoming locomotives in the smaller huts. Each gust shook the walls next to our sleeping bags and rumbled across the floors. The wind pounded against our heads like fists. None of us could sleep due to the constant battering and cold, combined with the anxiety over Ally McSeal's disappearance.

In the early morning on the second day of the first Herbie, I awoke with the vague feeling of mixed warmth and cold. Slowly opening one eye and then the other, I found that snow had forced its way through small nail holes and cracks in the walls and floor during the night. The high winds had pushed a fine spindrift of snow onto my cot, covering the foot of my sleeping bag, coating the walls, and blanketing the floor in several inches of fluffy powder. In the soft morning light my corner of the sleeping quarters had the cold, quiet aura of an ice cave. My toothbrush and cup were coated with a puffy spray of snow. My face towel and a pair of wool socks hung stiff and frosted on a nail beside my cot. Boots, pants, water bottles, and my watch were dusted white. It was charming until I moved my feet.

I groaned out loud with a trailing, "NOoooooooo. . . ."

I could feel the clammy moisture of melting snow seeping into my sleeping bag, soaking my socks and thermals. Shaking myself out of the sleeping bag like a wet seal emerging from an ice hole, I tried pulling on one of my frozen socks and then wedging my cold stiff foot into a snow-filled boot. Once thawed, I repeated the exercise with my other foot. Wincing and shuffling, I sought out one of the preway stoves to try to defrost my clothes and warm my frozen feet on the way to the kitchen to find something to eat.

Hard, crystalline snow continued to scrape along the sides of the buildings, adding to the nerve-wracking noise created by the rush of the wind. Nine hours of sleep had made little difference in the intensity of the storm. Just like the day before, we could only intermittently see the other buildings as the winds gusted and fine snow swirled around the camp. Blowing snow obscured the radio tower, the compass calibration hut, and the outhouse. Fortunately, in anticipation of the storms we had marked each with an identifying flag.

Recognizing that Captain Scott had proudly displayed the British flag and Roald Amundsen the Norwegian flag during their Antarctic exploits, our team had decided to follow in the tradition of the great Antarctic explorers and display our respective school colors. Atop the fifty-foot-high radio communication tower the maroon and white Texas A & M University flag faced into the blowing wind with ostentatious flapping. It was a three-foot-by-four-foot memorial to the Texas institution.

The University of California Santa Cruz display was by necessity more subtle but no less important. Before the expedition, it had been a disheartening search for a flag from Santa Cruz. Scouring the campus bookstore the week before I left for the ice, there was nothing to compare with the Texas A & M flag. Why was it that everything from Texas had to be bigger? There was no majestic flag for the mighty Santa Cruz Banana Slug, considered by many to be a king among school mascots. On the thin shelves, there were only the standard wimpy felt pennants that would be ripped to shreds at the first sign of a southern breeze, and decals that would have frozen and fluttered away. Little else displayed our beloved yellow invertebrate mascot.

In the end I took a utilitarian approach. Consequently, in the middle of a Herbie triple header, as the Texas A & M flag waved from a dizzying height above the camp, a pair of silk boxer shorts emblazoned with UC Santa Cruz slugs fluttered from an eight-foot-tall bamboo pole over the outhouse. It was difficult to miss the bright yellow banana slugs against a background of University of California dark blue. The slug shorts nobly weathered each Herbie, fraying another inch from the legs every day. By the end of a week of storms, they were down to skimpy briefs. Despite the beating, even in the worst blowing snow the needy could rely on the Santa Cruz slugs to lead the way to relief.

During the storms, the team huddled in the Jamesway and listened intently to the radio receiver, waiting for the steady beeping of Ally McSeal's radio tag. We went through daily chores always with an ear towards the receiver, hoping for the bird-like "chirp, chirp, chirp" that would signal Ally's appearance out on the ice somewhere nearby. At the same time, Randy periodically checked his e-mail for transmission signals from the satellite tag that she was wearing. Both tags remained frustratingly silent. Broken static was the only sound that was emitted from the radio receiver; the computer never responded to prompting.

Although disappointed and concerned, we were not surprised. As the winds persisted, the seals of Home Crack had all disappeared by seeking the calm waters beneath the ice. Only two pairs of snow-encrusted moms and pups remained on the surface braving the severe weather together. We recognized Lucky Pup curled up in the lee of his mom, who stoically protected him from the brunt of each of the storms. Ally, along with all of our instruments, had likely followed the other adult seals that decided to wait out the violent storms in relative safety under the ice. Constant overcast and blowing snow kept the seals hiding, muffling the radio and satellite signals from Ally's tags.

In the few hours of calm between the back-to-back Herbies we were obsessed in our efforts to track the elusive Ally McSeal, and set out on foot and on snowmobiles. Our only chance of finding her depended on the two tags on her back; the likelihood of actually seeing her in the blowing snow was extremely low, even if she had hauled out. During our desperate attempts, we used a handheld antenna and portable radio receiver that could be slung over one shoulder to search for her on the ice. Standing in the drifting snow, we tweaked the frequency and volume knobs of the receiver trying to zero in on the radio signal from Ally's tag.

For hours, we searched in teams of two to three people for the instrumented seal, driving across the rugged sastrugi that had built up on the sea ice after the storms. The rough ice and snow wrenched our backs and necks as we miscalculated the size of the drifts in the low-ground visibility. We pointed the radio antenna towards Home Crack, Weddell World, McMurdo, and Herbie Alley. The only response was the hard crackle of static from the receiver.

Finally, in an effort to improve the vantage point for the radio signals, we climbed to the top of the Erebus Glacier Ice Tongue, overlooking Home Crack. Razor-edged crevasses that had been created by the slow advance of the glacier down the mountainside made the climb precarious. It was all the more dangerous because fresh snow bridges concealed the dangerous fractures. One wrong step could have easily resulted in a broken ankle or a fatal slip between the wedges of ice.

After all of the effort, there was no familiar rhythmic beep of the radio tag. There were no seals on the horizon. It appeared that Ally and our equipment were truly lost.

Back at camp, Jesse placed a hydrophone in the dive hole under the laboratory floor to try to listen for Ally. Acting as a submersible microphone, the instrument allowed him to eavesdrop on the underwater "conversations" of the local Weddell seals. Jesse could sit for hours with the headphones on, stroking his ever-lengthening beard while recording the confusing mix of simultaneous cocktail party dialogues by the Weddell seals.

"Whrrrrrrrrrrr . . . chirp, chip, chip-chip," sang one seal.

"Chip, ship, chipp . . . gluuu-ug, CHUG," responded another from a distance.

The vocal seals chirped, clicked, trilled, and created booming sounds that echoed off of the ice all around the camp. Their repertoire was extraordinary when compared to the simple woofs, growls, and whines of my dogs. By comparison, terrestrial mammals reminded me of children just learning to speak, whereas Weddell seals were true masters of mammalian linguistics. Their vocalizations ranged from high-pitched canary chirps to thundering low-frequency pulses that dropped into lower and lower registers. Quick warning clicks to other seals sounded like castanets being played by a nervous Spanish dancer. Deep-throated chugs pulsed with the cadence of a beating heart until the conversation ended with a single boom, blasting with the resounding finale of a fireworks display. Often the final blasts were so powerful that Jesse's recorders would shudder in the presence of the low-frequency pulses.

The most pervasive and impressive single sound was the trill: a long, drawn-out, high-pitched whistle that echoed into the black depths in an eerie, wailing "WWHIiiiRRiiirr . . . iiiirrrr. . . ." The trills traveled across the ocean, up your boots, and down your spine, reminiscent of the long whine of dropping bombs released into the sky.

A survey of Jesse's Weddell seal recordings demonstrated their vocal repertoire and his amusement over their sounds. His titles included "The Cancerous Lung Cough," "Great Knockers," "Trills and Thrills," and "Strange Klink Klanks."

The Weddells showed little courtesy, talking over one another with increasing bravado as they approached one another. When Jesse and Bill installed a submersible camera near the hydrophone, we were able to watch as the seals interacted and vocalized. The clicks seemed to indicate territorial displays between males. Two male Weddell seals would face off immediately below our diving hole, vying for ownership. They circled each other, clicking continuously by popping their jaws until one of them thrust his bulky head forward in an effort to bite the other in the hind flippers or belly. The sparring continued, sometimes drawing blood until one of the males backed off, slinking into the depths while the winner floated up into the dive hole to relax and breathe in the calm of victory.

Chirps were warning signals used by the seals ascending from a dive. There was little doubt that they shouted, "Get out of the way, I need to breathe NOW!" Most often the other seals in the area complied with the demand by backing out of the breathing hole. Males and females spoke back and forth in trills, chirps, and a *Star Wars* R2D2-like "Hmmmmmm."

For all of their intensity, the sounds were made without the benefit of exhaling the way that humans and terrestrial animals do when they vocalize. It was amazing to me that Weddell seals were able to create the vast array of sounds with their nostrils clamped shut while holding their breath. Watching the vocalizing seals on the submersible camera, I could see head and chest movements associated with many of the sounds, but no bubbles to indicate that the animals had exhaled. Only when the seals emitted a long, low foghorn blow near the water surface would the water boil with their breath. Clearly, air was too precious to waste on talking during a dive, and the foghorn was used only near an ice hole or tide crack where the seals could quickly catch their next breath.

With all of the seals vocalizing at once, it was impossible to pick Ally out of the crowd. From Jesse's hydrophone we learned that a large number of Weddell seals were in the waters around our camp. We remained confident that somewhere below us Ally McSeal was in the group contributing to the conversations while outfitted with our expensive instruments.

Following the third Herbie and six days of on-and-off-again storms, the winds calmed and the sun showed bright and warm. In twenty-four hours we went from a Condition 1 whiteout to the best of the Antarctic spring. In the transition, air temperatures rose from -50°C to -5°C (-58°F to 23°F) and we were able to work outdoors without our bulky parkas. Surveying the damage from the winds, we noticed that one of the ice coolers used to store our food was gone as well as several flags and two shovels. Any of the items could have been buried nearby in a drift or blown seventy miles to the end of the ice shelf. In either case, it was unlikely that we would ever locate any of them again.

In addition to seven feet of snow, the Herbies blew in several unusual visitors to the camp. Two Adelie penguins arrived together, sliding along the soft snow on their white-feathered bellies. They appeared out of nowhere on the middle of the sea ice, rowing along by using their wings and feet as oars to propel themselves. Don Calkins was immediately taken with the little penguins and tried with moderate success to take a photograph. At first the Adelies stood their ground in front of the bear-sized man. The penguins reared up as tall as they could on three-inch-long legs, ruffled their head feathers into a black halo, and peered back at Don as if daring him to take another step closer. Don stood still, afraid to move a muscle that might scare the little black-and-white birds. Oblivious to the mismatch in size, the two brazen birds walked up to Don in a stand-off that had him backing up along the ice. The penguins only came up to his knees but they had him on the run. Having made their point, the pair dropped onto their bellies to once again skirt along the snow, each leaving a telltale flipper-and-belly trail in the soft powder.

Humbled by the experience, Don retreated inside to make lunch only to find that one of the penguins had circled around to the back of the Jamesway. A snowdrift allowed the penguin to climb up and peer inside the kitchen window. The Adelie watched curiously as Don stirred in the ingredients to one of the team's favorite lunches, turkey noodle soup—broth, noodles, carrots, and turkey breast. By the time Don had ladled out the steaming soup for the rest of the team, the penguin had taken off, quickly waddling across the ice after its partner. The penguin's speedy departure left Don chuckling, "I suppose it was rather rude to eat one bird in front of another."

After lunch, Matt and I prepared to survey Home Crack to search for Ally among the seals that had hauled out in the emerging sun. As we walked around the snowmobiles, we found that another visitor had been blown into camp. A lone seal had fallen asleep just fifty yards from our Jamesway along the side of the flagged road. The seal was partially covered by snow, creating a small bump that looked like the rest of the snowdrifts around camp. It was unusual to have a seal come so close to our buildings, and we assumed that it was a juvenile that had become disoriented in the blowing snow.

Worried that the sleeping seal would inadvertently be run over by a snowmobile or Spryte, we decided to help the animal along by pointing it in the right direction towards Home Crack. With the best of intentions we approached the dozing seal only to have it rear up, snarling at us before we had gotten within twenty feet. The vibrissae on its long snout stood erect, and there was frothy drool frozen on its wrinkled muzzle. Matt and I jumped back, only narrowly escaping the snapping animal.

Spinning around, the seal sized us up with small squinting eyes and then admonished Matt and me with a large, open-mouthed roar. We had never encountered such an aggressive seal. The animal growled menacingly and stood nearly upright on all four of its flippers.

On closer inspection, the angry seal had a pelt that was more brown than black, and a head that was longer and narrower than any Weddell seal. The snarling, spitting animal was a different species of ice seal altogether. Behaviorally and anatomically it was nothing like the docile, smiling Weddells we were used to; it was a crabeater seal.

Smaller than the Weddell seal, the crabeater gets its name from its invertebrate diet. Rather than fish, crabeater seals primarily eat krill, small shrimp-like crustaceans that live in the open Antarctic oceans. The crabeater seal usually lives in the pack ice where long leads and open water allow it to dive freely for its favorite food. Rarely are they found in areas of solid ice, and the threatening posture of the animal indicated that it was uncomfortable with its situation.

With its open-mouthed, snarling threat, I could see the seal's unusual teeth. Like the Weddell seal, the crabeater seal has a specialized dentition for living in the Antarctic. Instead of protruding front canines for reaming ice, the crabeater has three pronged molars that resemble pitchforks. When the animal's mouth is shut the teeth allow the seal to sieve out seawater after taking in a mouthful of the tiny krill. Strained krill remaining on the seal's tongue can then be swallowed without large amounts of salty water in each bite.

Specialized teeth or not, we did not want to get bit, so Matt and I backed off and left the aggressive crabeater seal to its nap. Eventually the seal moved off to find a diving hole to slip back into the water. From a safe distance we watched as the crabeater approached a small isolated hole in the ice that had partially frozen over in the storms. The seal wedged its long snout into the hole, pushed with its large floppy front flippers, spraying snow all around, and tried to squeeze its head down. But the hole was not wide enough. Without the reaming teeth of the Weddell seal, the crabeater was at a severe disadvantage; it had no tools for widening the hole other than brute force.

Despite its obvious physical limitations, the seal tried repeatedly to fit its bulky body into a hole the size of a teacup.

The animal snarled and twisted, finally giving up. Huffing in steamy breaths, the seal lay on the ice overheated from the exertion. An hour later the seal was at it again. After an afternoon of fighting with the undersized hole, the crabeater was defeated and headed for Home Crack in a snakelike crawl along the ice. The only chance for entering the water was going to be through a hole made by a Weddell seal. It took nearly a day for the crabeater seal to slither to the crack. Once there, the seal quickly found a Weddell dive hole and slipped into the water, never to be seen in our camp again.

Although Ally did not make an appearance, the day did end with one more visitor—a gentle snowfall. For once it was real snow, the type of fluffy winter snow illustrated in scenic Christmas cards. Rather than the harsh, gritty ice that blew in at seventy miles per hour, the falling snow was soft and drifted slowly down. The startling feature was how quickly the snow accumulated around our camp. It fell in mounting puffs the size and texture of cotton balls.

Textbooks state that Antarctica is a desert, with the distinction of being the driest continent on earth. The average reported snowfall is only one to three inches per year; Weddell World was obviously on the high end of the range. What appeared to us as snow during the Herbies was in fact recycled ice that had been blown across the continent. Actual precipitation is unusual. Because summer temperatures in Antarctica are never high enough to melt the snow that does fall, it accumulates year after year as it has done for hundreds of thousands of years. That is why the Antarctic is covered in white. Eventually the accumulated snow compressed under its own weight and formed two giant ice sheets covering the Antarctic landmass.

At Weddell World we began to experience the same effects of compression under the weight of too much accumulated snow on a local scale. Despite its original fluffiness, the snow turned to the consistency of cement within a day. It was the perfect texture for cutting into blocks and making igloos.

With the ice and snow of three Herbies and one true snowfall surrounding the camp, the team suddenly realized that Weddell World was in trouble. Our Spryte and the seal sled were buried in a huge drift next to four snowmobiles that could be identified only by the top edge of their front windshields. Fine snow had found its way into the Spryte through a thin crack where the door gasket was missing. Snow packed the entire cab from floor to ceiling as if a bad college prank had been played on us. The Jamesway had not fared much better. The soft sides of the building were dangerously drifted over with more than eight feet of snow climbing over the top in some places. Except for the side door leading to the kitchen, all entrances were solidly blocked. The back door with the chute and weighing station had completely disappeared in a seven-foot-high drift.

The snow was more than just an inconvenience. Inside the laboratory, Lee walked over to the diving hole and then frowned. Lying belly down on the floorboards, he leaned down towards the dive hole and placed a ruler between the surface of the water and the top edge of the ice. To our dismay, he discovered that the water in the hole had risen over sixteen inches. Saltwater was within two inches of spilling over the lip of the ice.

"We're sinking," Lee informed the group flatly.

It was difficult to imagine snow actually weighing more than a Spryte or the buildings in our camp. C-130s could land on the snow and ice without causing it to bow. In our case, the weight of all of the accumulated snow around Weddell World was bending the sea ice beneath us. As we sunk lower, the water in the dive hole rose progressively higher, threatening to overflow into the lab. To add to our problems, the flexion of the ice was not uniform along the length of the camp. This created a disturbing effect on the floorboards of the 128-foot-long Jamesway. Its floors began to creak painfully as the ice compressed and flexed unevenly. The noise was particularly apparent at night. From the comfort of our sleeping bags we would hear the floors moan and creak as if we were rocking belowdecks of a wooden ship sailing on the open ocean. Each night the creaking seemed to worsen, adding to our anxieties: How much strain could the old wood take? Could we actually sink into the ocean depths below?

With Weddell World and the entire expedition in jeopardy, the team had a new serious task to focus on—shoveling snow. The job that lay ahead was daunting. Tons of snow smothered the camp and all of the outdoor equipment. All we could do was put our backs into the job and start with the roof of the Jamesway and work our way down.

Half of the team dug all morning, trying to clear out the back chute and weighing station; the remainder worked on freeing the insulated blankets of the Jamesway roof. It was mindless, sweaty, tiring labor that was only interrupted by the occasional snowball fight that erupted when the wind shot a shovel full of snow into the face of someone nearby. Sputtering inhaled snow, the poor soul who had been covered would invariably pick up a boulder-size chunk of snow and throw it back at the offender. The snow boulder tossing generally escalated until both people were rolling in a drift laughing, grimacing, and trying to stuff as much snow down the other's shirt as possible. The others barely acknowledged the tussle since snow packing served to cool both of the folks down. Afterwards, the shoveling could begin again in earnest.

At noon we assessed our progress to find that we had barely made a dent in the drifts. The only encouraging advance was with the doors, which now could be opened with ease. A set of snow stairs had to be carved in five-foot-deep drifts to climb up and out of the Jamesway, but at least we could escape from more than one exit. Following a quick lunch, we were all at it again regardless of the accepted futility of our efforts. There was little else to do except dig and then dig some more. To ignore the snow would have guaranteed the demise of the camp.

The team continued to shovel into the afternoon, bent on the task of saving Weddell World. We would have worked well into the night if it had not been for the appearance of a road train headed down our flagged road. We looked up from the snow caverns that we had dug into the drifts to watch the approach of a giant machine working its way slowly towards us. It took a few minutes for us to recognize what we were seeing. Like the cavalry riding over the horizon, it turned out to be Ralph and the massive bulldozer that we had traveled next to during the flight to the ice. He had driven the lumbering machine for hours across the sea ice from McMurdo Station to our camp.

"Need a little digging?" he shouted cheerily from the heated cab as he rumbled into camp.

Without stopping to wait for an answer, Ralph started to plow out a lane next to the Jamesway. The front blade of the machine was as wide as a pickup truck, taller than any of us, and could have easily scooped away the Spryte with our entire team inside of it in one quick swoop. The sheer size of the machine was impressive, but it was Ralph's skill at handling it on ice that was extraordinary. With the dexterity of a surgeon Ralph maneuvered the giant yellow bulldozer within inches of the Jamesway walls, avoiding the tie-down cables, flags, ropes, and fuel hoses that could have easily been entangled in the front blade. He made short order of the drifts that lined each side of the building and then set his blade on the snow mounds behind the weighing chute.

For two days Ralph, his bulldozer, and our team dug through the snow, finally freeing the camp. For the first time in a week we were able to walk without tripping into a snowdrift between the Jamesway and the outhouse. The ice below was smooth, blue, and flat. However, it was also cracked. Severe winds from the Herbies had apparently been too much for the ice, creating a series of hairline fractures that crisscrossed and marred its slick surface. We considered ourselves lucky that none of the fractures appeared to extend the full seven-foot thickness of the sea ice.

With the snow piled in a giant berm several yards away from Weddell World, the sea ice, cracked as it was, could rebound. The ice was still solid enough to retain its springiness. Free from the weight of the snow, the ice sprang back to life and began to float higher on the water, carrying our entire camp up with it. The progress we had made was immediately obvious from the change in the height of the seawater in the diving hole. Once again Lee took a ruler to the side of the hole, to find that we had gained nine inches. We now had eleven inches of free-board. Looming disaster had been averted and we were safe from sinking—at least for the moment.

The end of the storms and the emergency snow shoveling left an exhausted research team in its wake. Physically and emotionally we were reaching the ragged edge. The team was already operating on little sleep due to the constant battering by the storms from the previous week. During that time, we had envisioned the entire expedition sinking with the camp and felt that we had only narrowly escaped. If it had not been for Ralph and his bulldozer, Weddell World would likely have ended up flooded with seawater and iced over by now. Coupled with overused muscles from the exercise and tension, the team felt a fatigue so intense that we lay wide awake in our sleeping bags, paralyzed, waiting for our bodies to finally relax. None of us had bothered to change clothes. Instead we had kicked off our boots and flopped on top of our cots, just glad to be off of our feet.

An early evening sun shown in a window that had been covered in snow for days, casting the bunkroom and the team in a warm orange glow. I tried to feel my hands, which were torn up, callused, and permanently curved from holding a shovel handle. Stretching each finger, I could feel the worn tendons sliding over every joint. My left arm did not want to fully extend and my lower back was gratefully numb. Aches were sure to come, and I hoped that I would be asleep by the time they arrived.

Below the floorboards, I could hear the long trills of Weddell seals calling back and forth in the distance beneath the ice. They conversed so loudly that I could eavesdrop through my sleeping bag and seven feet of ice now that the rush of the wind was gone.

CHAPTER 12

THE HUNTER'S
BREATH

November 8–15

At midnight most of our weary team was still awake, lying on
their cots, when the muffled trill of Weddell seals calling
beneath the camp was interrupted by a rhythmic "chirp, chirp,
chirp." The sounds pulsed with metronome accuracy, echoing from
the laboratory over the low static of the radio receiver.

Still reeling with exhaustion from the previous days, no one
reacted. But the chirping continued and through sheer persistence
began to register with us. Slowly the significance of the sounds tri-
umphed over our fatigue, causing everyone to stumble into the lab
one by one. Checking the frequency on the radio receiver, we were
suddenly jolted awake and ecstatic. The signals were coming from
Ally McSeal's radio transmitter. She had finally come home.

Grabbing binoculars, I scanned Home Crack from a frosted

window and counted seven large seals hauled out. From the strength of the radio signal, Ally was surely one of them. The entire team excitedly pulled on boots, parkas, and gloves over their sleep-wrinkled clothes. With parkas still unzipped, we revved up the snowmobiles and headed to Home Crack full of high expectations. It didn't take long to find our girl. After missing for six days through a series of horrific storms, Ally was rolling in the soft fresh snow next to the ice crack with the other seals. There was no chance of mistaking her profile with the VDAP pack.

To avoid scaring her back into the water, we abandoned the snowmobiles and approached her slowly on foot. Bill rambled on excitedly about the batteries in the VDAP still having enough power, and then stopped short.

"What the . . . ?" he sputtered.

"It doesn't look right," Randy said slowly.

We crept closer to the seal, feeling our high hopes and excitement sink lower and lower, finally diminishing into bitter disappointment. Ally McSeal had returned to us but the instrumentation appeared to be in shambles. The camera that should have been on her head dangled on a long cable that trailed behind her. The neoprene blanket holding the VDAP was torn and most of the sensors were barely hanging on. Two speed sensors were packed with snow, the tiny turbines frozen in place and unable to spin properly.

All of our expensive instrumentation looked as though it had been run over by Ralph's bulldozer.

There was little doubt about what had happened. High winds and blowing snow had caused a number of changes in the sea ice during the past week. The few breathing holes that had existed at Home Crack before the Herbies had frozen over in the storms. In many places the crack was snow-bridged. Although Ally, along with most of the seals, had sought the safety of the water during the storms, it had been necessary to repair their escape holes in order to breathe. Undoubtedly the tooth reaming and body squeezing required for Ally to finally haul out had shaken the camera loose and scraped the instruments along the sharp ice lining the seals' escape holes. What we didn't know was when the damage had occurred. Ally could have spent the previous six days vigilantly reaming to keep breathing holes open or had made a onetime Herculean effort to break through the ice at the end of the storms. There was no way of telling until we opened the VDAP to download the data and retrieve the videotape.

Bill ran up quickly to see if he could determine the extent of the damage. The VDAP was his baby, shaped by his ideas and born of his hard work; it hurt to see it so tattered. He first tried to revive his confidence by checking for salt water in the camera head. If it was flooded then there was little chance that any video images would have been recorded. Shaking and peering into the unit as Ally kept an eye on him, Bill could tell nothing. The front lens merely frosted over in his warm hands. Realizing that trying to assess the damage outdoors was pointless, the team helped Bill begin the process of removing all of the instruments from the seal.

Ally McSeal sat patiently while we swiftly removed the VDAP, sensors, and the neoprene blanket. The hose clamps, cable ties, Velcro, and glue that held the damaged instruments onto the neoprene pad were loosened or cut. The neoprene blanket was then removed by peeling it back like a Band-Aid. With the rest of our equipment already on the ground, it took less than fifteen minutes to collect everything, including the speed meters, stroke sensor, and radio and satellite tags. The pieces were placed gently into backpacks and then hand-carried by the somber crew back to the laboratory.

As we left Ally at Home Crack she resumed rolling in the soft snow, oblivious of the emotional roller coaster we had just ridden. She seemed to revel in the warm sun on her belly and the feel of fresh snow on her back, scratching everywhere that the neoprene blanket had been.

Back at Weddell World, Bill, Randy, and Markus methodically inspected the damage to the camera and the sensors. From outward appearances, it was too soon to tell if any data had been recorded. Rather than risk further damage to the frozen instruments, they decided to let the equipment warm slowly overnight to room temperature in the laboratory. If salt water had leaked inside then the damage was already done. Trying to open the cold-stiffened connectors would only exacerbate the problem and ruin the VDAP for use on other seals. We had to remain patient and let the VDAP and sensors equilibrate to our world.

By the time we finished covering the snowmobiles for the night and hung up our snow-soaked clothing by the kitchen preway stove, it was 3:00 A.M. Bright sunshine streamed into the lab as we stood around the frozen, battered VDAP. In many ways the ragged condition of the instruments reflected how we all felt.

It was going to be hours before we would know if Ally McSeal was a success or a failure as a marine biologist and underwater videographer. In the quiet of the moment, exhaustion finally overcame the group. Each of us wavered in the warmth of the stove, no longer able to stand on our feet. With the pressure of Ally's disappearance, the violent storms, and the sinking camp alleviated, we finally allowed our bodies to relax. Sore muscles and tired bones welcomed the comfort of the sleeping bags as we abandoned ourselves to a deep slumber.

Late the following morning, excitement mounted as the VDAP microprocessor was downloaded and the videotape rewound. There had been no flooding as we had initially feared. Instead, the computer monitors displayed line after line of numbers as the data were transferred. In its raw form, the numbers were indecipherable. Translation would come later and would require the calibration curves that the team had developed for each of the sensors in the previous weeks. At the very least, we had the satisfaction of knowing that something was recorded during Ally's long journey.

The moment that everyone waited for was the playback of the videotape. If the camera and videorecorder had worked, there would be six hours of images. The entire team gathered around the television monitor in anticipation.

For the first thirty seconds the screen was flat blue, with only the time code ticking away in the corner. We girded ourselves for disappointment. As the seconds passed, we stubbornly remained in our chairs hoping that *something, anything* had been recorded by Ally.

Just as we were beginning to lose faith, the monitor flashed white then black. Suddenly we saw that we were underwater. The nose, eyes, muzzle, and long whiskers of Ally were clearly visible and filled the bottom of the screen. An expansive view of under-ice Antarctica filled the top half. Not only had the VDAP worked, it had performed magnificently.

I was captivated by what I saw. For hours I watched the television screen intently, riveted to my chair as Ally McSeal provided me with a remarkable journey through her underwater world. She took me to the bottom of McMurdo Sound, traveling from the ice surface through black water and finally to the ocean floor. With the aid of the LED array, I could see objects appearing out of the dark in front of the swimming seal. For me, it was like a spotlight cutting through the night. I watched as the seal cruised along the gravelly bottom, skimming past giant sponges, gelatinous tulip-shaped organisms that were practically invisible, and thousands of brightly shining starfish sitting on black volcanic rocks. It was as if the world had been turned upside down, with darkness and brightly lit stars lying on the bottom of the ocean instead of in the sky. This was the closest to nighttime that I had seen in over a month.

The rest of team was equally enamored. As Ally swam even deeper, we saw long, sinuous, white sea worms that were over four feet in length slithering in slow motion along the sea floor. Spidery crinoids, lacy fans, and peculiar plant-like animals that inhabited the cold clear waters whizzed by as she swam along. Transparent jellyfish, tubby nudibranchs, striped sea cucumber–type creatures, and dots of marine snow faded in and out of the picture while the seal continued on her underwater sojourn. So many of the animals that Ally encountered were larger than herself. She could fit her sleak head into the top openings of the sponges, which she did periodically in pursuit of tiny fish. There were so many rooted creatures growing out of the darkness it was as if she were navigating through an overgrown forest. The bottom of McMurdo Sound was inhabited by such a rich array of organisms that it rivaled the biodiversity of a tropical rainforest to us. How all of these different species were able to survive in the darkness and the cold was a complete mystery.

The seal did not appear interested in all of the odd-looking animals, paying little attention to any of them. There were many times when at least one of the team members groaned in disappointment as Ally swam steadily by an especially peculiar creature; if only she could have stopped for just a few seconds to give us a little longer look. Only on one occasion, when she mistakenly bumped into one of the sponges, did she acknowledge its presence by shaking her head and backing up. She did not waste time sightseeing on her dive. Instead, she continuously scanned her head back and forth, always searching, always moving forward. The prey she was hunting did not live at these depths. She was merely passing through.

In time we were almost able to read Ally's moods through her whisker movements. When relaxed and cruising her long whiskers lay flat against her muzzle, swinging passively with her head. On those occasions the view in front of her showed only black empty water. She would travel for minutes on end like that, swimming through the waters of McMurdo Sound, scanning with her eyes and cocking her head in a systematic searching pattern. Her head rocked back and forth like a slow-bobbing toy in counterbalance to the propulsive strokes of her hind flippers.

Her casual behavior when cruising contrasted markedly with her head movements when Ally found something worth investigating. Another seal in the vicinity or the presence of a fish would cause the whiskers on her muzzle and eyebrows to stand straight up on end. Her muzzle would crinkle and each vibrissa would point so stiffly into the water that the whiskers of a hissing cat paled by comparison. Often Ally's vibrissae were so rigid she seemed capable of spearing a fish or a competing seal with them.

With her whiskers erect, we knew that she was about to encounter something or someplace unique under the ice. It took a second or two from the time her whiskers went up to the point of encounter. The seal was definitely ahead of us in terms of perceiving what would come next. In anticipation we would wait and then the water in front of her would fill with huge looming Weddell seals, the rugged underside of the Antarctic ice, flashing schools of fish, the fin rays of a giant cod, or even an ice cave. We couldn't predict exactly what we would see next—we knew only that something was coming and that we probably had never seen anything like it before.

The data from the sensors that Ally carried were equally astounding. The depth gauge alone revealed a physiological capability that was beyond that of other diving birds and mammals. Her routine dives would have left sea otters, bottlenose dolphins, sea lions, and even some whales bobbing breathless at the surface. As a breath-holding marine mammal, she was an Olympian. During the storms, while we had sat in the Jamesway huddling for warmth, Ally McSeal had been diving a quarter of a mile deep below us. By comparison, a human diver on standard scuba is limited to depths less than 120 feet. Ally was diving ten times deeper, reaching over 1,200 feet.

I wanted to know how her biology allowed her to hunt at such depths. The hydrostatic pressure she experienced when diving is known to cause a medical condition called high-pressure nervous syndrome in humans. Our nervous system is not built to work at depth and once past 200 feet, the increased pressure of the water column causes misfiring between nerves. Hands shake, speech falters, vision blurs, and coordinated movements become increasingly more difficult the deeper we go. Without the aid of a submarine, we could never visit even the middle layers of the ocean. In contrast, the Weddell seal is completely at home diving to depths and temperatures that would have killed another mammal, including us.

Ally hadn't done just one spectacular dive, but had repeated her performance over and over again as if there were no skill to it at all. With every dive the seal had covered a distance equivalent to swimming up one side of the Empire State Building and down the other—all accomplished on a single breath of air. Each dive for Ally McSeal was an astounding display of athleticism.

> *The exercise physiologist in me tried to figure out what makes Ally so different from us. How is she able to swim, explore, chase fish, and hold her breath all at the same time? In the end, I concluded that the difference is what I call the Hunter's Breath. Every molecule of oxygen in the seal's lungs, blood, and muscles has to be budgeted carefully for her to catch up with a fish meal at depth and then make it back to the surface. Each dive is a calculated risk, a turn of underwater Russian roulette played with the Hunter's last breath of air.*

Ally's breathing when she was between dives was regular, deep, and easy to count on the television monitor. I could determine her respiration rate by simply counting the number of times her nostrils opened and shut in the bottom of the screen. Her nostril movements were almost hypnotic as she lay quietly on the surface. Exhale, inhale, and breath-hold for several seconds. Exhale, inhale, and breath-hold. Exhale, inhale, breath-hold. Like other seals, she had a three-phase respiratory pattern instead of the two-phase, inspiration-expiration pattern typical of humans. For those of us watching the video, the contrast with our own breathing pattern was obvious. We constantly breathe in or out. If we are not inhaling, then we are exhaling. The seal breathed out, breathed in, and then added a prolonged period of breath-hold. Some scientists believe that this holding pattern enables seals to absorb more oxygen from the air in each breath, making them very efficient. We found it impossible to mimic her breathing pattern for long. This was due in part to the unique design of Ally's nostrils. No simple hole system would do for the diving seals. Instead, muscular ridges enable the seal's nostrils to open widely for a quick intake of air and clamp tightly shut to prevent water from rushing in when they are on a dive. As a result, seals don't have to "hold their noses" when they submerge; the muscles surrounding their nostrils do all of that automatically.

The seal used her breath-holding ability to her advantage in a unique hunting path below the surface. Take a breath, dive to depth, hit the bottom of McMurdo Sound while skimming along the gravel past the invertebrate life, ascend, and burst into a breathing hole in the ice. On the surface she would poke her nose just above the water line to take several deep breaths. After a single, long exhalation she descended into the dark once more to repeat the entire pattern. Each dive took anywhere from twelve to twenty minutes, depending on whether she hit the floor of the Sound or not.

Watching the videos, it was difficult not to begin to hold our breath in empathy as the seal began her descent. Within two minutes we were all gasping for air while the seal was barely getting started on the dive. She still had ten to eighteen minutes more of breath holding to go. As she descended, we could see the breathing hole fall farther and farther away, giving some of the people watching the video a distinct feeling of desperate claustrophobia as they realized that fresh air was moving progressively away from their grasp.

Although she was holding her breath, Ally had a variety of tasks to complete while underwater. Some dives were for hunting while others were for scouting out the area. A third type of dive was longer than the rest and tested her endurance as she explored how far she could travel before having to return to her original breathing hole. She could travel into new territories as long as there were cracks or holes in the ice that she could push her head through to catch a breath of air. Without breathing holes she would have to navigate without error back to her starting point. On these exploratory dives, misjudging her direction of travel would be fatal, and we found that Ally's reverse track matched her outbound line with incredible pinpoint accuracy.

Most importantly, the seal had to budget her time. A mistake in calculating how long her breath would last would result in drowning just like any other mammal that stays underwater too long. The difference is that Weddell seals can easily make their breath last nearly twenty minutes underwater.

With her limitations in mind, I studied the videotape of Ally McSeal, trying to piece together how she was able to guarantee that she had enough oxygen while she hunted and explored. The beginning of each dive was characterized by a period of hyperventilation. The seal would take several deep breaths before embarking and then head down to the depths. I could almost predict whether she would be going on a deep dive or a shallow swim by counting the number of breaths she took immediately prior to descending. A few breaths meant she would be back to the surface quickly. Loud, deep breathing before a dive meant she would be heading for the darkness below.

On the return part of the dive the seal's huge eyes constantly scanned the underside of the ice. Vision was essential for the seal to detect the best breathing holes as well as to navigate around the Sound. From the video each member of the team noticed that bright sun shining from above lit up the holes in the ice like beacons. Thick ice appeared dark when viewed from beneath. The shadows created by Weddell World could also be seen as dark outlines on the underside of the ice. There was the long rectangle of the Jamesway, and the small square shadows of the outhouse and compass calibration hut. Even the area of ice cleared by Ralph's bulldozer could be detected as a light gray landing strip.

In contrast, ice cracks appeared as long white scars overhead. Looking up from the depths the pressure ridges, cracks, and snow-drifts formed road maps of light and dark that Ally could follow to find her way back. The trick for under-ice navigation was always head towards the light. That was where air would be found. It was an exciting discovery that, like most scientific discoveries, led to more questions than answers.

We watched as Ally approached one of the larger ice holes, the light getting bigger and brighter as she ascended. She had been holding her breath for over twenty minutes and was in need of air. After following her on the entire dive from her initial descent to the bottom of McMurdo Sound, where she caught several fish, and finally on her prolonged ascent we knew that she had to be nearing her limit in terms of available oxygen. Closing in on the breathing hole, Ally's whiskers suddenly stood at jagged attention. She obviously had spotted something that was out of the field of view of the camera. Her muzzle crinkled, causing her stiffened vibrissae to fan out on end. Throwing her head back she let out a series of sharp chirps. As she vocalized into the water, the seal's head and whiskers vibrated with the chirping. She ended her sentence with a last high-pitched burp and forward head thrust.

The seal stopped swimming, and floated motionless in the water just below the breathing hole. Her whiskers remained at full attention with her head and eyes stiffly focused above. Then we saw the cause for her rigid behavior and vocalizations. Above Ally was a pair of flippers hanging beneath the breathing hole. Her chirps had warned the other seal of her approach and the need to breathe. The other seal had not complied with her request. And now the two animals were in a standoff. The giant body of the other seal completely filled the breathing hole, blocking Ally from any access to air.

"Chirp, chirp, chirrprppp, Wwwwwhhhhirr . . . iirrrr . . . irrr?" Ally called as she backed down a little farther and tried another series of sharp, high-pitched chirps, this time ending with a question mark trill.

The only response from the other seal was a slow dip of its head below the ice to see who was calling. The seal looked at Ally in silence. Its head was larger that hers and had a fleshy white scar across its muzzle. I knew that muzzle. Scarface! The team had purposely not chosen him for our study, and here he was anyway. From his attitude, we presumed that he had set up a territory in one of the few breathing holes in the area. Scarface was not budging. After a long stare the scarred seal continued to breathe at the surface, ignoring Ally's vocalizations.

Usually, the social tone around the Weddell seals' breathing holes was more amiable. At the end of most of her dives Ally shared a breathing hole with three or four other seals. The animals lined up under the ice like cars coming to the pumps of a filling station. They jockeyed for position, would gain access to the hole, take several quick gulps of air and then allow the waiting seals to take their turn breathing. Alternating turns the seals would slide past each other belly to belly in order to squeeze into breathing position. While one seal inhaled and exhaled deeply taking in the cold air, the others would float against the under-ice surface waiting for their chance to do the same. The process was repeated several times until all of the seals had taken their fill of fresh air. Then they would individually go about diving only to return to the breathing hole when they needed. From a human perspective, the behavior of the breathing seals appeared quite civilized and efficient.

However, on this occasion the situation grew desperate for Ally, who had been left waiting below the breathing hole for over five minutes. She was approaching thirty minutes since her last of breath of air. Lactic acid was surely building up in her muscles and blood, and would exhaust her if she did not replenish her oxygen stores soon. The team wondered what she was going to do.

In other years, Ally could have just backed down from the confrontation and found another crack or breathing hole. However, this year backing down was not an option; there was nowhere else to go. B-15 had created an ice sheet that was so tight there were too few breathing holes for all of the diving Weddell seals that needed to use them. She had to breathe here or risk drowning in an attempt to find another crack in the ice. Between her and air was the hind end of Scarface with his hind flippers dangling limply beneath the hole.

Ally made one final attempt to communicate with the other seal by swimming directly below his flippers and chirping loudly upward.

"CHIRP, CHIRP, CHIRPPP!" echoed sharply through the water.

The male seal did not even respond with a downward glance. Finally, Ally took more serious action. Sinking a few yards below the seal she let out a long foghorn blow with the last of her air. She blew out a large bolus of air from her nostrils along with the warning tone. The bubble mass ascended, boiling into the bottom and tail of the seal blocking the hole. We couldn't be sure if the bubbles caught him by surprise or merely tickled his flippers; they definitely got his attention. Scarface gave a quick look down, but Ally was already was on the move. She swam up from the depths and grabbed one of his dangling flippers in her teeth.

What happened next was all a blur on the videotape. We could see flashes of gray and white spots from the belly of the male seal and a rush of small bubbles. The two seals entered into a tumbling fight just below the breathing hole. White ice alternated with black depths on the video as the seals rolled over and over. Using her jutting front canines, Ally swung her head back and forth in a reaming action normally reserved for scraping ice. Scarface responded with an open-mouth display of teeth. It was as if his entire lower jaw had unhinged in rattlesnake fashion, creating a wide dark gape that filled the screen in front of Ally's face.

The two seals threatened and snapped, parried and sparred for less than sixty seconds. It was all over before we could even figure out if the seals were fighting right side up or upside down. From the sudden burst of sunlight in the camera lens we instantly realized that Ally was victorious. She had won the use of the breathing hole.

After the combined exertion of the dive and the fight, Ally gasped for air. She spent several minutes recovering in the breathing hole that she had worked so hard to gain. There was no fear of retribution by the scarred male seal; he was long gone after his defeat. Scarface had drifted slowly away beneath the ice, leaving Ally in peace. Consequently, she never bothered to look down at her vulnerable flippers hanging from the hole.

Floating with her head out of water while resting in the breathing hole, we caught a seal's perspective of Home Crack. We could see the sun shining overhead and the surrounding snow mounds at ground level. In the distance we could just barely make out several other seals that had hauled out onto the snow.

The six-hour videotape ended all too quickly, leaving Ally still resting in the breathing hole, and us wanting more. We wanted to know if Scarface had returned to the breathing hole to challenge Ally. Was she able to hold her ground or did she eventually give in? We hoped to see more of the peculiar animals that inhabited the floor of McMurdo Sound. Did the whiskers of the seals act like sensitive antennae, "feeling" the water for the wakes of fishes and other creatures that lived in the dark-water column? Was that the secret of hunting in the dark at depth? Listening to the throaty chugs of the seals echo off of the ice, we wondered if the animals used a form of sonar to test the thickness of the sea ice before they approached the surface. That would certainly be a useful tool for seals that had to make a living under ice. We had so many more questions now that we had been given a glimpse below the ice.

Ally's adventure had exceeded our expectations and was

cause for celebration in camp. A lot of hard work by humans and seal alike had gotten us to this point, so the team took a moment to salute Ally McSeal and the people who made it all happen. Randy broke out a bottle of champagne that he had been saving under his cot for the occasion. With a satisfying "clunk" of our plastic camp mugs, we toasted teamwork and persistence, the National Science Foundation, our new discoveries, and especially the first Weddell seal to carry the VDAP into the wild, open water under the Antarctic ice: Ally McSeal.

Jesse added his special brand of Texas flavor to the celebration by treating us to American night at dinnertime. For most of the afternoon he prepped and cooked, keeping his menu a secret. Pots and the front door banged periodically as he walked in and out of the kitchen with ingredients in his arms. Despite the commotion, we could not figure out what he was doing. Finally, in the evening he revealed his culinary masterpiece: pizza pies!

The team sat around the kitchen table with a newfound respect for our acoustics expert. The sight of four, fresh pan pizzas topped with ground meat and shredded cheese was beautiful after all of the rushed camp stove dinners we had eaten during the past weeks. It went beyond the fact that the food wasn't burnt, which usually occurred in our hurry with the propane stoves. The pizzas surprised us by stimulating a rush of memories of pizzas back home. In that wonderful moment, gathered around the aluminum folding table in the warmth of the Jamesway kitchen, the team reveled in the camaraderie and success of the day. With the aroma of oregano and pizza dough surrounding us, we also took a long, overdue minute to remember the friends and family who waited back home. Surely, these were the best pizzas ever created.

But American night was only beginning. Before we had finished dinner, Jesse went outdoors to haul in a huge metal pot. The top had been taped shut to prevent skuas from getting into it, and, according to Jesse, "to seal in the ingredients." He began scooping out the contents into individual mugs, handing one to each of us. At first we looked skeptically into the mugs. Pink contents were flecked with red in a mushy sauce. It looked like something that even scavenging skuas would refuse. We turned expectantly to Jesse.

"Strawberry milkshakes!" he announced proudly.

Tentative tastes were followed by loud slurping and requests for second and third servings. We were in paradise. Jesse had hit upon one of the biggest morale boosters on the frozen continent: ice cream. Even in the galley in McMurdo, ice cream was considered a major treat. The fat and sugar was what made it so appealing, irrespective of the cold. What we couldn't figure out was how Jesse managed to get ice cream out at Weddell World. After considerable urging he finally admitted that it had taken an afternoon of experimenting and tasting to create the ultimate Antarctic shake. I copied the recipe in my journal so I wouldn't forget American night on ice, knowing full well that I could never duplicate it.

Jesse's Antarctic Strawberry Shakes
1 bag frozen strawberries
1 bottle vanilla extract
1 can condensed milk
1 can evaporated milk
1 bucket fine Antarctic snowdrift (be sure to use a clean shovel)
Lots and lots of granulated sugar

Over the following weeks of the expedition we occasionally saw Seal 19 (Ally McSeal to her human friends). She often spent her days sunbathing near Home Crack with the other seals. She took little notice of our presence unless we ventured too close to her sunny spot, and was oblivious of her participation in our science and underwater exploration. As near as we could tell, her biggest concern was which side of her body to face into the bright sun.

One week after removing the VDAP and sensors, Ally visited us at the dive hole in the laboratory floor of Weddell World. She stayed for several minutes, using the Jamesway as a private breathing hole while she stretched out on the water surface to rest. When I went in to check on her, I found that from all outward appearances she was well fed and healthy. Some might have argued that she had even gotten bulkier, judging by the way she had to squeeze her bottom through the dive hole.

Without actually putting it into words, I thanked the seal for a research job well done.

She just snorted at me, exhaled, and went for another dive.

CHAPTER 13

SINK OR SWIM

NOVEMBER 16–20

With the success of Ally McSeal, our research began in earnest. We repeated the entire process—from seal selection at Home Crack, to transfer by sled to Weddell World, to outfitting with a VDAP, to release in the dive hole—with three new seals: Seal 20 (Godzilla), Seal 21 (Ms. Apnea), and Seal 22 (Ms. Zodiac). Personality and circumstances dictated their names. Seal 20, otherwise known as Godzilla, was the only male seal of the group. He was large, confidant, and a challenge in terms of weighing. Godzilla was the archetypal territorial male: big, and preoccupied with his own agenda. If he did not want to move there was little you could do about it other than wait him out. It took so long for Seal 20 to make up his mind to inchworm from the sled into the chute behind the lab, get weighed, and get instrumented that we decided never to work with another male Weddell seal again. As a result, our next seals, Seals 21 and 22, were mild-mannered females.

Both were relatively small, with Seal 21 being the heftier of the two. Seal 21 was nicknamed Ms. Apnea due to her penchant for sleeping and her unusual snoring pattern. She would snore with long breath holds (medically termed apneas) between each inhalation and exhalation and then noisily wake herself up.

Seal 22 was much more active than Seal 21 and also one of the smallest seals from Home Crack. She had the temperament of a curious, fidgety cat always looking around and poking her nose into everything. During her initial fitting for the neoprene pad that carried the VDAP instrumentation, it quickly became apparent that she was much smaller than the other seals when the blanket draped onto the floor.

"Think we have enough neoprene?" Bill understated.

He took scissors to trim down the pad to tailor it to her petite size and pointed out, "She looks just like a Zodiac boat!" The resemblance between the pontoon-shaped, neoprene-covered seal and a small inflatable boat was unmistakable. From then on Seal 22 was called Ms. Zodiac.

While we worked indoors with the seals, big events were occurring out on the sea ice. We first noticed the changes inside of the Jamesway. Several taller members of the team had the distinct feeling that the roof was getting closer. At five foot seven, even I could now reach the top of the wooden ribbing in the kitchen area if I stretched up. Either the top of the building was getting lower or the floor was getting higher. With each passing day, doors became more difficult to open, and screws in the floorboards started to work their way out of the plywood. Don Calkins finally had to saw off several inches from the bottom of the kitchen and back doors in order for us to be able to open them.

We also detected an increase in the intensity of wood creaking that was now part of the background noise in camp both day and night. With each shift of the sea ice below, the Jamesway moaned, shuddering in fits of movement beneath our feet.

Outside, the constant November Antarctic sun was altering the face of the ice. Hairline cracks along the glacier edge next to Weddell World opened up into crevasses. Ice ridges behind the camp that we had never even noticed before seemed more prominent. Even the leading tip of the Erebus Glacier Ice Tongue was changing. When we had first arrived, the glacier had bit solidly into the sea ice. Now it lapped into a slushy, blue melt pool. The signs were ominous, and we realized that it was only a matter of time before the ice became too unstable for us to remain in Weddell World. At most we had only a few more weeks.

The response of the team was to intensify the research pace.

From the moment he took off from the dive hole in the lab, Godzilla verified that the sea ice was opening up. Rather than stay at Home Crack, he swam all over McMurdo Sound with our instruments, zigzagging from hole to hole. At first we heard the radio signals from his tags nearby, then they were gone. Days later they seemed to emanate from the opposite side of the glacier, and sometimes to the west across the Sound. It was obvious that breathing holes and cracks were opening up everywhere, turning the sea ice into a Swiss cheese of breathing opportunities for the seals. Godzilla could now range anywhere there was a hole or crack. Our biggest fear was that he would move out into the open ocean. If he traveled north he could carry our instrumentation all of the way to Southern Australia or Chile. In either case we would never be able to retrieve the instruments if he made it to open water. Instead, the blanket carrying the sensors and VDAP would simply fall off when he molted his fur, causing our hard-earned data to drift away.

After missing for almost a week, Godzilla took us on a wild chase across the sea ice to find him and the VDAP. Snowmobile searches with the handheld radio receiver and antenna failed repeatedly. The seal had moved outside of the one-mile transmission zone of the tag. Finally, an e-mail message from the Service Argos satellite provided a "hit." Mapping the lat-long coordinates from the message, the team realized that Seal 20, our Godzilla, had swum over five miles away to the base of the Erebus Glacier. Staring at the worn map spread out on the kitchen table, we could not figure out where the seal had landed—we had never seen a crack in the area that he was supposed to be in. From the satellite coordinates it looked as though he was in the southern icefall at the base of the glacier—new territory for us.

Because of the unpredictable offshore currents and the increased activity of the glacier, the team questioned the stability of the sea ice in the area. We decided to play it safe and travel on smaller, lighter snowmobiles rather than rumble in with the heavier Spryte. But the condition of the sea ice did not make it an easy ride. A teeth-shattering hour later, the snowmobile team dead-ended in a wall of broken ice boulders at the base of the glacier. A tower of blue ice hung precariously above our heads, creaking and crackling in the sun. Although the ice above appeared solid, pieces scattered on the ground in front of us were larger than school buses and could have crushed us instantly. It was difficult to believe that our seal was anywhere nearby. There were no obvious open-water cracks; instead, there was a good chance of being hit by falling ice if the seal lingered too long in one spot. Our own team members jumped with each crack of the glacier wall in fear of an avalanche of ice that was about to let loose. We were afraid to talk too loudly, concerned that our voices would echo off of the fragile ice above and initiate a tumbling cascade.

While we waited nervously and silently below the glacier, Markus switched on the radio receiver and pointed the antenna. Instantly he picked up the missing seal's signal loud and clear. Godzilla was somewhere nearby in the outfall of the glacier.

With a direction to aim for, our train of snowmobiles gingerly picked its way through the jumble of ice, passing huge icebergs that had calved off of the glacier. There was no clear path, only twisting routes around the frozen boulders and over blue and white pressure ridges of deformed sea ice. We maneuvered blindly in the hopes that we wouldn't be blocked into a frozen dead-end or worse.

Eventually we found a hidden bowl created by a circle of fallen ice and the shoreline of Ross Island. A three-foot-wide tidal crack meandered the length of the protected area. With the wind unable to penetrate the ten-foot-high walls and with access to open water, the area was idyllic from a Weddell seal's perspective. The bowl was far enough from the active end of the glacier and the walls high enough that they prevented any boulders of ice from rolling through and mowing the seals down.

Females with newborn pups had taken advantage of the protection, using the ice grotto as a nursery to care for their growing newborns. All around us fuzzy gray pups nuzzled their mother's bellies in search of warm milk. The moms lay docilely on their sides, offering their teats, while the pups nursed with muffled intensity. Sunlight streamed in, adding to the warmth of the maternal setting.

And, in the middle of the mother-pup pairs, as out of place as any young male in a nursery, was the elusive Godzilla, resting by himself in the shallow of the bowl. He sunbathed sleepily, dozing in deep breaths with all of our instruments still intact.

Abandoning the snowmobiles, our team crept up on the seal and quickly removed the VDAP camera and the rest of the sensors before he knew what was happening. Unlike with Ally, the instruments looked as good as on the day we deployed them. The cables had held fast and the camera lens was still facing over the seal's muzzle. Everything, including the seal, looked in great shape.

Godzilla shook off the disturbance with a nod of his blocky head and then continued with his nap in the Weddell nursery. We carefully retraced our path on foot to avoid awakening him or the moms and their pups. As we passed the jagged walls of ice and slid along the torturous path leading out of the ice bowl, there was little doubt among us that this was an ideal place for Weddell seals to seek solitude. It was also one of the most dramatic areas on the west coast of Ross Island.

But as beautiful as the ice bowl was, we tempered our desire to return to take photographs and honored the privacy of the seals. No member of our team ever returned to the Weddell seal's nursery grotto. It would remain their secret hiding place.

When we finally reached Weddell World with the VDAP and sensors, we could barely wait to download the data and view the videotape. Ally McSeal had whetted our appetites with her travels among the deep-sea creatures. We wondered what new things we would discover with Godzilla.

As we reviewed the data from the sensors, we immediately realized that our twentieth seal had split personalities, ranging from Olympic diver to slug. Diving vicariously through the videotape, we were immediately plunged to the bottom of McMurdo Sound on the back of the seal in an impressive dive of over 500 meters (one third of a mile deep). His total time from last breath and descent into the inky darkness to bottom cruising and ascent back to the surface was more than forty minutes. The excursion surely pushed him outside of the bounds of his aerobic capacity.

It was humbling to see a mammal, built internally like humans, hold its breath for so long and dive so deep. Weddell seals have a heart, lungs, blood, and muscles that are much like my own, but the seals travel to depths that I could never hope to achieve. Riding on the back of the seal through the VDAP, I could sense the subtle differences in our biologies. While my heart rate raced in excitement, the seal's heart rate quieted at depth. My breathing intensified; his was stopped. The seal swam effortlessly through the blackness, carrying me along as an unskilled passenger.

Previous scientific studies had given us a few important clues about the biology behind the Weddells' diving abilities. Weddell seals had earned their reputation of elite diver based on several unique physiological features that allow them to go for prolonged periods without breathing. Like other mammals, seals carry oxygen in their blood hemoglobin and in a related molecule called myoglobin, residing in their muscles. Weddell seals are able to pack three times more oxygen into these tissues than a human or a dog, with the result that they travel underwater with the equivalent of an internal scuba tank. All of this on-board oxygen allows the seals to hold their breath for twenty minutes, ten times longer than the average human.

As if that isn't enough, Weddell seals can push the envelope by switching gears into anaerobic metabolism. Using the same biochemical pathways as a sprinting athlete, submerged seals buy precious time, especially when breathing holes are scarce. However, anaerobic metabolism comes at a hefty price, called lactic acid. If a seal pushes its dive duration beyond twenty minutes, lactic acid begins to accumulate in its muscles and blood, causing the same burning sensation and fatigue experienced by human sprinters—"No pain, no gain" is as applicable to diving seals as it is to exercising humans. For seals, specialized buffering mechanisms in the blood help keep the detrimental effects of the acid at bay but result in an enormous payback in terms of recovery after the dive. Like cheetahs that lay panting and exhausted after a high-speed chase, deep-diving Weddell seals must spend long recovery periods resting on the water surface, gulping in air until the lactic acid clears from their tissues and the scuba tank is once again replenished with oxygen. The danger during these times comes when another air-starved seal nips at the recovering seal's flippers.

Weddell seals are champion divers that can remain submerged for over eighty minutes; however, they perform these extreme dives sparingly. Ally McSeal had proved to be a conservative diver, keeping most of her dive durations within a safe aerobic twelve- to twenty-minute range when she hunted. Seal 20 lived up to his namesake Godzilla; at times he was unstoppable in his activities and was bad-tempered with those that crossed his path. Although he managed fewer dives than Ally, his repeated forty-minute dives pushed him into the elite athlete category.

As impressive as the seal's aerobic and anaerobic reserves are, there is an upper limit to what can be carried on board. Another strategy is to increase fuel efficiency during diving and make the oxygen reserve last longer. Much like a well-tuned car, Weddell seals appear to be masters at stretching out their fuel tanks to cover more miles per gallon of oxygen. One way they accomplish this is by squeezing more oxygen out of their blood. In fact, elite diving mammals such as Weddell seals do this so efficiently that the resulting arterial oxygen tensions are so low that any human would be rendered unconscious under similar conditions.

Another way to prolong a dive is to conserve the total number of heartbeats. Once again Weddell seals excel by dramatically slowing their hearts in a physiological response termed bradycardia when they submerge. From the heart-rate sensors, we found that before a dive the heart rate of Weddell seals is similar to that of an out-of-shape human adult, around eighty-three beats per minute. This compares to a bradycardia of only twenty-nine beats per minute when the seal is diving. Depending on the type of dive, the seal's heart rate could drop even lower, to what seems like suspended animation levels to us.

From the videotapes we could see that the diving seal was far from quiescent when its heart rate plummeted. Paradoxically, the heart rate of the Weddell seal decreased when the animal was exercising its hardest under water! This is completely opposite to what happens in terrestrial mammals.

The faster we run or swim, the faster our heart races, reaching 200 beats per minute—over three beats per second—when we max out. It would have been ludicrous to suggest that an African lion's heart rate decreased when it was on the prowl actively hunting for food. Yet here was an actively swimming seal, hunting, chasing, and eating fish, with a heart that beat less than every other second. Clearly the cardiovascular system of the diving Weddell seal is plumbed differently than our own. During a dive the seals systematically shut down blood flow to oxygen-consuming tissues, such as the liver and kidneys, that are not essential for underwater hunting.

These organs can wait to be flushed with blood when the seal is breathing on the water surface at the end of the dive, when there is plenty of fresh air available.

The end result of all of these heart-rate and blood-flow adjustments is a heart pumping less blood to fewer body parts. To the seal, the ebb and flow of blood provides a distinct advantage in terms of oxygen conservation and fuel efficiency. The effect on our team was an anxious, edge-of-our-seat wait between successive heartbeats on the seal's extreme dives.

In addition to all of these remarkable physiological changes, diving Weddell seals proved to be exceptionally proficient at moving through the water with hydrodynamic ease. I had finally found the champion of all swimmers in Godzilla.

His smooth, torpedo-shaped body produced almost no wake as he slipped through the water. Two enormous hind flippers, which Matt and I had measured with a digital camera and ruler, provided the propulsion. Godzilla swam like other phocid seals by swinging the posterior third of his body with paired hind flippers held straight back.

Size is everything when it comes to swimming fins and propulsion. This is one of the reasons that seals will always win a race against a human swimmer in the next lane of a pool. The surface area of even the biggest kid's foot in my swimming classes was less than 38 square inches (250 cm²). In comparison, the surface area of the hind flipper of an adult Weddell seal, when the toes are closed, is 114 square inches (750 cm²), about the size of a tennis racquet and three times the size of a human foot. The flippers expand to twice that when the seal spreads its toes and exposes the interdigital webbing as it swims. We are sorely outclassed footwise, and it is little wonder that swim-fin manufacturers look to marine mammals for inspiration in design.

Big feet are only part of the story. The real secret behind Godzilla's swimming proficiency was revealed by the accelerometer sensor that Markus had placed on the seal's tail. With each stroke of the massive hind flippers, a high-pitched tone that had the same undulating wail of a British ambulance was recorded on the audio track of the videotape. Listening to the tone and watching the seal's movements, we discovered that the seal budgeted the number of strokes that he took during a dive, even to the point of turning off his stroking engine during his longer, deeper excursions.

Based on how much energy the seal put into moving his enormous flippers, I calculated that he had enough oxygen on board to take a total of 1,400 strokes during a dive. That was only 700 strokes down and 700 strokes up, regardless of how deep the seal dove. Rather than take stroke after stroke to keep moving as I had to when swimming the length of a pool, Godzilla would take a few strokes then glide, take a few strokes then glide, and finally continuously glide for minutes on end. By the time the seal reached 100 meters (328 feet) during his descent, he was free falling through the black water column without moving a muscle or expending the oxygen of his scuba tank for swimming.

So that's how he does it; that's how he can dive for so long on a single breath of air. I replayed the videotapes over and over again. The next question was, What was changing as the seal descended that allowed him to stop swimming but still move forward at over two meters per second? The seal was careening through the water as fast as an Olympic gold medallist and not even bothering to take a stroke.

Finally, it all started to make sense when I realized that each long glide began at just about the same depth for the seal.

Simultaneously watching the depth gauge and listening to the tail accelerometer, I realized that the seal's flipper motor nearly always turned off between 70 to 100 meters (229–328 feet) in depth. At these depths the surrounding pressure on the seal's body was seven to ten times greater than that experienced on land. The hydrostatic pressure was high enough to cause the animal's chest to cave in and the air in its lungs to compress.

Air in the blood forms bubbles at these depths. For humans and other terrestrial mammals, such changes are potentially devastating. Compression of the lungs of diving humans occurs sporadically, with pockets of air stuck in the lower reaches of small, well-vascularized airways. If nitrogen in the air forces its way into these blood vessels during rapid changes in depth, the gas can coalesce into bubbles. This, in turn, leads to decompression illness, a devastating and potentially lethal condition known to human divers as the bends.

Unlike their terrestrial cousins, seals do not experience the bends. The protection is due to special cartilaginous rings that reinforce the airways of the lungs. When compressed by high pressures at depth, the lungs of seals collapse systematically and completely, slowly moving the air into the upper reinforced airways. Eventually all of the air is sequestered in the large, nonvascular upper airways of the trachea and nasal passages. With no air in contact with the lower airways, no air can be forced into the blood, no bubbles form, and consequently there is no trouble from the bends for diving seals.

From the swimming behavior of Godzilla, it was easy to recognize that there is another benefit associated with the seals' collapsible lungs. On the water surface, inflated lungs acted as positively buoyant balloons that enable the Weddell seal to float lazily. As the lung air was systematically compressed into a smaller space during the descent of a dive, the buoyancy of Godzilla changed from positive to negative. At 100 meters (328 feet), the hydrostatic pressure was so great that lung compression was complete; suddenly, the seal was negatively buoyant. The effect was like placing lead weights in a diver's pockets. Instead of being buoyed up, the seal began falling like a rock though the water column. Deeper and faster the seal fell until he finally had to flatten out his body in skydiver parachute fashion to stall his rapidly increasing speed. There was no need to waste any of his precious few strokes and oxygen reserves to swim to depth; Godzilla could simply glide and parachute his way down into the darkness.

As I rode dive after dive with Godzilla on the videotape, I became increasingly impressed with his ability to take advantage of these buoyancy changes and use them to conserve his scuba tank. He knew how to angle his body precisely to glide in any direction in the pursuit of fish. By relaxing and gliding for over half of the dive, the seal could save his final bit of oxygen for chasing and eating fish that lived on the bottom of the ocean and then ascend. On the ascent everything happened in reverse, with the lungs reinflating as the hydrostatic pressure decreased. By the time the seal reached the shallows the inflated lungs helped float the animal back to the surface with barely a stroke needed.

All of this is made possible by the specialized anatomy of the seals' lungs that enables them to prevent the bends. Behavior, anatomy, physiology, and physics combine in such a marvelous synergy that this unassuming mammal is capable of athletic feats below the Antarctic sea ice that humans can only dream of. It is no wonder that the Weddell seal is always grinning. More than ever I was convinced that these marine mammals are the ultimate swimmers.

As the videotape began to wind down, Godzilla finished several long dives and then descended into the darkness for over fifteen minutes. Unlike the other dives, he suddenly stopped, parking himself in front of a sponge and a few starfish. He lay on the bottom of the ocean without breathing, moving a muscle, or making a sound.

"Is he sleeping?" Bill asked.

As if to answer the question, the seal rolled his eyes and peered up through the water. From his position on the ocean floor, Home Crack appeared as a thin white scar across a mottled gray surface above him. The dark outlines of several seals were backlit by sunlight streaming through the crack in the sea ice. Some of the seals were obviously paired off. Depending on their gender they could have been sparring or courting. It was too far away to tell.

November is prime mating season, which begins with the larger, most aggressive adult male seals setting up territories around breathing holes in the ice. Scarface was just one of the many older, experienced males vying for female attention in the area. Most of his bite injuries had occurred from the jaws of other males battling for the same breathing hole and for females.

Female seals are attracted to the holes or to the territorial males, depending on whether you believe in resources or in brawn as the more important factor in the mating game. Younger males that were unable to fend off the likes of Scarface were relegated to the sexual sidelines for the season, unless they could sneak in at the last moment. Often the sneak-in males suffered gaping wounds near the base of their flippers and genitals, delivered swiftly and deliberately by the aggressive territorial seals. The injured sneak-in males would then haul out, bleeding on the ice trying to avoid further conflict, and heal their wounds in relative solitude.

From his position beneath the crack it appeared as though Godzilla was on the losing end in the fight for female seals this year. Rather than battle the other territorial males, he had sunk into the depths to watch the courtship activities from below. His only chance for mating with a female would be as a sneak-in. But he didn't move.

"I think he's sulking," Randy laughed.

Unexpectedly, Godzilla suddenly lashed out at one of the starfish that happened to be within his reach. He bit at the invertebrate, shook it in his mouth, and then spit it out. Just as quickly he went back to lying motionless on the ocean floor, only to repeat his attack on a nearby sponge moments later. There was no attempt to eat the animals. The seal just seemed to want to rustle things up, like a disgruntled teen tormenting siblings after being jilted before the big prom.

We never got the chance to find out how the mating season ended for Godzilla. His videotape ran out after just two hours of play, interrupted by a malfunction in the camera. Upon inspection it turned out that the camera unit had flooded during one of the seal's big dives. Whether the result of scraping the housing along the ice, high pressure at depth, or just banging the camera during fights with territorial seals and starfish, the recording stopped midway in the action. In view of his retreat into the seal nursery where we found him, we suspected that Seal 20, the Godzilla among our research seals, had sought out the softer, quieter company of female Weddell seals rather than the confrontational territorial males of Home Crack.

Ms. Apnea, Seal 21, was the next seal to work with us and she treated our team to an amazing six-hour tour of the underside of the Erebus Glacier Ice Tongue. Her initial dives were through a maze of ice caves that had formed beneath the glacier. It was an extraordinary place that no human had visited, for no scuba diver could have safely entered such a tortuous twist of ice. The seal explored the caves, sliding along on her belly and squeezing into unpredictable holes. The sea ice beneath the glacier had been folded into great white sheets that rose and fell into smooth caverns and blind alleys, a product of the ice tongue sliding down Ross Island and the ocean currents swelling from below. Bits of black volcanic rock formed long ribbons frozen into the rolls of ice that eventually spread out in a dark gravel path along the ocean floor.

Once inside of the ice tunnels, there were few features other than the smooth undulating walls. No invertebrates inhabited the caves. The only fish present were dead, and probably deposited by seals. Only on one occasion did Ms. Apnea come upon another seal. The animal floated mid-water, motionless in a deep fold of ice, peering out of the dark with the stern demeanor of a statue placed in a hidden alcove of a curtained frozen cathedral. Neither seal acknowledged the other, except for a silent furtive sideways glare.

As Ms. Apnea continued her journey along the underside of the glacier, she periodically tested the integrity of the ice overhead seeking a place to breath. Stopping briefly, she would push upwards with her nose against the ice sheet to see if it would give way under her urging. If the ceiling did not budge then she would move on, looking for another area.

Twenty minutes later Ms. Apnea surfaced in an underwater tomb of ice. The floor was a pool of water big enough to allow her to float while a pocket of air trapped beneath the glacier formed a breathing dome. She remained for several minutes floating and slowly breathing as if contemplating her next dive. Diving in such close quarters required calculated moves. If she swam too far into the glacier there was a chance that she would not be able to reach another air pocket in time for her next required breath. Each dive had to be navigated and budgeted judiciously so that she reached a new breathing space or was able to return to the abandoned pocket of air. Often there didn't appear to be enough room for the seal to turn around if a backwards retreat was required.

Despite the risk, the seal pushed on exploring new areas of the glacier's belly, using a series of submerged caves and air pockets to rest and breath. We now understood why we had lost the signals from her radio and satellite tags as soon as she had left Weddell World. She had spent most of her time hiding beneath the glacier where neither tag had a chance of transmitting a signal to us.

In contrast to the previous three seals, locating our fourth seal of the field season was easy. When we first released her, Seal 22 (Ms. Zodiac) had swum slowly under the camp for three hours, carrying our instrumentation and all of our high expectations with her. She had been so active in the camp she seemed ready for adventure. Would she take us to the bottom of McMurdo Sound like Ally and Godzilla, or beneath the glacier like Ms. Apnea? Would she hunt for fish and encounter other seals in her travels? There were so many possibilities in terms of where she could take us and what she would show us about the world beneath the sea ice that the team could barely contain their excitement.

Instead, the seal was true to her unfortunate nickname. Ms.

Zodiac went into dry dock. She beached herself by hauling out on the ice and proceeded to stretch, roll, and sleep in the sun by Home Crack. We didn't need to scout by radio or satellite tags. We did not have to track signals during a backbreaking snowmobile trek. All we had to do was look out of the side window of the Jamesway; we could see Ms. Zodiac lying in the sun with all of our instruments among the other dozing seals.

For several days we watched her laze about at Home Crack. In some ways we couldn't blame her. The weather was the finest offered by Antarctica, with cloudless blue skies, soft breezes, temperatures hovering just below freezing, and a warm sun that never set. On these windless days we wore just a windbreaker over our sweaters, which gave the team a refreshing sense of lightness.

We were jolted back to polar reality as the snow and ice softened under our feet. Every new, sharp creak of the Jamesway reminded us that our time on the ice was growing shorter with each sunny day. The other buildings at Weddell World showed the strain and were beginning to list to one side as the pressure ridges next to the glacier grew higher. What had once been flat ice now buckled in ridges over twelve feet high. The sun-softened sea ice bowed beneath the buildings, forced by the glacier moving behind the camp.

Soon nothing with a rounded edge could be placed on tables, for fear of the object's rolling onto the floor. Pens, pencils, lip gloss, flashlights, and Swiss Army knives eventually ended up lost in the dusty corners of the tilting buildings. Because the Jamesway was the only structure in Weddell World anchored to the ice, its floorboards took the brunt of the strain. The wooden floors continued to moan in response to the shifting ice, making the building appear alive and in agony. Plywood sheets bowed and finally ripped from the understructure, shearing the heads off wood screws with a loud "snap" when the strain became too much. The groans and splintering of the wood only added to our apprehension regarding the completion of our research.

Finally, we knew that we had to accept our losses and remove the VDAP and sensors that we had worked so hard to place on Ms.

Zodiac. It was clear that she was going nowhere in the foreseeable future; she had displayed no interest in diving or hunting, the very behaviors that we wanted to study.

She could have been waiting for a suitable territorial male or wanted to avoid the mating scene altogether. Maybe she was just taking advantage of the sunny weather. The explanation didn't matter. The seal had made no moves towards the water for nearly a week, and the likelihood that the VDAP camera would record anything other than sleeping seals was low. With each shift of the ice, time was running out for us. There were other seals to be studied as long as we could retrieve our instruments from Ms. Zodiac.

When we approached the snoozing seal, I noticed that she had been lying on the ice for so long that she had inadvertently created a snow angel from multiple impressions of her body and hind flippers in the ice. Her body had gotten so hot from lying in the constant sunlight that she had melted herself into a huge tub. We had to watch our footing to keep from slipping on the melting ice and falling onto her.

Like the other seals in our study, Ms. Zodiac snorted at the intrusion of her nap and then went back to sleep with the other seals after we removed our instruments. What the seal lacked as a scientific explorer she certainly made up for as a world-class sunbather.

Our decision to remove Ms. Zodiac from the study had been the right one. She stayed on the ice by Home Crack for several more days until blowing wind and low clouds forced her into the water. True to form, however, she went right back to lazing in her usual bathtub spot in the sun immediately after the storm blew through.

Not all of the seals of Home Crack were as lethargic as Ms. Zodiac. All around the sleeping seal, the ice crack was alive with seal moms conducting swimming lessons for their young pups. The coaxing, splashing, and insecurity of the youngsters brought me back to my college days as a swim instructor. There were the eager pups that dove headfirst into the water after their moms, and then there were the timid ones that cried on shore.

While watching the activities, I discovered that it took considerable practice and growth before a Weddell seal pup developed into an expert swimmer and diver. Young seals lacked coordination and the first dips usually ended up in a water-whipped froth of flailing flippers. It would take another year before the muscles and blood of the seal pups contained the same oxygen stores as their moms. The first dives by the pups were by necessity short due to their comparatively small scuba tanks.

Internally, the hearts of the pups already showed signs of the roller-coaster heart rates characteristic of their parents. Their small hearts bounced from a high of eighty-five beats per minute when breathing to lows of thirty to fifty beats per minute when holding their breath, even while sleeping on the ice. At the very least, the cardiovascular system of the young seals was primed for underwater activity.

After several weeks of sleeping, drinking milk, and growing stronger on top of the sea ice, all of the pups had gotten noticeably larger. They had ballooned from skinny little furry sacks to rotund fuzzy balls with necks so fat that they could barely move their heads. Only one month old, the pups already weighed over 91 kilograms (200 pounds), most of it consisting of a two-inch layer of blubber that encased them like one of our down parkas. Now that they had enough insulation to keep warm in the water, it was time to learn how to swim like a seal.

Lucky Pup was sleeping as usual, with his belly facing into the sun, when his mother tried to nudge him towards the ice crack for his first dip below the ice. Like the other pups, he cried loudly as his mom, and his source of milk, headed for the water. But she was persistent. Rather than give in to his cries, she dipped her head into a large, open pool near the crack and slipped her body smoothly into the water. Lucky Pup was instantly curious about the sudden disappearance of his mother and crawled over to the edge of the pool. As he dipped his whiskers down, his mother popped her head up to meet him nose to nose. Lucky Pup yelped until he recognized her whiskers and her smell. Still he backed off, calling all of the time, trying to get her to haul back out onto the ice with him.

His mother would have none of it. At first she called to him repetitively and loudly from the water, trying to verbally coax the little pup in. Lucky Pup answered each of her calls with a throaty "Mmaaaaaww," but did not budge.

As if her patience was wearing thin with an obstinate child, the seal mom began reaming the edge of the hole furiously. She tore at the ice with her teeth bared, churning the water into white foam. Intermittently she would stop, call to her pup—who answered back without moving—and then continue to ream at the ice edge. Within several minutes the mom had created a sloping ice stairway that would allow Lucky Pup easy access into and out of the water. Lucky Pup did not even turn around. Instead, he rolled onto his back, flopping his large hind flippers behind, and continued to call for his mom without looking back at her.

With her pup several yards away from the hole and refusing to get wet, the mom dove. Before I had a chance to guess her next move, I heard her. Chirping and trilling, the mom called to Lucky Pup through the ice. The vocalizations were so loud that I could feel each one vibrate through the bottoms of my boots. There was little doubt that the pup could both feel and hear his mother's calls beneath him. With each call, Lucky Pup called back into the air but did not move a muscle.

With her options exhausted, the mom returned to the surface. She rose high in the water of the open pool trying to spy hop and locate Lucky Pup. He kept an eye on her from a distance but did not venture anywhere there was a chance of getting wet.

After bobbing in the water for several minutes, the mom finally hauled out slippery and wet onto the ice. She rolled in the snow several times to dry her fur, and then joined Lucky Pup lying belly-up in the sun. Together they slept stretched out with our champion sunbather, Ms. Zodiac, under the intense Antarctic sun, delaying the swimming lesson until another day.

CHAPTER 14

THE COST OF
A HOT MEAL

NOVEMBER 21–30

With three previous field seasons behind us, we had learned to recognize the symptoms of fatigue in our teammates and ourselves. Like clockwork, weariness began to be manifested in a series of accidents by the third week of November. Air temperatures had gratefully risen into the plus column hovering around 16°F (-9°C), but caused a thin layer of melt water to form on the surface of the sea ice. We now had to contend with a slick skating pond that was impossible to stand on when we worked with the seals. Slipping and sliding as we cautiously walked towards the instrumented seals, each member of the team eventually took a hard fall. In time our bodies were spotted in what felt like a never-ending series of bruises.

Nearly all of the injuries were minor—the usual bruises and scrapes from falling caused by a combination of fatigue, overconfidence, and pure bad luck. Dull thinking also contributed to the accidents. We just were not as mentally sharp as we should have been. Both our bodies and minds wore out faster while living on the ice; healing was definitely prolonged in the cold. Continuous pounding and wrenching maneuvers that at one time had seemed thrilling on the snowmobiles were taking a toll on our backs, necks, shoulders, and elbows. Cuts and scrapes from handling tools and seals in the cold ached as they slowly healed. The tips of our fingers had frozen and thawed so many times that the edges of our nails had curled and the pads were callused and hard. Our feet were callused, too, from months of wearing the heavy bunny boots.

In our own individual ways, we started to show signs of wear and tear. I was bruised, ace-bandaged, and noticeably slower in the morning. Lee and Don were quieter, and Randy prone to afternoon cat naps. Markus used larger espressos and Jesse more hot chocolates to keep going. One of the key lessons we had learned over years of Antarctic work was that each team member had a unique breaking point, something that could push them over the edge. An unexpected fall that used up the last bit of adrenaline, a snippet of bad news from home, or an unguarded side comment could mark the end for a team member. If pushed too far they could withdraw from the group, seeking their own company and thoughts. To prevent that from happening, we learned to accept our differences and kept a wary eye out for potential rifts.

Personal fatigue was set aside as the pace of scientific research and survival continued nonstop. Our lives were commanded by the protracted field season caused by deteriorating ice conditions and the free-ranging behavior of the Weddell seals. Instead of paying attention to our bodies, we pushed harder and harder, accepting that emotional and physical healing would wait until after the expedition.

Observing how quickly we ran ourselves down made me question how expeditions managed to drive on for month after month during the Heroic Age of Antarctic exploration, in the time of Robert F. Scott and Ernest Shackleton. The men of Scott's *Discovery* expedition and Shackleton's *Endurance* expedition had lived and survived with minimal supplies under the harshest of Antarctic conditions for years. My respect for those explorers reached new levels after trying to work on the ice for a single field season. Had our 21st-century lifestyle made us that soft, or had we simply underestimated the draining effects of living in the polar environment?

Shackleton demanded a regular schedule of work and exercise for his men as the ice trapped the *Endurance,* even if it meant playing hockey on an ice floe. Black-and-white images taken by Frank Hurley, the photographer on Shackleton's expedition, show men strolling along the ice pack, romping with sled dogs, and playing soccer so intensely that several appear bare-chested on the sea ice. The captain excused periodic short tempers and turned small pleasures into moments of celebration.

Like Shackleton, we tried to monitor the temperament of the team and relished the small victories, accomplishments, and pleasures. One of the greatest pleasures for our team came in a cardboard box from the Berg Field Center in McMurdo. Delivered by a group of carpenters passing by on their way to another field camp, the box contained "freshies." These were perishable fresh food items that were flown into McMurdo by cargo plane. In town such deliveries were sporadic and dependent on the weather and flight schedules; it could be weeks during the summer and months during the winter between salads. Isolated in a field camp, you might never see fresh fruit or vegetables for the entire field season.

By the end of November, eating at Weddell World had developed into a necessary chore made up of basic brown foods. Breakfast was cold cereal with powdered milk, if it at all. Lunch was a quesadilla and Oreo cookies. Dinner was brown fried meat, rice, or pasta. The cold, dry Antarctic air had drained most of the flavor from the foods, making eating a sensation of texture rather than taste. Supplies were running down and meals had become repetitive.

Delivery of the freshies box had an instant impact on the morale of the team. Opening the cardboard box, we ogled the contents as Lee brought forth several fresh onions, potatoes, withered carrots, a frozen wilted head of lettuce, four apples, and—to our complete amazement—an entire pineapple. At first we just stared at the yellow-green fruit. How it had made it all the way to our camp in one piece and how we had been so fortunate to receive this gift was beyond our comprehension. Its gnarled yellow skin and spiky green topnotch conjured up sandy white beaches, tropical green hillsides, and humid air laden with ginger and plumeria. It would have been sacrilege to take a knife to such a miraculous delivery. Instead, we gave the pineapple a place of honor as the centerpiece of our dining table. Each meal was eaten in its presence, whether it rested on the aluminum table or cast its pungent odor from a nearby shelf. For several days we caught a faint whiff of the fruit whenever we passed closely by. Just seeing the pineapple was enough to make us smile; it was as out of place in Antarctica as we were.

The pleasure of owning the pineapple was short-lived, however, as the daily freezing and thawing of the building ravaged the tropical fruit. It began to lean to one side and the odor turned noticeably sharper even to our deadened noses. By the time we finally decided to eat it, the yellow meat had rotted to brown inside of the skin. We tried carving out the most edible portions and were left with little more than the tough fibrous core, wrinkled brown skin, and dry withered leaves. Perhaps we should have greedily eaten the pineapple the first day that we took it out of the box. However, most of the team agreed that it had been infinitely more satisfying to live with the fruit and dream for a week than to have consumed it in one sitting.

As we continued our analysis of the videotapes from the diving seals, we discovered that dietary variety was as significant for the Weddell seals as it was for us. The seals hunted and overwhelmed tiny fish that were only a few inches long. They wrestled with underwater giants that appeared as large as sea dragons in the brief glimpses provided in the video images. Flashes of eye shine and the roll of a spiked dorsal fin belonging to an enormous deep-dwelling fish added to its menacing, mysterious appearance. So big that only parts of the body could be caught by the camera lens, we could tell that the monster fishes were the largest prey in the dark waters. Usually these fish were savvy and large enough to give the hunting seals a wild underwater chase when detected.

We also learned that eating required considerable skill by the diving seals, with each type of fish demanding a unique hunting style. This was most apparent for Seal 23, our most successful underwater huntress. Seal 23 was the largest Weddell seal that we handled, weighing in at over 455 kilograms (1,000 pounds). Her rotund shape as she lay on the ice near the tip of the glacier had been our first clue that she was a successful predator. No seal could have gained her size without eating a tremendous number of fish. With the failure of petite Seal 22 (Ms. Zodiac) to even enter the water, the team decided to choose the largest female seal we could find as our next candidate for the VDAP camera. It took all of our collective strength to help wedge Seal 23 into the seal sled and keep her moving in one direction in the chute leading towards the lab. If she had tried to turn around, there was a good chance that she would have gotten stuck, a predicament that the team didn't even want to consider.

Once she was outfitted with our instruments and camera, Seal 23 was reluctant to leave the warmth of the Jamesway. We splashed in the water of the dive hole with our hands trying to encourage her to go for a dip. Instead, she blinked and turned over on her side to sleep. There was nothing for us to do but wait. After sleeping through the night and into the next morning, Seal 23 finally launched herself and our instruments on what would have been Thanksgiving Day in the United States. Hence, she was christened Mayflower.

To our dismay, Mayflower miscalculated her dive and aimed her head in the wrong direction when she finally dipped into the hole. Her tail ended up hovering over the four-foot-wide dive hole while her front lodged on the ice shelf. Too broad to turn around, she was stuck. Mayflower peered over her shoulder as best she could, with her thick neck bulging, but remained unsure about the location of the diving hole behind her. She lay in the water on the ice shelf, briefly twisting to her right and then her left—to no effect. Finally, by feeling with her hind flippers she began to wedge her back end down into the hole as if she were trying to squeeze into a tight girdle. She twisted and pushed and eventually exhaled, which allowed her to slip her bulky chest slowly down through the seven-foot-thick ice and into the open water below. It was the first back-flippered dive entrance ever performed by one of our seals.

Free to dive and feed, Mayflower proved to be a hunting champion. She dove repeatedly to 400 meter (1,312 foot) depths looking for fish to eat. On the ocean bottom she shunned the diversity of incredible sea creatures that she encountered. Without stopping to even taste the porous giant sponges, soft-bodied starfish, and prickly spiderlike crinoids, the seal swam steadily through the dark water. After ignoring the bottom dwellers, she focused her hunting on Antarctic silverfish, *Pleuragramma antarcticum,* small anchovy-like prey that were about six inches in length. Her strategy when hunting these small fish was to dive to the ocean floor, skirt along an underwater ridge, look up using the back lighting of the sea ice and sun above to silhouette her prey, and then ascend into large aggregations of the *Pleuragramma.*

Swimming into a ball of fish, she began to pick them off like popcorn. On the video we anticipated each fish by the spiked appearance of her whiskers. First the spiky whiskers rose to attention, then there was a flash of silver followed by gulping movements of the seal's head. It was as if Mayflower's whiskers enabled her to "feel" the location of each individual fish just before the kill. Fish after fish were swallowed as the seal ascended through the fish ball. After her feast she floated up to the water surface to catch a few breaths of air and then repeated her performance. It was a remarkable display of eating that the high metabs certainly related to, with over twenty silverfish slurped down on each dive. By the time she was finished she had consumed over a hundred fish, a bellyful even for a 1,000-pound Weddell, before stopping a moment to digest her meal.

If it were not for the specialized digestive system of the seals, we never would have thought that a seal could pack in so many fish in a single meal. One of the most impressive internal features of the seals as well as other marine mammals, including dolphins, whales, and sea lions, is the length of their small intestine. Compared to terrestrial mammals, mammals that hunt in the ocean are clearly built for eating. A medium-size dog has a small intestine that can be stretched to three meters (ten feet), while a similarly sized harbor seal has a small intestine that is over five times longer. The small intestine of humans is five meters (sixteen feet) long. Weddell seals and bottlenose dolphins have small intestines that are thirty meters (over ninety feet) in length, about four times longer than that of an African lion. Stretched from one end to the other, the small intestine of the Weddell seal can span the length of a basketball court. With plenty of room for holding and digesting her prey, Mayflower could gulp down silverfish by the dozens with ease.

But silverfish were only the appetizers. Near the water surface, Mayflower hunted for larger prey in the form of "borks." *Pagothenia borchgrevinki* "bork," for short—are buggy-eyed, dark-spotted fish with a Mohawk ridge of fins along the top. They live among the ice crystals formed by the platelet ice, hiding just below the frozen surface of the sea in -3°C (27°F) water. The water is so cold among the platelet ice that the fish rely on cellular antifreeze. Without this antifreeze, the cells of the borks would crystallize and burst, instantly killing the fish.

From the video we could see that the borks had adapted to their unusually chilly environment and flitted with ease among the ice crystals that formed frozen chandeliers on the underside of the sea ice. Our hunting seal also noticed the movements of the fish, which were easily backlit against the surface. Floating just below the platelet ice, Mayflower jerked her head right and left, following the borks as if she were a fox tracking a field mouse. Like a fox, she pounced. Mayflower pushed her head into the ice, trying to grab at the escaping borks, which wedged their bodies as far up into the ice crystals as possible. Because of her size the seal couldn't move any farther forward, and the borks remained barely out of her hungry reach. Just when we thought that the small fish had outwitted the seal, she did an extraordinary thing—Mayflower blew a long series of bubbles out her nose. The unexpected blast of air was not a howl of frustration as we first thought. Rather it was an amazingly effective way to flush out her prey. Startled borks suddenly scattered in the presence of the bubbles. Some escaped over the head of the seal, shooting past the camera with a wild, fish-eyed gawk into the lens. Others had the misfortune of swimming right into her hungry, waiting mouth.

The bubble trick had one drawback—it sacrificed part of the seal's scuba tank. As a result, Mayflower used this hunting strategy when only she was close to a breathing hole where she could quickly replenish her oxygen supply. To ensure immediate access to air, the seal usually informed others occupying a breathing hole of her approach and need for air. Throaty chugs and long, high-pitched trills caused the other seals to move out of the way. None of them were willing to challenge Seal 23, the Mayflower.

Following several days of hunting, Mayflower hauled out on top of the ice near a blue melt pool at the end of the Erebus Glacier Ice Tongue. This time, when our team headed out, we had a different plan for the seal and our instruments. The seal had been so successful a hunter and so confident around us that we decided to take one more risk. Rather than remove all of her instrumentation as we had done with the previous seals, we simply replaced the batteries and videotape. In doing so we gained the opportunity to see what Mayflower would do next, far surpassing the six-hour glimpses we usually obtained for each seal. The risk was that the seal might tire of the game and finally swim away with the equipment and data.

And that is exactly what Mayflower did. To our disappointment she left, presumably to seek a quieter resting place. Like Ally

McSeal, Godzilla, and Ms. Apnea, the seal disappeared, leaving us with no signals to follow. The situation was worsened by the quickly deteriorating sea ice. With countless breathing holes and cracks perforating the ice, extensive travel was possible for the submerged seal, and the possibility of reaching the open sea had become a reality.

After seven days, we began to think that our luck had finally run out. In desperation Matt, Randy, and I tried to track down the missing seal by searching the icefalls on the northern side of the Erebus Glacier Ice Tongue past Little Razorback Island. If Mayflower had hauled out to the north it was possible that we would not be able to receive the signals from her radio tags through the glacier. With a bit of luck we thought we could intercept her if she was heading towards the northern open waters. So we headed out with the handheld radio receiver and antenna to find her.

It was early evening, and it had already been a long day of radio tracking the instrumented seal. Dinner was long past. But the sun was shining brightly, night temperatures were warm, and conducting one more snowmobile foray into the Sound was better than sitting at Weddell World hoping that the seal would return on her own.

The trip was especially rough due to the effect of the erratic winds that swung around the glacier tip and Big Razorback Island. In addition to the increased number of holes, cracks, and pressure ridges, the texture of the ice had changed, alternating between the remnants of rough sastrugi, and flat, bright-blue glare ice. While the ice ridges were back wrenching, it was the blue ice that proved to be more dangerous. Scoured by numerous windstorms that had blown across the open ice during the previous months, the blue areas of sea ice were slicker than glass and offered no relief for traction. Walking on the slippery ice was difficult enough; driving a snowmobile across it was nerve-wracking. The front ski of the snowmobile wobbled constantly on the ice, threatening to twist out of our control at any second, and our arms and hands quickly tired from the white-knuckled grip on the steering. For our own safety, we avoided blue ice whenever possible.

On this particular evening, the three of us ignored the flagged road in order to travel the shortest distance between the glacier and our destination. We headed in a straight line for Little Razorback Island across the open ice. A season of winds by the island had sculpted and hardened the snow into ridges that caused the snowmobiles to buck and jolt. The clarity of the air made the distance appear deceptively short, and by the time we arrived at the northern icefalls forty-five minutes later our arms and shoulders were aching from the effort.

We checked the area for our seal; finding no signs of her, we began the ride back to camp. Long shadows stretched across the ice, revealing a flat, snowy course that tracked the edge of the islands. We considered our options.

"Let's follow the edge of the islands," suggested Matt.

"I vote for anything smoother," I added, rubbing my sore elbow.

"Smooth it is," Randy agreed.

We opted for a longer but hopefully less-demanding ride for the return trip to Weddell World. Our plan had us skirting Ross Island, cutting behind Inaccessible and Tent Islands, and then circling around to the south side of the glacier to finally arrive back at Weddell World. In addition to being a more pleasant journey, the track would allow us to survey the back sides of the islands for Mayflower.

In the glow of the early morning sun, the sky turned a deep marine blue that outlined the perimeter of the glacier and the islands. Deep crevasses had formed between the sea ice and the snow-drifted shorelines of the islands, creating a series of frozen ridges. In our frozen world it was as if the ocean tides had risen up, crashed onto the shore, and then chilled instantly into a rolling wave that never completed its curl. This was the endless summer wave that the surfers of Santa Cruz spent a lifetime searching for.

The going was smooth along the side of Ross Island. We then crossed the open sea ice and were just beginning to round Inaccessible Island when we came upon an eight-foot-high pressure ridge. The ridge was just one of several ice formations in the area. Irregular currents had created ridges and gaps in the sea ice that had opened and refrozen during the season. The fractured ice had turned into a jigsaw puzzle of flat and rough areas. To negotiate the features we began standing on our speeding snowmobiles, zigzagging in thrilling maneuvers between the icy obstacles. Unless a lead was obviously open, the rule of thumb when traveling on the ice was to keep moving. Slowing down or sitting on a pressure ridge only increased your chances of breaking through the melting ice.

At one point a chunky pressure ridge separated me from the two others. Too high to see over and too wide to drive across, I quickly found a small gap that appeared to be the ideal crossing point. Revving the snowmobile faster I crossed the ridge with ease, and quickly banked a hard left turn to join the others. I reveled in a feeling of self-assured cockiness at having squeezed out of a clinch. However, the high-speed, overconfident maneuver was a bad mistake on ice. Hidden on the opposite side of the pressure ridge was a sheet of blue ice glistening in the sunlight.

My snowmobile hit the smooth ice sheet and began an out-of-control sideways skid, and then a 360-degree spin. Before I could even sit down and get the machine steadied, the front ski hit a small patch of snow. Acting as if the gears had suddenly been thrown into reverse, I was immediately thrown off the machine like a bucking bronco. Landing on the ice with a hard crunch, I kept sliding, only briefly opening my eyes long enough to see the snowmobile tumbling towards me. The sensation was one of rolling and watching a succession of orange, black, orange, black, orange, black as the top and bottom of the machine turned over and over on the ice.

All I could think was, "That is really going to hurt when it hits me," as I continued to tumble and slide uncontrollably along the ice.

Finally, I skidded to a stop. I had no idea how long or how far I had traveled, but when I looked up I saw that my snowmobile had landed upright nearby and was still running. I breathed a sigh of relief once I realized that we hadn't collided, and lay back looking straight up into the sky. Any injuries would be due to hitting the ice. For a brief moment I thought that I had imagined everything that had just happened. Then I felt the ache in my head, shoulder, and elbow. I was sitting on the ice holding my head, dizzy and nauseous from all of the tumbling, when Matt rode up. He had witnessed the whole accident and started firing questions at me.

"What day of the week is it?" he asked.

Dammit, I thought. I never knew what day of the week it was in camp.

"Do you remember your name?" he asked getting increasingly worried.

All I could think was that my ears were ringing, my head ached, and that it was a dumb question.

"Who is the current president?" he tested me. It was my last chance to respond before he considered pulling out a radio and calling for a helicopter medevac.

Finally, I snapped, "I really don't care."

I was more angry than hurt. By this time Randy had arrived to help. My clothing and gear were scattered all around the ice. The backpack I had been wearing to safeguard my new Nikon camera had been thrown off, smashing a polarizing filter and zoom lens. A plastic box of Tic Tacs was the other casualty in the pack, spilling the little white mints all over the ice.

After picking up my hat and ski goggles, which had been thrown off during the tumbling, I shakily got to my feet. We were in the middle of an ice field, miles from camp, and the fun of the evening had been rattled out of me. Matt traded snowmobiles since mine now had a shattered front windscreen and crumpled steering bar. We headed slowly to find the flagged road behind us for the longer, but quieter trip back to camp.

At Weddell World the rest of the team took turns checking on me, staying up into the early morning hours to make sure that no serious problems developed with my head injury. Under normal circumstances I would have shaken off the attention, but I was too tired to resist. Jesse offered me a mug of hot chocolate and talked until we were too sleepy to care what was being said. I had complete confidence in my teammates; they would look out for me the same way that I would look after them. We were a working scientific team, expedition members, friends, and survivors. At last I fell asleep to the reassuring sounds of Weddell seals trilling below my cot, able to momentarily forget my bumps, bruises, and aches.

The next morning I was taken along with the battered snowmobile to McMurdo Station for a quick checkup. The hospital consisted of an unassuming, white, one-story building with a plywood cutout of a penguin by the front door. I passed the cheery cartoon penguin wearing a Santa hat and carrying a sign that read, "Dr. Penguin says Get Well Soon," and entered the makeshift reception area and clinic. Fortunately my visit was short. The doctors of McMurdo General Hospital let me escape with a simple elbow brace, a packet of ibuprofen, and orders to slow down. I thanked my father for "hardheaded Welsh ancestors," and went right back to the sea ice and Weddell World. Two days later my snowmobile was fixed and I was out on the ice conducting surveys again, albeit with a few less acrobatics.

By Thanksgiving Day in Antarctica the team was so battered and bruised that we decided we were in need of special cheer. For the first time during the expedition, we took a break to join the celebrations in McMurdo Station. With all of the camp work completed by mid-afternoon, we hopped onto our snowmobiles, forming a train down the flagged route back to town. Sun and gentle winds made the ride pleasant. There was a tinge of sadness among the team members as we recognized that the trip to town also started our transition back into "real" life. After interacting primarily with our small group for so long, we were going to have to learn to be social again.

At first it was difficult to break out of our clique and converse with others. They didn't know our inside jokes, and we didn't want to know theirs. In many ways, we were the outsiders. We were the peculiar sea-ice folks, the beakers that wore bunny boots in town and smelled of diesel fuel and Weddell seal shit. The members of our group tended to quietly stare, giving the impression of standoff-ishness to those we met in the hallways.

We cleaned up the best that we could, with a hot shower and a clean set of jeans and underwear. There was little doubt that we were underdressed compared to the McMurdo crowd in their ties, suits, and dresses. Regardless, our team was in their cleanest and ready for a feast.

The chefs in the McMurdo galley outdid themselves for the holiday. Turkey, dressing, and three kinds of cranberry sauce were accompanied by fresh stuffed pumpkins from New Zealand, salad fixings that we had not seen in weeks, and five kinds of dessert. After eating camp food for nearly two months, the amount of food and the variety of tastes were overwhelming. We tasted everything and nearly made ourselves sick in the process. The holiday spirit was in the air, and a bottle of wine on the table soon melted our "camp reserve." Carpenters, electricians, and the radio personnel whom we checked in with daily stopped by to ask how things were going in camp. The doctor and lab assistant who had helped with my injuries came by our table to see if I had slowed down on the snow-mobile. There were holiday hugs and handshakes from scientific colleagues. We toasted the Antarctic, Weddell Seals 19 through 23, and Gerry Kooyman, who had been our mentor and introduced us all to the ice. It was a grand time.

Two hours later we changed back into our smelly cold-weather gear, with our insulated pants feeling a little too snug. The snowmo-bile ride back to Weddell World was considerably slower than the ride into town. We didn't want to ruin the post-festive glow. Nor did we want to jostle the enormous meal that we had just consumed. At the time I wished I had the intestinal capacity of the seals. We sat back on the cold black seats, let the evening sun shine on our smiling faces, and rode contentedly along the smooth flagged road across the eleven miles of sea ice back to camp.

As soon as we stepped into the Jamesway, the team was back to work. Unbeknownst to us, the seals at Weddell World had had their own plans for Thanksgiving feasting. While we were gone one of the local seals had come up in the diving hole in the lab and deposited six Antarctic silverfish. The fish had undoubtedly been the topping of an overzealous hunt and had been vomited whole while the seal was resting on the water surface. Too satiated to take another bite, the seal left the remains of its dinner floating in the hole. For us, the seal's gluttony represented an unusual opportunity. Markus quickly dip-netted the fish and for the first time we saw what the seals had been eating on the video. Until now our view of these slender fish had been as flashes of silver before being swallowed by the seals. From the video sequences, we had the impression that they were the size and shape of anchovies. These fish specimens proved it. The silverfish left by the seals were four to six inches long, with transparent fins and delicate silvery scales.

I was impressed with the size of the eyes of the little fish; the giant eyes almost dwarfed their heads. In this regard the predator and prey were quite similar. Interactions between Weddell seals and silverfish occurred in the dark depths of Antarctic waters over 200 meters (656 feet) below the surface of the sea ice. Both the hunter and its quarry had eyes designed for capturing what little light could penetrate to these depths.

Large eyes as well as large intestines seemed to be prerequisites for hunting at depth if you were a marine mammal or if you were trying to escape as their prey. Looking at the mucous-covered fish vomited by the seal brought new meaning to the old saying, "Your eyes are bigger than your stomach."

Before Randy and I had even finished measuring and photographing the silverfish, we heard splashing in the dive hole in the back of the Jamesway. Rarely were Weddell seals so rambunctious at night, and several of us went to investigate. We found the floorboards and walls soaked with seawater from a fierce struggle that was taking place in the dive hole.

With a loud splash, a flipper hit the surface of the water. Then the water boiled as two bodies somersaulted. Another flipper slapped the water surface, initiating another round of tumbling and splashing.

From the intensity of the battle and the amount of water that was being sprayed across the lab it appeared that two Weddell seals were fighting over possession of the breathing hole. In the foaming water we saw the flash of a large white head that was followed by the dark head of a small female Weddell seal. We soon realized that the other combatant was not a seal, but was large nonetheless.

As the struggle subsided and the water settled in the dive hole we discovered that the seal's mouth was clamped around the gills of a giant fish. She was holding on with all of her strength, unwilling to move a muscle for fear of another bout of struggling by her prey. The fish was very much alive, slowly moving its fins but otherwise momentarily passive under the seal's vice-like grip.

On the water surface, the female seal breathed through her nose in long hard exhalations and inhalations. She huffed in exhaustion, lying out on the water surface next to the fish but never letting go. Her quarry was an Antarctic toothfish, also called Antarctic cod, *Dissostichus mawsoni*.

At last, we were face-to-face with the monster fish we had only glimpsed in the videotapes. If anyone had walked into the camp at that moment, our mouths would have resembled that of the giant gaping fish, as we stood gawking over the dive hole.

The fish was over five feet long, mottled with large black-and-white scales, and was huge relative to the size of the seal that was trying to eat it. With its massive head and gills, the fish made the seal look like a puppy holding onto a bone that was much too big to fit into its mouth. The enormous cod had finally succumbed to being captured but had not been killed. On the water surface it gasped for oxygen, revealing rows of jagged, vicious-looking spiked teeth.

Exhausted from the chase and capture, the seal was too out of breath to finish off her prey at that moment. Remaining clamped onto the gills of the fish, the killer seal took her time gaining strength for the final blow.

After several minutes the seal loosened her grip on the fish, letting it right itself and swim slowly around the surface waters of the hole. But before the fish could gather itself for an escape, the seal pounced on it grabbing the gills once more, and shook the giant fish from side to side. We realized that the gills were the only purchase that the seal could gain on the huge fish. The tail would have been too powerful to grab, and the body was too large for the seal's mouth. Long white scars down the length of the fish told of the underwater struggle with this seal and perhaps others. The raking tooth marks left little doubt that many predators had tried to grab this fish over the past ten years of its life. Until today, none had been successful.

The actual kill began with a vigorous shake as the seal bit into the thin gill plate that covered the side of the fish's head. Unbelievably, the seal was able to lift the entire fish up and out of the water only to slam it down again, the black mottled tail fin flying through the air. Over and over she lifted and smashed the fish down, swinging its head back and forth. Except for a few fin movements the cod remained limp.

When the seal tired of the activity, she sunk below the hole with the fish in tow. From the vantage of a submersible camera, we watch as the female seal swung the fish back and forth trying to rip the head from the body. Whenever the seal let go of her prey, its limp body sank into the depths. Then the female had to swim down to retrieve the dying fish and drag the body back into the diving hole. On the water surface, the seal would take in several deep breaths, before resuming the thrashing.

For an hour the seal worked on decapitating the fish by grabbing and thrashing, swinging, diving, and breathing heavily on the surface. At last the giant head of the fish broke at the spine, leaving the tail and organs in the mouth of the seal. As a reward for all of her work, the seal immediately ripped a chunk of the white flesh off and swallowed the piece whole in a single noisy gulp.

Tiring of our voyeurism, the seal took her dead prey beneath the ice hole to continue eating. Suddenly we realized the reason for the seal's prolonged, concerted effort to decapitate the fish. This time when the submerged seal let the tail of the fish go it did not sink. Instead, the tail floated slowly to the underside of the ice where it rested against the brash crystals. The cold water was the equivalent of a refrigerator for the Weddell seal. By decapitating the cod, the meaty tail was positively buoyant and could be stored for another meal. Such a large prey item was too large even for a Weddell seal to eat all at one time. However, by caching the tail near the ice hole the seal could feed at her leisure for over a week. The only danger would be "fridge raiding" by another seal.

For the moment the female seal took advantage of her own Thanksgiving feast, feeding on the oily white flesh, the stomach, liver, and intestines of the fish. She gorged for nearly ninety minutes as we had just done in the galley at McMurdo Station. Most of her eating was done on the water surface. She ripped off a succulent piece of fish, swallowed it whole, and then dove for a brief time between courses. By the end of the evening she had the bulging stomach and sleepy-eyed, satiated look of the rest of the team. At that point she drifted slowly underwater to digest her meal in peace, leaving the fish tail on the water surface.

"Why don't we take a few measurements while she's gone," suggested Markus.

With the seal diving and digesting somewhere below, the team had a rare opportunity to measure the size of the fish tail that remained floating on the water. Considering the effort that had gone into capturing, killing, and decapitating the fish, the seal had only begun to eat the huge muscular tail.

Randy and Markus worked together to drag the remains of the

fish carcass onto the floor of the lab. Even without the head, it was four feet long and weighed over sixty pounds.

"How about a muscle sample?" I asked. Later I would analyze the caloric content of the tissue from the fish. Much like the nutritional labels on food items, future chemistry tests on the fish meat would allow me to determine just how many of these fish a Weddell seal could eat in a year based on the animal's daily caloric needs.

As we cut into the flesh of the fish, Randy said, "You know, fresh cod goes for over sixteen dollars per pound in Houston seafood markets."

From our calculations we had almost a thousand dollars worth of fresh fish in our hands. With that in mind, we decided to take a larger muscle sample, one that was big enough to feed eight people for dinner.

The next evening, we marinated the extra muscle samples in lemon juice and poached them on the camp stoves. The soft flesh was exceptionally oily compared to other fish that we had eaten, and had the light taste and texture of Alaskan halibut. It was no surprise that Weddell seals could put on such a thick blubber layer given the amount of fat that was in the flesh of the fish. As the newest inhabitants of Antarctica trying to keep warm, we found the fatty fish quite satisfying.

If it had not been for Thanksgiving the day before, the fish would have been the freshest meal we had experienced in months. We savored dinner even more because of the way we had obtained it. As we sat around the kitchen table polishing off the fish, we could not think of another instance where a wild animal had brought such a tasty dinner to humans.

The female seal came back for the cod the following day. Despite our sheepishness, it was difficult to know whether or not she recognized that pieces were missing from her fish. We did notice, however, that she took the remains of her fish tail out of our dive hole and deposited them in an undisclosed location that was outside of our view and hungry reach.

CHAPTER 15

RACING
THE ICE

DECEMBER 1–7

The ice meant everything to our expedition. It dictated where we could go and how long we would remain at Weddell World. We were acutely aware of its various faces, and the language of the ice dominated our daily conversations. Sastrugi, brash ice, anchor ice, permanent ice, and free ice were the vocabulary of our world.

As it softened and cracked under a persistent summer sun, the sea ice began to severely buckle and open up in long, tortuous leads that were often invisible under a thin covering of snow. Larger fissures had developed by Hutton Cliffs, Turtle Rock, near the Barne Glacier, and across the flagged road back to McMurdo. The shoreline transition zone between the island-locked station and the sea ice had turned to salty mush that necessitated constant attention in order for cargo vehicles to travel back and forth to the sea-ice runway of

213

the airport. Preparations were already being made to move the airport from its site near McMurdo Station to a more stable area miles away on the permanent surface of the Ross Ice Shelf.

Over the handheld radios we heard that a snowmobile from another expedition had gotten caught in one of the pressure ridges near the Weddell seal nursery at Turtle Rock. They were stuck in the same area in which our California colleague had lost his life in the sunken Spryte nearly ten years ago. This time the driver and the snowmobile escaped a watery demise, but the event served as a chilling warning to our team. Eventually the gaps in the ice would be too large to drive any of our vehicles across and our expedition would be forced off the ice. We were already making long traverses along the wider cracks and pressure ridges to find safe crossings. The time was quickly approaching when no amount of traversing would allow us to make it back to McMurdo safely by way of the sea ice.

Within the confines of the Jamesway, the ice seemed especially dynamic and ready to shake us back onto land. Every day the building moaned louder with growing pains, and shuddered under the conflicting pressures of the blowing wind and creeping glacier. Stable appearances by the ice were the ultimate deception. The truth was the sea ice was alive and undulating in slow motion with the rise and fall of each tide. At the same time it was slowly being dragged along the glacier tongue, buckling as it resisted.

The plywood floors of Weddell World mimicked the surface of the ocean, with great swells and hollows in the wood along its 128-foot length. In many places the wood screws were sheared in half. Most of the pressure was directed towards the center of the Jamesway, causing the floorboards of the kitchen to heave several feet and the dining tables to tilt. As the building shifted, the indoor ice sumps—our pride and joy—were rendered useless. Pipes shifted and the sumps filled with snow and froze over. The indoor shower and sinks were destroyed. The slant of the floors also disrupted the flow of diesel into the preway stoves, cutting off heat to some parts of the building. Fortunately rising air temperatures and intense sunlight provided warmth from the outside that nearly balanced the loss of the stoves inside.

But we read the signs. Antarctica was slowly reclaiming our campsite.

The eerie creaking of wood under pressure from the surrounding ice was reminiscent of Shackleton's ship, the *Endurance*. As in previous years, there was a copy of Shackleton's book, *South: The Endurance Expedition* in our camp. Between its covers was the spirit of the O.A.E.—Old Antarctic Explorer—and his relationship with the *Endurance*. This year, as we turned to the pages that described the final hours of his ship, we felt as though we had fallen into a similar trap. Shackleton's words were too familiar when he spoke of wooden decks "shuddering" and "jumping" under the squeeze of moving ice. The beams of the great ship had arched and the stanchions buckled and shook as a million tons of pressure from the sea ice crushed her. Eventually the force of the shifting Antarctic ice caved in the sides of the wooden vessel and sank her. As we read and reread Shackleton's words, the team realized that if we waited much longer Weddell World would suffer the same fate as the explorer's ship.

The sea ice surrounding the camp had already become too dangerous to walk on, and even short hikes had to be approved by the team. What was once flat ice now rose over twelve feet in a series of long ridges. From the kitchen window the ice appeared to be rolling in a series of frozen waves surging towards the Royal Society Mountain Range. The tops of some of the ridges had blistered and broken open where the pressure had become too great for the nine-foot-thick ice. Peering into the open blisters, when we dared to crawl up the side of a ridge, revealed deep-blue crevasses that dropped to open seawater below. Weddell seals could have hidden in the center of the blisters, although we never saw an animal take advantage of it while we were looking down.

Weddell seals gathered around the edges of turquoise-blue melt pools, lying with their round spotted bellies pointing assertively up towards the sun. With summer at its peak, there were now more Weddell seals gathered in one spot than we had seen the entire field season. Lone males, single females, and moms and pups congregated in loose packs to lie in the sun on the sea ice. The tip of the Erebus Glacier Ice Tongue had turned into the southernmost summer beach vacation, with blue skies and bright sunlight, warm bodies scattered around the edge of crystal-clear water, and sunbathers asleep in various awkward poses soaking up the rays. The only missing element was a brightly colored beach towel to define each seal's spot on the frozen beach.

We also welcomed the warmth of the sun, only to hide from its intensity when exposed skin quickly burned and turned raw red. With the ozone hole hovering over the South Pole, the escaping ultraviolet (UV) radiation was too much for our pale skin and eyes. Once again we were forced to cover every inch of skin, this time to protect it against sunburn, skin cancer, and snow blindness rather than frostbite.

With sunscreen and dark polarized sunglasses as part of our survival gear, I had to wonder about the animals. How could Weddell seals, with their exceptionally large eyes adapted to seeing at dark ocean depths, withstand such intense solar radiation when they hauled out? I had no definite answers, but with other scientists reporting cataracts in the eyes of Adelie penguins, I suspected that the animal residents of Antarctica were also feeling the effects of the ozone hole. Only time would tell the extent of the damage.

In contrast to the languorous scene by the melt pools, our team recognized that we were in a race against the ice. All too quickly we were reaching the point where all of our equipment and the camp buildings were going to have to be removed. If we waited too long Weddell World would either sink or drift out to the open ocean when the ice broke up later in the season. Neither prospect was appealing.

Locating the instrumented seals was becoming more difficult, and traveling to their haul-out sites a test of nerves. The camp was breaking under the strain, and conditions were so tenuous that it was time to finish our research.

Racing the ice was something of a tradition in Antarctic exploration and, like the others before us, our team accepted the risks. Expeditions succeeded or failed based on the behavior of the ice, and how well the team members could anticipate its impulsive moods. Shackleton's *Endurance* expedition had proven that. But never was the contest between men and ice more apparent than during the greatest Antarctic race of all, the quest for the South Pole. In January 1911, Robert F. Scott and Roald Amundsen led separate expeditions to be the first to reach the Pole. Sea ice blocked Scott's ship from reaching Hut Point on Ross Island, forcing him to winter at Cape Evans—less than ten miles from where Weddell World resided ninety years later. Amundsen was able to establish his base camp sixty miles closer to the Pole in the Bay of Whales.

Each team set out to reach 90° south in fall 1911—Scott using ponies and manpower to haul sleds over the ice, while Amundsen relied on dog teams. The most direct route took Amundsen over uncharted ice regions of the polar plateau. Scott and his team chose instead to travel across the relatively flat permanent ice of the Ross Ice Shelf and then up the Beardmore Glacier.

The ponies proved to be a liability for Scott's team, breaking through the ice cover and causing the men to sink into the snow, which slowed their progress significantly. In the end, Amundsen won the race for the Pole, leaving Scott and his team in cold, bitter disappointment when they arrived thirty-three days later. By January 26, 1912, Amundsen was back at his base camp and ship, ready to depart and announce his victory to the rest of the world. Scott was still struggling with the remnants of his team until March 29, 1912, when he entered the last words he would ever write in his diary.

The bodies of Robert F. Scott, Henry Bowers, and Edward

Wilson were found frozen on the Ross Ice Shelf the following November. Other members of Scott's expedition had anxiously awaited his return to the base camp just 170 miles away. Months later they located the bodies of their comrades in a snow-drifted tent.

Speed across the ice supplied by dog power ultimately contributed to the success of Amundsen. The efficient use of sled dogs allowed the Norwegian explorer to complete his drive for the South Pole in just over three months, thereby avoiding the extreme cold weather of late February and March. Scott's team labored for five months on the ice, the delays forcing Scott and his men to endure exceptionally cold conditions that year. Meteorological measurements taken by recent expeditions have been compared to the weather data recorded by Scott's team. These comparisons have shown that late February through March 1912, when Scott was struggling to return from the South Pole, was 10° to 20°F colder than average temperatures on the Ross Ice Shelf today.

There is little doubt that the persistent, unanticipated cold added to the frostbite, exhaustion, and hypothermia that led to the end of the great Antarctic explorer and his men. Their colleagues buried them where they lay by collapsing the tent over their bodies on the ice. Antarctic lore has it that the frozen mummified bodies remain entombed in the snow somewhere on the ice to this day, slowly advancing seaward with the Ross Ice Shelf. One day Scott, Bowers, and Wilson will be buried at sea when the leading edge of the ice shelf eventually breaks off. They are destined to remain a part of Antarctica waters.

The fates of Shackleton's and Scott's expeditions were well-known to our team and only bolstered our response to the movements of the ice. In a concerted effort we made a final push to find our seals and to complete our expedition before the relentless pressure of the ice overwhelmed the camp.

Our first task was to find Mayflower. The seal had continued to elude our team by remaining underwater, still diving while the videotape and batteries in her instruments ran out. There was little that we could do to convince a hunting seal to stop diving, so we were forced to simply wait for her to finish her journeys and haul out.

In the meantime, the team decided to take one last gamble.

We had a spare VDAP unit that had been reserved for switching out the system if the batteries or a sensor failed. This was our backup for the instrumented seal. Rationalizing that we had no use for a backup with Mayflower, we decided to deploy the spare VDAP on one last seal for the season. Thus, we added Seal 24, which we named Sunday, to our study. For the first time we had two Weddell seals cruising somewhere below the sea ice with our camera systems. It amused us to think that if Sunday happened to pass Mayflower there was a chance that one seal could videotape the other wearing the VDAP as it swam by.

By the time Seal 24 was outfitted with the VDAP, the melt pools around the glacier had thawed into one long, open lead. The surface of McMurdo Sound was riddled with watery potholes. There were so many places for the seals to breathe that the instrumented animals soon led us on a cat-and-mouse chase around the glacier trying to find them. We began to think that we had pushed too hard and too late into the field season.

At first the satellite tags showed the two instrumented seals moving in opposite directions. Mayflower was heading north towards the open sea. Sunday was headed south towards the glacier icefall where we had found Godzilla hiding among the nursing seals. Before Sunday reached the icefall she switched direction again, now swimming west into the dangerously cracked area near Turtle Rock.

Each day we waited like anxious mothers, hoping that one of the seals would return to Home Crack where we could easily retrieve our instruments and move off the weakened ice. But the seals had other plans.

With the sea ice breaking down too quickly we had to take

action. We split our team into two snowmobile parties, one that would head north and another that would drive south. The plan was to conduct a series of transects across McMurdo Sound, honing in on the seals using the radio signals. The one-mile range of the signals meant that we would have to be nearly in visual contact with the seals in order to find them. Fortunately the weather was on our side, and we counted on the warmth of the sun to entice the seals to haul out on top of the ice.

Within the first hour the northern party passed right by Mayflower sunbathing with a group of females next to one of the glacial melt pools. Surrounded by ridges of blistered ice, the seals lounged in a cove that was hidden from wind and view. The ridges had muffled the radio signals from Mayflower's tag, initially fooling the search party, which zoomed right by. Only by luck and curiosity did the team backtrack to peek over the ridge, and eventually found the missing seal with our VDAP.

Scrambling quickly over the ridge, the team soon had the camera and instruments in their hands. Mayflower remained the epitome of tolerance during the equipment retrieval, having been through the routine several times during the multiple deployments. Like the other seals we had worked with, she continued her nap after rolling onto her back and giving it a thorough scratching on the ice.

The second hard-earned videotape from Mayflower maintained her status of elite underwater huntress. She continued to gulp down silverfish and nip at the tails of Antarctic cod although she never actually was able to catch one of the giant fishes.

She spent hours cruising beneath the frozen surface of McMurdo Sound in search of prey. The seal introduced us to a unique cold-water ecosystem that lived on the ocean bottom comprised diverse, alien-looking creatures defying definition. None of us were invertebrate specialists, but we quickly recognized that we could map the location of the slow-moving inhabitants by using Mayflower's underwater tracks as a guide. Like a panther pacing along a worn path through a forest, the seal followed the same underwater trek during her hunting excursions. We began to recognize the placement of odd-shaped rocks and individual starfish as the seal passed them on multiple dives. From the internal clock of the VDAP we could time the walking speed of individual starfish by recording their location each time the seal swam by—usually measured in agonizingly slow inches per hour.

Lee realized that he had all of the information he needed to create a virtual Antarctic environment. In plotting the seal's three-dimensional movements, he could re-create the underwater ecosystem of the Weddell seal. The virtual environment would be filled with fish and deep-sea creatures placed in their exact location as seen on the videotapes. Shallow-water inhabitants could be separated from the deep-sea dwellers by noting the depth at which Mayflower encountered them during her travels. Lee especially enjoyed the fact that this would be the first time that a seal had mapped out its own environment.

Mayflower also briefly followed in the tracks of Ms. Apnea and twisted through several frozen caves on the underside of the glacier. In the confined spaces, she wrinkled her muzzle in long, echoing trills as she warned other seals of her presence. With no fish to be found she hastily retreated from the caves and back into open waters.

All in all, Mayflower provided us with another spectacular glimpse of the daily life of the Weddell seal, and was deserving of her long, uninterrupted vacation in the sun at the tip of the glacier pools where she had taken up residence.

There was only one more instrumented animal left out on the ice—Seal 24, Sunday. While the northern snowmobile team had been busy with Mayflower, blowing wind had thwarted attempts by the southern team to locate Sunday. Unexpected gusts kicked up fine snow from the slopes of Ross Island and obscured the ground. From Weddell World we watched though binoculars as a cloud of snow rolled like a heavy fog down the slopes and across the ice. Turtle Rock, Hutton Cliffs, and the sea ice bound to their edges disappeared in a white haze. Putting our desire to search for the instrumented seal on hold, we restlessly paced in camp to wait out the localized windstorm. The sea ice surrounding Turtle Rock was dangerous enough in good visibility; we were not foolhardy or desperate enough to attempt travel in a whiteout.

By afternoon the winds had subsided and three of us, Randy, Don, and myself, geared up once more for the trip south. Home Crack had grown wider and longer, necessitating an extra mile traverse along its length to reach solid ice. As we passed by we recognized a few of the hauled-out seals from their size, whiskers, and new color-coded flipper tags. Ally McSeal, Ms. Zodiac, and Lucky Pup and his mom all wore a single plastic tag that dangled like a pieced earring between the toes of their hind flippers. The individually numbered tags had been placed on the seals by another research team monitoring seal movements across the Sound. The seals would be followed until they headed to sea at the end of the summer, and hopefully would be identified by the plastic tags when they returned next year.

For now these seals represented the few faithful ones that had remained at Home Crack. The rest of the Weddell seals had already scattered to more open waters in other areas of the Sound, some even moving towards the ice edge and the Ross Sea.

Once past Home Crack and out of the influence of the glacier, we immediately hit rough sastrugi that tried to tear the steering out of our hands. We slowed to a crawl, driving methodically up then down each snow ridge, maneuvering the front ski of the snowmobile to prevent getting caught sideways in a trough. After an hour on the rugged terrain we had crossed Erebus Bay and entered the severely cracked area by Turtle Rock. Nearby was the pressure ridge that had snared the snowmobile from the other expedition the week before. Below us, frozen in the depths, was the Spryte that entombed our colleague. We moved cautiously, fully aware of the paralysis that would have come if we stopped to considered the dangers. There was nearly a quarter mile of ocean below our feet.

Near Turtle Rock, a season of turbulent winds had scoured down the sastrugi to glassy smoothness. Travel was easier and the clarity of the ice enabled us to anticipate the location of the numerous cracks. Most of the fissures were less than five inches wide, which allowed us to pass with ease as long as we were careful not to turn the snowmobile's front ski into the depression. Wider cracks, even if they appeared frozen over, had to be cored. Here was where the hours of sea-ice training from Happy Camper School finally paid off. From just a couple of holes drilled into the ice, we could "read" the history of a crack and determine our ability to pass. At the larger cracks, we religiously stopped, took out a handheld ice auger, and drilled several test holes into the ice: first the thickest part near the edges to determine the width of the crack, then a series of holes towards the center of the frozen lead to determine how long ago the cracked had healed. A few calculations, based on the thickness of the ice and the length of our snowmobile track, and then we could decide how to proceed.

All of these stops and calculations made the search for Sunday a slow, labor-intensive process across Erebus Bay as we rode, stopped, radio-tracked, and ice augered. We tacked from right to left and back again, zigzagging to avoid the wider cracks and pressure ridges. Finally we entered the coastal, ice-torn area surrounding the small island that got its name from the humped shape of its upper ridge. This was the first time that we had seen the island up close, having purposely avoided Turtle Rock since it was a traditional birthing and nursing site for Weddell seals. We turned off our snowmobiles one hundred feet from the shoreline to avoid disturbing the moms and pups, opting instead to walk through the uneven, pressure-ridged ice towards the seals.

On first approach the Turtle Rock nursery appeared as busy as usual. The dark bodies of moms and pups peppered the area while grunting, scavenging skuas flitted between them. The mottled brown seagull-like birds had been in the area since October, timing their arrival with the birth of the pups at Halloween. Feeding on discarded placentas had made the skuas fat during the early part of summer. Now they searched for other remains around the nursery.

Even among these scavengers there was a semblance of politeness, with the number of birds limited to the amount of available food. What was immediately troublesome as we moved on foot closer to Turtle Rock was how many agitated skuas circled the seal nursery.

Stepping warily across the cracks, Randy, Don, and I walked towards a group of seals on the western side of the small island. We passed several sleeping adults along the way, although Sunday was not among them. A lone male lying on his side next to an ice ridge had attracted the attention of several skuas. The birds flew off as we approached, grunting in agitation after landing several feet away to watch our movements. It was not surprising to find that the seal was dusted in white following the morning's windstorm. However, with the sun shining overhead the snow should have already melted from his face. We walked warily beside the male, and shuffled our boots to get his attention. There was no response. Dry snow crunched loudly under our footsteps as we moved towards his head. This usually roused the sleepiest of seals, but had no effect on the animal. Using the blunt edge of an ice axe I prodded the hind flipper of the seal only to realize that it was stuck to the ice. The seal was dead.

Skuas had already determined this and had been trying to pick off anything to eat from the frozen carcass. Except for the peck marks from the scavengers, the seal had few external wounds that could have resulted in his death. He had none of the large, gaping gashes of territorial disputes; there was no blood on the snow. I could find no telltale discharges from his eyes or nose that would have indicated a systemic infection. On closer inspection his pelt was in near perfect condition and his sharp, clean teeth the picture of health. This was not the profile of a seal that had succumbed to old age complications. Because he was frozen solid and we carried little in the way of surgical tools, performing a necropsy was out of the question. We were left only with questions as to why an apparently healthy adult seal had died on the ice.

Our team left the carcass and crossed a small pressure ridge, moving into a small, protected bowl. Once again there was a disturbing flurry of activity from skuas as we approached two mom-pup pairs. The birds took off with their characteristic low mumble and stood in a circle around us. One pup was intently nursing, and the other was sleeping next to his mother. Moving slowly to avoid disturbing the seals, we soon realized that something was very wrong. Both moms had been in the same position for so long that their whiskers had frozen into the ice. Even the laziest of seals would not have allowed this to happen during a nap.

For all of our good intentions about keeping quiet, it was clear that there would be no reaction from either of the moms. Both had recently died lying on the ice with their pups still beside them. The nursing pup cried as it tried in vain to extract milk from the teat of her unresponsive mother. She was a little female that used her head to nudge at her mother's flaccid belly. Alternately suckling on one exposed nipple and then the other, the little female gained nothing for all of her effort.

The second pup had given up trying to feed and huddled quietly next to the body of his mother. He looked up with large, wet Weddell eyes and pressed his soft gray body closer into his mother's side as we passed. Skuas had discovered the carcass, and the pup could only lie helplessly in the shadow of his mother as the birds pecked at her lifeless pelt.

Taking off a mitten, I laid a hand on the side of each of the female seals to find that the bodies were still soft. Unlike the adult male that we had just passed, the mothers were not yet frozen. Death must have occurred in the past twenty-four hours, and I doubted that the pups even had time to realize that their moms would never answer their cries.

As heartbreaking as it was to watch the desperate seal pups, there was little to do other than hope that they were old enough to survive on their own. The unspoken rule of field biology is to let nature take its course, although some times were more difficult than others to live by it.

The best that we could do was keep the skuas at bay, if only for a moment of relief for the seal pups. Fortunately, both of the moms had done an excellent job fattening their offspring right to the end. The pups were large and healthy enough to fend off the skuas for themselves. Had they been younger or weaker, the scavenging birds would have tried to peck at their soft skin and eyes. In this regard, the moms, even in death, still protected their pups. The skuas would be kept busy for weeks with the carcasses of the moms, leaving the pups in peace to finish growing until it was time for them to go to sea.

In trying to understand what had happened to the seals, it was difficult not to draw a line of logic between the oppressive influence of B-15 and the carcasses lying in front of us. All three carcasses had one suspicious thing in common; they seemed exceptionally thin. The death of a lone seal could have been rationalized as a natural event—sometimes animals just die in the wild. Three apparently healthy adults dying at the same time in the same location seemed more than a coincidence. I considered this the raw aftermath of the massive iceberg.

For the entire summer season, B-15 had severely limited the movements of the Weddell seals and ourselves. Locating a field camp had been nearly impossible at the end of September. We had been backed up against a glacier that now threatened to crush the buildings. The timing and location of Weddell seal haul-out sites had also changed, births had occurred in unusual areas, and fewer seals had made it into McMurdo Sound this year. Our videotapes showed that the sea ice of the Sound at the beginning of the summer was so tight that submerged seals had fought for the right to steal a breath at Home Crack and in hidden air pockets on the underside of a glacier. I had no way to explain how pregnant Weddell seals had been able to swim under solid ice to make it all the way to Turtle Rock to have their pups. Perhaps they had been the daring ones willing to take the one-way extreme dive to reach the traditional nursing and mating sites. In the end the two moms and the lone male had paid with their lives.

Perhaps the dead seals had not been able to find sufficient

amounts of prey in such an isolated area. Without the normal system of breathing holes across the Sound, their hunting forays would have been severely impeded. The seals had been left with the unsatisfactory choice of running out of air or forgoing a meal. For a male defending a territory and trying to mate, the situation would have been challenging. For a female trying to feed herself as well as a growing pup, the demands would have been especially untenable. Regardless of any other factor affecting the seals, B-15 had made survival on the Antarctic ice more difficult this year. Only in the past weeks under the intensity of the late summer sun had the ice finally opened up to provide adequate breathing holes for the hunting seals.

Sadly watching the two seal pups struggle on the ice next to their dead mothers, I traced a theoretical cascade of events from the ozone hole and atmospheric warming that had led to the calving of the ice shelf and the creation of B-15, to the unprecedented blockage of ice movements around Ross Island resulting in limited choices for pregnant and hunting seals, and finally to their untimely deaths. Two generations of seals would be impacted if the orphaned pups did not survive the next few weeks.

In fact, it had already happened. Surveying the surrounding ice, we found bloody evidence of several late-term abortions all around. With all of the focus on the dead adults, we had overlooked the desiccated, skeletal remains that had been scattered by the skuas. In this spot alone at least six pregnant seals had given up their unborn pups to ensure their own survival. It was easy to recount their recent history from the remains on the ice. The seals had swum over eighty miles, pregnant and heavy, under near-solid ice to reach Turtle Rock. There they had hauled their rounded bellies onto the ice, squeezing through a rough tidal crack formed on the west side of the small island. The seals had supported a growing fetus for nearly nine months, traveled miles underwater, and battled ice and snowstorms only to lose it all. Once they had aborted, the females left the area, abandoning the carcasses to the ravaging skuas.

Was the arduous journey too much for the pregnant seals? In other species of seals and sea lions, abortions could occur in the face of an unusual environmental challenge. El Niño events, storms, anything that disturbed feeding by the pregnant animals could trigger a late-term abortion. The mom's natural strategy seemed to be, "Better to survive yourself and invest in a youngster next year when environmental conditions might improve and your pup will have a chance."

As I stood among the skuas sorting through the scattered bones of aborted fetuses and watched the futile efforts of the two orphaned pups as they tried to nurse, I realized that the devastating effects of the iceberg would be felt for years among this small population of Weddell seals. I could not have predicted the chain of events as they unfolded in Antarctica, but I had to question if somehow I could have prevented them. As a biologist, I always felt one step behind. Humans have such a poor understanding of what animals need to survive in this world that we rarely appreciate our impact on them until it is too late.

But nature often provides an unexpected solution if allowed to act on her own. In the short time that I had been recounting the events of the day, the orphaned pups had found each other. They snuggled side-by-side, taking comfort in each other's presence, and took turns warding off the skuas.

Nature had surely found a way for these two to survive.

There was still much to do before we could leave the ice and think about going home. Sunday was still missing, seal surveys had to be completed, and the final thermal measurements had to be made. Hiking one last time to Home Crack with our infrared camera and thermometers, Matt and I found that the pups had grown noticeably bigger in the past weeks. Fuzzy gray puppy pelage hung off the youngsters in tattered rolls, revealing new, spiky adult hairs below. The variety of colors and spotting were impressive. Some of the pups appeared as black and speckled as the volcanic rock on the surrounding islands, while others were as light and silvery as the snow.

The moms had done such an impressive job of providing milk that their pups now rivaled them in bulk. While the youngsters had grown noticeably rotund, their mothers had deflated into hollow shells comprised of little more than spotted fur draped over sagging bones. During the past six weeks the moms had transferred almost their entire blubber layer through fatty milk to their offspring. They had barely eaten in all of that time and had been transformed from the meaty-looking sausages we had observed in early October to dried-out jerky on ice. It was time to go to sea to feed. There was only one more chore—complete swimming lessons for the pups— for survival was measured by what a Weddell seal could do below the ice, not on it.

In another attempt at lessons, we saw Lucky Pup's mom dip below the water surface by sliding into a large hole at Home Crack. This time Lucky Pup poked his head into the water a little too far over the edge. He slipped in almost by accident after her. Following the initial splash Lucky Pup flailed his front and hind flippers ineffectively, bobbing up and down in the water but not moving forward or downward. Splashing and churning the water, he called for his mom who remained watchful from below. She stayed at a distance encouraging Lucky Pup to submerge with her, but never rose up to assist the flopping pup.

As it was, help was not necessary. There was no chance of the little seal drowning, for Lucky Pup was so fat that he floated. After nursing so intensively for six weeks, he had put on a thick layer of blubber that not only kept him warm but also buoyed him up in the water.

After several minutes, the chubby little seal realized that he was positively buoyant and began to calmly float from breathing hole to breathing hole along the crack. His movements were less like swimming and more like scraping along the underside of the ice in short spurts underwater. When he arrived at each hole he blurted out a short call for his mom mixed with a big gulp of air. Finally, he lay resting his chin on the side of the ice hole that he had originally fallen into. His mom rose to the surface beside him, nuzzled his nose, and then resubmerged.

Lucky Pup looked down into the clear water unwilling to follow his mom on her dive and called for her as he struggled to get out of the water. But the sides of the ice hole were too slippery for his wet flippers. His hind end thrashed the water in a propeller motion with little progress. Nearly exhausted, he flopped forward on his fore flippers with all of his strength, only to slide back beneath the water surface. Before he could catch his breath to let out a cry, Lucky Pup's mom reappeared. This time rather than surface beside her struggling pup she pushed his bottom from below. With the benefit of her gentle nudges Lucky Pup gained purchase on the icy slope and slid with the slippery pop of a squeezed watermelon seed onto the snow.

Inchworming his way quickly from the hole, Lucky Pup took another deep breath and stopped for a moment. He looked around trying to orient himself, shaking the water off of his head. Finding an open space on the ice, he pulled himself forward with his fore flippers while flopping his hind flippers side to side until he claimed a spot to resume sunbathing. He turned his belly to the sun only to find that the drying salt water on his new coat caused his skin to itch. Using the index digits on his huge fore flippers, he began to scratch and rub, starting with the top of his head and continuing down his belly in one long scratch. The activity caused his uneven coat to stick out raggedly in all directions, reminding me of the scruffy-haired young boys whom I had pulled out of the pool on more than one occasion during swimming lessons. They didn't have a care in the world as long as they could lie in the sun and scratch.

In just a few short lessons in the ensuing days, Lucky Pup gained his confidence in the water. He began to dive in short bouts on his own under Home Crack, sometimes with his mom and sometimes independently. We noticed that Lucky Pup's mom kept a safe distance away, often leaving the pup on his own for long periods as she hunted underwater.

This was the last time that Matt and I saw Lucky Pup and his mom together. Her job was finally done. The next day she was off to resume her adult life while Lucky Pup's adventures as an elite diver beneath the Antarctic sea ice were just beginning.

CHAPTER 16

WORLDS APART

In the end, Sunday made it easy for us to find her and our equipment. As the summer reached its peak she took to sleeping in the sun among the moms, pups, and territorial males on the opposite side of the Erebus Glacier Ice Tongue. She had fooled our team by turning north from the Turtle Rock area and traveling over to Big Razorback Island. There was no telling what had instigated her change in direction. Maybe it was the competition for limited fish with the nursing moms at Turtle Rock. Perhaps she had come upon the seal carcasses and taken them as omens of poor hunting grounds. Regardless of the reason, Sunday reversed her direction, passed beneath Weddell World along her underwater transit, and ended up nearly in our backyard just across the glacier. On a good day we could have hiked over the top of the ice tongue and seen her lying by the tidal crack next to the island.

Big Razorback Island was the longer and taller mirror image of Little Razorback situated on the northern leading edge of the Erebus Glacier Ice Tongue. What appeared to be an island was actually the jagged upper lip of a submerged volcano that jutted straight up out of the ice. Huge tidal cracks surrounded the dark peak, making it the perfect place for young and old seals to cool down in the long open leads after sunbathing. This late in the season, older males had staked out underwater territories along the cracks in an effort to entice females into mating. Pups were quickly weaned and left on their own as their moms turned their attention towards a potential tryst. Black volcanic debris sliding down the island created a gentle sloping bottom beneath the ice. In the clear water red and pink starfish littered the ground, forming a celestial backdrop for the underwater courtship rituals of the seals.

As interesting as the videos from Sunday's VDAP could have been (only once has the copulatory behavior of the Weddell seal been observed), we were sorely disappointed. When the team finally reviewed the data and video from her journeys, we discovered that Seal 24 was appropriately named Sunday; she spent most of her days relaxing. The seal either slept on her side hauled out on the ice, which provided a sideways view of Big Razorback Island, or she dozed just below the tidal crack with a view of dormant starfish. Towards the end of the tape our last seal of the season began to cruise slowly around the shallow pools socializing with other adult seals. Mating, not eating, was clearly on her mind. But before she had found an acceptable suitor the batteries in the VDAP gave out, leaving this part of the seal's biology a secret and our team feeling like frustrated, failed voyeurs.

We were done for the season.

With the last VDAP and all of the sensors in our hands, and Seals 19 through 24 back to sleeping with the other Weddell seals, our primary task was to safely shuttle gear, data, instrumentation, and people into McMurdo Station and then home. Safeguarding the computers containing our research data and the boxes of videotapes detailing the underwater journeys of the seals was paramount. One of our biggest fears was that these would freeze, leaving us with little more than anecdotes for all of our work. Consequently, the team members were relegated to the vertebrae-crunching, neck-snapping snowmobiles and sastrugi, while the computers and videotapes rode across the sea ice to McMurdo in the stable comfort of the Spryte's heated cab with Jesse at the controls.

The movements of the glacier had already initiated camp breakdown. We just needed to finish the job. In the previous months we had eaten through more than a ton of food, leaving little other than a few canned goods and dehydrated meals to carry back to the Berg Field Center. Everything else, including our sleeping bags, cots, clothing, tables, and chairs, was piled into sleds and hauled in by snowmobile or open-bed Sprytes.

The last ritual to be performed was the lowering of the flags. Both the Texas A & M banner and the UC Santa Cruz silk shorts had braved a season of windstorms and snow. Numerous Herbies had taken a toll on the flags, fraying the edges of the Texas banner and shortening the UC slug underwear to the crotch. In their individual ways the flags had served the team well, helping us to navigate back to camp and to the outhouse through blinding snow and disorienting whiteouts. The members of the expedition autographed the tattered flags, which were carried by Randy and me back to our respective universities to be proudly displayed in our laboratories.

In less than two days Weddell World was reduced to the shell of an old Korean War Jamesway and a couple of empty wooden huts. A team of carpenters with a bulldozer dismantled the remains of the camp. Nothing was left except for the frozen sump holes, and even those would be erased when the sea ice finally melted completely and broke out of the Sound during the next few months. With the roar of four snowmobiles and one Spryte pulling the seal sled filled with gear, the team left Weddell World, the Erebus Glacier Ice Tongue, Mount Erebus, and Home Crack for the last time. Ignoring the noise, the seals of Home Crack barely lifted a head from their naps to acknowledge our departure.

Arriving from the sea ice, we learned the hard way that the daily pace in McMurdo Station was slower and more regimented than we were accustomed to. Meals came at scheduled intervals and sleep occurred at regular hours, something that we had not experienced in months. At first many members of the team resisted the pace and the scheduling with the result that we often missed meals. Events seemed to move painfully slow in town. Despite the exhaustion we still craved the adrenaline rush of not knowing what was going to happen next.

There was also an inherent fear of slowing down. We were afraid that the moment the pressure was relieved we would be unable to pull ourselves together for the finish. We had pushed our bodies close to the limit; mentally and physically, we were done in. As soon as we let our guard down we knew that we would fall asleep for a long, long time.

Rest and recovery had to wait, however. Scientific instruments had to be checked and packed for overseas shipment, data needed to be compiled, and videotapes duplicated. With all of the work that had gone into collecting the data during the previous months, we became paranoid about losing it. No one person or computer was trusted. We made copy after copy of the tapes and spreadsheets to make sure that we could reconstruct the entire season of work if someone's computer failed or a cargo box was lost in transit. Raw data would be hand-carried in computers and notebooks on all of the flights back to the United States.

We continued to push ourselves in McMurdo Station, all the time wishing we were back out on the ice with the seals and the real action. Weddell seals were surely up to something interesting and we were missing out on all of it. Was Ally McSeal still cruising the bottom of the Sound and fighting with Scarface over breathing holes? Had Lucky Pup swallowed his first fish yet? Had Sunday, our love-struck seal, found a mate? We still had so many questions.

News from the United States filtered in through satellite television and newspaper clippings in town. We had been sheltered from all of the post–September 11 emotions and found ourselves confused with the onslaught of events. Anthrax scares had come and gone, and the United States was in the thick of retaliation. While the world tried to cope with the burden of terrorism, the Arizona Diamondbacks had stolen the World Series out from under the noses of the New York Yankees. George Harrison had died, and Harry Potter and Hobbits were movie stars. Information flooded in so fast that we immediately forgot much of it. Months later we would be asking, "What happened with anthrax?" and "Who played in the 2001 World Series?" Movies and television programs had come and gone, elections had occurred, and we had no idea what people were talking about.

For years gaps in our knowledge about current events during conversations would be passed off with a, "It must have happened while I was on the ice."

We experienced a rise and fall of emotions associated with preparing to go home, understanding a world that we had lost touch with, and wishing to escape back to the wild and the seals. While seated at meals in the galley, colleagues recognized "the big eye" as our team members intermittently stared blankly into space, losing track of the conversation. They remarked, "You've got a thousand-foot stare in a ten-foot room," and would leave us to our own thoughts.

Our minds were buzzing with what had just happened during the expedition and what would happen as we re-entered our lives at home. Reality was in the past or in the future, which often caused us to pay little attention to the present.

Jesse was the first to make the transition by cutting his fuzzy hair and beard. All of us had grown shaggier as the expedition wore on, but Jesse had gradually bloomed into a Jimi Hendrix–like figure. His brushy auburn hair sticking out at all angles from beneath headphones, hats, and parkas had been a source of entertainment and fodder for numerous jokes by the team. Clean-shaven, he suddenly looked *Texan*. Only when he rubbed the spiky hair on his head like one of the wet seal pups and boomed out his deep Walter Cronkite laugh did I recognize him.

The rest of us followed Jesse's lead, cleaning up the best we could. As the smell of diesel fuel and oily, fishy Weddell seal faded from our skin, hair, and clothes, our thoughts turned increasingly towards family. Suddenly nothing seemed as important as seeing family and friends for Christmas. We were going home.

After three days in McMurdo, the team boarded an ancient olive green C-130 propeller plane that provided the military-style flight back to New Zealand. Seating consisted of the same red-webbed slings lining each side of the gray fuselage that our bottoms had experienced on the way down. Once again a burley loadmaster in camouflage gear offering a brown paper bag masqueraded as the stewardess and in-flight meal. Unlike the energy-charged flight south, the flight north was subdued, longer, and noisier. No sooner had we crammed in the foam earplugs and the plane skied off of the ice than the team fell into a deep sleep, grateful for eight straight hours of nothing to do.

The opening of the cargo hold doors of the C-130 in Christchurch was just as memorable as it had been when we landed in Antarctica three months earlier. A rush of warm, moist New Zealand air rolled across my skin and reminded me that wind isn't always harsh, dry, and cutting. We each had the same dumbfounded look of Dorothy when she first landed in Oz and threw open the kitchen door. The shock of colors amazed us. We swore that we could actually smell the color green.

Breathing in deep inhalations, we tried to fill our heads with the spring green chlorophyll of the trees, flowers, and freshly mowed grass. One by one we stumbled out of the plane to stand on the hot tarmac and take in the vegetation, cars, and bustle of people. Before we became too overwhelmed, we were whisked by bus to the international terminal of the Christchurch Airport to pass through customs along with the other tourists entering the country. Australian, Japanese, Korean, British, and American visitors stared at our bulky parkas and ridiculous bunny boots as we tripped across the carpets, but politely said nothing. The Kiwis at the passport check stations took our blabbering about the humidity and colors in stride, having seen the wide-eyed, shocked polar behavior before.

While standing in line I watched the nonstop activities of a five-year-old boy holding the hand of his mother. His movements seemed so fast and his voice so incredibly high and piercing that I couldn't keep up with what he was doing or saying. He hid behind his mother's skirt, peeking out in response to me. Only then did I realize that I had been staring, and that it had been months since I had seen anyone under the age of twenty. I had forgotten how fast kids move and how small their features are.

At the downtown bed-and-breakfast our team welcomed the uninterrupted hot showers, fresh linens, and the smell of flowers in vases. I plopped onto the bed, enjoying the feel of a mattress, and watched the lazy buzzing of a fly as it circled the room in the warmth of the late afternoon. It wasn't that I had missed insects in Antarctica, it was just remarkable to see one after so long.

Everything seemed new to us. As the team headed out to dinner, we stopped on the sidewalk to turn our attention to the sky above as it turned from indigo blue to black. Darkness descended like a blanket, leaving us with a slight feeling of being smothered. Months of living in constant daylight made us uncomfortable in the oppressive dimness of the evening. Shadows thrown by the surrounding trees only added to the closeness. Our uncertainty dissolved with the rising stars as they began to outline the vastness of the skies. An old southern hemisphere friend, the Southern Cross, made its appearance on the horizon and assured us that at least the heavens had not changed in our absence.

Ignoring the indigestion that was sure to come, we chose the spiciest Thai restaurant in downtown Christchurch to celebrate our arrival from Antarctica. Over fiery hot pad Thai and coconut chicken soup, stories from the ice began to surface. The stress of the howling winds during Herbies and the mountains of snow sinking our camp already seemed so far away. We laughed about my snowmobile accident and Bill's shattered Frisbee, which never did fly right after Happy Camper School. Admitting that we had each snuck onto the cargo scale at the CDC when we returned our Antarctic clothing, the group demanded to know who had gained and who had lost weight on the ice. Despite the ravenous consumption of butter, chocolate, and pasta to stave off the cold, I had lost four pounds. The same was true for most of the high metabs. To their disgust the low metabs had each put on five to ten pounds that would require months of dieting to lose.

While finishing off the last of the fried rice, we marveled over what the seals had shown us, sometimes letting the conversation lull into silence as we remembered. There were personal victories and challenges that were destined to remain secret among the team members. For those we vowed, "What happens on the ice, stays on the ice." The celebration was for the team and the bond between eight people that had been forged over a season of hardships and exciting scientific discoveries.

Walking back from the restaurant, satiated and tired, we passed the monument to Captain Robert F. Scott in a downtown park. He stood stoically in parka and massive mittens among the willow trees and the Avon River, a bigger-than-life stone statue that towered over us. There was a tinge of sadness among our group as we walked by. We had made it back from the most desolate and unexplored continent on earth, something that Scott and his colleagues have not been able to do. Except for fleeting words in his diary, the details of his adventures had been lost with him. We would never know what he could have accomplished. In an odd way we were jealous of Captain Scott, for he would always remain a part of Antarctica both in body and in spirit.

It seemed a cruel joke that our first steps back in the United States took us through Los Angeles in the middle of the Christmas rush. The view from the airplane window was daunting as we landed in a city so densely inhabited that the flipper-to-flipper contact of an Adelie penguin rookery now seemed spacious. Under a backdrop of plastic snowflakes and fake snowmen, the team moved all of the expedition cargo through customs.

The international terminal had the old, familiar industrial smell and echo of sanitized tile. Structurally, little had changed in our absence. However, the tone of America was different. We had noticed the change even before boarding our flight in New Zealand. Rather than a single security checkpoint, U.S.-bound travelers were subjected to a second screening at the gate immediately before boarding the plane. Passports and boarding passes were triple-checked and random passengers pulled from line for pat downs like criminals. Temporary fencing herded us like cattle through narrow chutes while under the scrutiny of the most unsettling change of all—uniformed, armed guards. How in three months had paranoia reached such proportions that all of this was now considered normal? No one had told us. We were surrounded by acne-scarred twenty-year-olds in green military camouflage loaded down with heavy machine guns. They lined the gates and security checkpoints, twitching nervously.

Uniformed customs officials at LAX were also jumpy and unsmiling as they tried to come to terms with our mountain of cargo boxes, scientific instruments, and personal gear. Eight people, thirty-seven cargo bags and boxes, and a train of nineteen luggage carts snaked through the customs barriers. Travelers from other international flights began to line up behind our group and grumbled at the delay. We viewed the mass of humanity with both trepidation and suspicion, seeking the comfort of our team members.

We huddled together like penguin chicks braving a snowstorm. Despite the harsh conditions in Antarctica, the remote location now seemed more secure than home, and the unpredictable forces of nature kinder than the hands of man. In Antarctica, the simple, common goal was survival. We had learned that taking care of each other allowed us to meet unimaginable challenges. Here people were suspicious and angry.

To others there was little doubt that we were traveling as a unit. We knew each other's bags and limitations in strength; we were assisting each other in a way that was not typical of most travelers. Most telling was our habit of announcing our next move to the group. Whether it was a trip to the restroom or to a shop, we always let at least one other person know where we were going. It would take several days before we would realize that it was no longer necessary for someone to track our every move in the event of getting lost in a snowstorm.

The intrusion of advertisements and cell phone conversations threw us off, which annoyed people who were trying to quickly push through. Cell phones rang and a hundred conversations took place simultaneously. To us Weddell seals vocalizing over one another beneath the sea ice had been more polite. Eventually we would become numb to the overwhelming flood of sights and sounds, closing out the people around us. For the moment, we felt raw and vulnerable, and our team took comfort in each other's presence, huddling closer together.

As we pushed the train of luggage carts through another X-ray checkpoint I asked in understatement, "We don't exactly fit in, do we?"

Lee tried changing into a button-down, long-sleeve shirt to better dress the part. The rest of us splashed water on our faces, hoping the chill would ease the jet lag and the feeling of isolation. Only Bill seemed unaffected. Full of energy and excited at the prospect of Christmas with his family, he ignored the oppressive military presence and stares of the tourists to buy a new Frisbee and toys for his one-year-old daughter.

All too quickly our team members began to disperse as blaring overhead speakers announced the gates for upcoming flights. Parting was awkward and rushed, so we didn't bother to say much more than a mumbled, "Have a nice holiday," followed by a quick hug or handshake.

I watched with a growing sense of loneliness as Randy, Lee, Jesse, and Markus headed to another terminal for Texas. Don was off to find Alaska Airlines, and Bill with a bagful of toys like Santa Claus ran to catch a commuter plane south to San Diego. Finally, Matt and I walked in the opposite direction, trying to navigate through the crowds to find the American Airlines terminal for San Francisco.

On the short flight to the Bay area, I had one last moment to myself before the excitement of family reunions and frenzied holiday celebrations took over. I was going to miss my seven colleagues, each with their unique strengths and weaknesses. We had capitalized on our individuality, and in a spirit of cooperation and comradeship survived the most inhospitable place on earth. We had seen amazing things and collectively experienced the thrill of exploring the unknown. To me, this was as significant as any of our scientific findings: by valuing the differences that made each of us unique, we achieved great things.

In the months that followed we slowly recovered our personal and physical lives, all the time longing to be back out on the ice. My first lap swim at the pool was followed by a trip to the medical clinic to find that I had not escaped the snowmobile accident as well as I had thought. My collarbone had been fractured in two places and was slowly healing. The fact that I had ignored the pain while I was on the ice only reinforced what the team already knew—adrenaline and single-minded focus had driven us through to the completion of the expedition. For all of the eventual scars, the experience was well worth the pain.

CHAPTER 17

THE LAST LOOK

The first seal to arrive at Weddell World in 2002 was Mr. Pink, a medium-sized, rotund adult Weddell seal with a roll of fat below his chin. He earned his name from the color of his identifying flipper tags rather than any comment on his masculinity. Mr. Pink had shown up at the campsite within five minutes of us drilling our diving hole, before the walls of the Jamesway had even been assembled for the season. We had decided to place the camp even farther away from McMurdo than the previous year; this time, a half-mile behind Tent Island towards the deepest waters of McMurdo Sound. With the groaning of the splintering floors still ringing in our ears, we moved Weddell World as far away from the Erebus Glacier Ice Tongue as possible.

An extensive tidal crack system surrounding Tent Island supported a large colony of seals that we would be able to study. A series of large breathing holes at the cracks would also allow the seals to easily make the trip between our dive hole at camp and the island in a single breath. Tent Island Crack would be our new Home Crack.

B-15 still hovered on the opposite side of Ross Island and had been joined by another giant iceberg, C-19. Working together, they had effectively clogged the annual winter ice movements in McMurdo Sound for the second year in a row. The original Home Crack had disappeared along with Ally McSeal, Ms. Apnea, Ms. Zodiac, Sunday, Mayflower, Godzilla, and Lucky Pup and his mom. Without a home base to come back to, there was little chance of meeting up with any of them this year. More than likely they had moved out to sea in February and were making their way to new, more accessible seal colonies.

As the team once more stocked the camp with all of our scientific equipment, food, and sleeping gear, we realized that it had been nine months since we had all been together. This expedition would be our last; the last year of funding on the NSF grant, and therefore our last chance to work with the Weddell seals. We were determined to make it our most successful year yet. The faces were the same except for the absence of our Alaskan grizzly, Don Calkins, who had turned his attention to the Aleutian Islands in Alaska. While the rest of us journeyed to the Antarctic, Don was kept busy in the North Pacific trying to understand the reason behind the population declines of the Steller sea lion, the largest otariid on earth. North or south, there always seemed to be some marine mammal in need of attention.

Mr. Pink had swum the half-mile distance from Tent Island to Weddell World, popping his head up with an explosive exhalation that sprayed slushy brash ice all around the newly drilled site, much to the surprise of Andy the ice driller. Surveying the hole by turning in a 360-degree circle, Mr. Pink immediately settled in. His first job was to clean house, which according to Weddell seal protocol meant removing any local competition.

Despite his effeminate name, Mr. Pink bullied several other

adult seals out of the hole before they could even catch a breath. Few seals were willing to challenge Mr. Pink as he stared them down with huge, glaring brown eyes. His strategy whenever another seal dared to approach was to raise his shoulders slowly out of the water and then hover threateningly over the intruder. The other seal would not even make eye contact with so imposing a figure. They just slunk away into the depths without a drop of blood shed in the encounter.

With a "Possession is nine-tenths of the law" demeanor, Mr. Pink remained oblivious to us and the camp construction all around him. He rested in his dive hole as we chainsawed the ice around him. He watched casually as the carpenters and our team assembled the Jamesway laboratory above him and the hole. He didn't blink an eye at the hammering to put in the floorboards of the lab and secure the electrical lines. His noisy upstairs neighbors were simply ignored while he reaped the benefits of blizzard-free accommodations.

If roaring chainsaws had been unable to chase Mr. Pink off, we knew that there was little chance of our physically removing him. So we carried on our work as if he wasn't there. Except for Jesse.

For Jesse the stubbornness of Mr. Pink was an unexpected gift that he welcomed wholeheartedly. The animal behaviorist had spent the entire previous field season making underwater recordings of the Weddell seals' vocalizations. Although he had collected a remarkable library of chirps, whistles, bangs, and booms, he had been frustrated in his attempts to follow the conversations or to identify whether it was the male or female seals that did all of the talking. With the arrival of Mr. Pink and his territorial ways, Jesse had the perfect experimental setup. Over the next few months we would bring female seals into the Jamesway lab as we had done in the previous year. Each seal would be outfitted with a VDAP camera and sensors, and then provided access to the dive hole in the laboratory floor. The seals would then head into deep water to hunt and interact with other seals while the instruments recorded their travels.

The presence of Mr. Pink added an entirely new dimension to the study. With the right placement of his underwater cameras and hydrophones, Jesse would be able to capture the sights and sounds of the instrumented females as they encountered Mr. Pink on their initial descent from the dive hole. It was the ultimate under-ice blind date. To make it in the world of seal mating, Mr. Pink would have to prove his masculinity and attractiveness to the females; and if all went well, Jesse would be one of the first scientists to catch a view of the submerged courtship between Weddell seals.

Seizing the opportunity, Jesse quickly installed his underwater instruments as soon as the Jamesway was completed. To add to the feeling of a master control center, he opened his last packing crate to reveal his prized possession for the expedition, a plastic deckchair. Days of sitting on a frozen metal folding chair during the previous field season had made more than one impression on the scientist. This year he would relax in the comfort of the deck chair while manning his electronics station.

As soon as his hydrophones were sunk below the camp, Jesse settled in with the same resolve as Mr. Pink. Hour after hour he stared into the video monitors, sipping hot chocolate and listening intently with headphones to the vocalizations of the territorial seal as well as the distant seal calls from Tent Island. For days he waited for something to happen. Jesse was so focused that if it were not for the ridge of fuzzy hair that stood up over the top edge of his chair, we would have barely noticed him in camp.

After nearly a week Jesse finally announced, "Mr. Pink appears to be the strong silent type."

The stereotype held as long as he was the only seal in the area. Left on his own, Mr. Pink rarely vocalized into Jesse's hydrophones. However, the seal rivaled Luciano Pavarotti if threatened. On those occasions, Mr. Pink would release a long, low warning trill to keep other seals out of his breathing hole. These occurred day and night, often lulling us to sleep when the activities of the camp quieted down at the end of the day.

Rarely did it ever come down to a tussle with another seal. Only the most foolhardy animal desperate for a quick breath of air following a dive was willing to risk tangling with Mr. Pink. The intruding seal would surface and then immediately gulp in enough air to make it back to Tent Island. If detected, Mr. Pink would begin a series of loud jaw claps, snapping and swimming threateningly immediately below the dive hole. When the intruder tried to make his escape Mr. Pink would encounter him, circling and biting with the vengeance of a toothy shark. The sparring would continue until the intruding seal found an opening that would allow him to speed past the snapping teeth of Mr. Pink and head into the depths.

From our camera view the fighting resembled a choreographed boxing match filled with vocal threats rather than actual landed punches. The seals circled and spun, snapped, chirped, and boomed at each other.

Inspection of the post-fight losers told an entirely different story. Matt and I encountered one such loser lying on the ice while we were conducting seal surveys and taking thermal measurements. The infrared camera image showed the extent of the damage. Each bite lit up as a bright, hot dot in the picture, making the wounded animal appear more like a Dalmatian than a Weddell seal.

We also found that the male seals fought dirty. The penile orifice and the soft tissues between the hind flippers and the armpits were the most vulnerable and sensitive areas; they were also the most likely to get bitten. Chewed up and exhausted, the losers would lie in the sun, turning the snow pink with their blood before attempting another dip into the water.

I suspected that the penchant for sunbathing by Weddell seals had a lot to do with these wounds; our infrared images now confirmed it. My own nicks and cuts seemed to take an inordinate amount of time to heal in the Antarctic. Any scrape that would normally heal within a few days back home lingered red and raw for weeks on the ice. Physicians had told our team that reduced skin circulation in response to the cold caused the delay. In fact, much of the effort by the medical community studying tissue repair was now directed at developing heated bandages, radiant heat dressings, and laser therapies that would increase blood flow to a wound. With increased blood flow, injured tissues receive additional heat and oxygen, both of which promote healing.

It occurred to me that the sunbathing Weddell seals had already discovered the benefits of radiant wound healing. If an injured seal remained in the water, its skin was cold and poorly vascularized. By lying in the sun, the skin was warmed and blood blow to wounds increased, as evident from the glowing areas on the chewed-up, Dalmatian-spotted seal. What I had presumed was a loser's retreat was, in reality, a novel way to quickly heal before the next underwater battle.

Despite his intolerance towards males, Mr. Pink's passion for females knew few bounds. It was Seal 25 that first revealed his softer side.

As our first instrumented seal of the season, Seal 25 was also the inaugural blind date to enter Mr. Pink's dive hole. She was a healthy adult female seal from Tent Island with exceptionally dark fur and white curling whiskers on her muzzle. We transferred her by seal sled, and weighed and instrumented her with the VDAP camera in record time. She came through the Jamesway so fast that she was never given a name—she would always be Number 25.

We waited for her to take the plunge into the dive hole. As Number 25 dipped her whiskers and flipper tips to test the water, there was a low rumble from below. Jesse immediately turned up his audio and video recorders. Swimming slowly onto the screen just beneath the dive hole was Mr. Pink. He had seen the shadow created by Number 25 and was noticeably agitated. All of the past intruders into his territory had come from the depths. A seal arriving from above was completely unexpected, but he was still prepared to fight.

Mr. Pink's patrolling movements increased in intensity while

Number 25 slowly considered a swim, oblivious to the growing tension below her. Mr. Pink finally ascended at top speed into the dive hole, popping his head out of the water and directly into the dripping face of the instrumented seal. To our surprise it was not Mr. Pink that started the verbal assault.

It was Number 25 who let out a roof-shaking, "Owhooowwll."

The howl stopped Mr. Pink in his tracks. Whether it was something in her breath, her smell, the tone of her voice, or her manner that signaled him, there was little doubt that he instantly realized that Number 25 was not an intruding male. She was female, and by virtue of that a much more interesting opponent.

With renewed interest and a much softer attitude, Mr. Pink slowly circled the waters below the dive hole as if trying to decide his next move. Periodically he popped his head up to encourage the other seal into the water much like a mom would entice a pup. He nudged her toes, and cocked his head but to no avail. There were no hovering threats, no sounds uttered. A less rambunctious Mr. Pink floated below the water surface, looking up expectantly at the female seal.

But Number 25 was not moving. She stayed perched on the edge of the dive hole without tossing a glance in Mr. Pink's direction.

When his advances continued to go unnoticed Mr. Pink dove out of the range of our camera and out of sight of Number 25. Sensing that the way was finally clear she dipped her head into the water, scanned beneath the hole, and then took the big plunge with our VDAP and sensors.

Despite her smooth entrance into the dive hole, Number 25's actions had been witnessed by the ever-attentive Mr. Pink, who had been hiding off to the side. As soon as she hit the water Mr. Pink let out a series of low-throated chugs that increased in power with each successive boom. What began as a low-frequency thump, thump, thump, with the cadence of a heartbeat, gradually reached such volume and power that the television signals from the underwater camera were interrupted. Booming like a massive bass drum, the sounds pulsed slower and slower through the water with such growing force that the television monitor flinched in response. We could feel the impulse of each vocalization through the floor of the Jamesway, and knew that the sounds had to be reverberating through the chest of Number 25. Jesse rushed to turn down the volume on his hydrophones for fear of breaking the speakers and his eardrums.

The instrumented seal responded to the thundering calls by slowly floating back to the surface of the dive hole. She remained silent, returning none of Mr. Pink's vocalizations. Rather than chance the bullying, Number 25 waited in the hole while Mr. Pink finished his vocal display below. Eventually, he ran out of air and was forced to find another ice hole to catch his breath. In the silence of the moment, she made her escape. With Mr. Pink gone, she casually swam off to find something to eat, never to return to Weddell World or her suitor.

On his return to the empty dive hole Mr. Pink seemed torn between defending his territory and his honor. If he went off in search of Number 25 he ran the risk of losing control of the dive hole. If he stayed, all of his courting was for naught and another male seal would likely sway Number 25 during the short Antarctic mating season. In the end, Mr. Pink chose to stay put and was soon back to sleeping alone on the water surface of his bachelor dive hole.

Like Mr. Pink, we did not wait for Number 25 to return before moving on. In the past we had been willing to risk only one or two sets of instruments on the seals at any one time. This year, with five VDAP systems at our disposal and facing our final expedition, we planned to maximize our time on the ice by deploying four VDAP units simultaneously. The change in protocol meant little to the individual seals. To our research team it meant that we would operate on a breakneck schedule of seal captures, instrumentation, monitoring, and tracking that was three times more hectic than we had ever attempted.

Before the water in the dive hole had even settled from Number 25's big plunge, the team was off to find Seal 26 and Seal 27 for our study. The seals were brought to the Jamesway, custom-fitted with the neoprene blanket and instruments, and quietly slipped into the water. Each time Mr. Pink tried his best to woo the females to stay. Each time they left without a second look.

By the time Seal 28 arrived Mr. Pink was ready. All it took was a shuffle of boots in the laboratory for Mr. Pink to set up station below the dive hole. Like the other females, Seal 28 remained perched on the side of the dive hole dangling a fore flipper over the edge testing the waters. She was in no hurry to leave. We had found Seal 28 to be independent to the point of being stubborn. Not particularly large, she often moved and acted like a male. Her size and personality caused Bill to name her Vasquez, the petite, rough-and-tumble, machine-gun-toting alien fighter from one of our favorite camp movies, *Aliens*.

For over twenty minutes Mr. Pink circled in the cold water below waiting for the seal to dive. Vasquez yawned and continued to dangle and dawdle.

As he had done with Number 25, Mr. Pink ascended in a determined line straight up into the dive hole. We fully expected him to pop up in front of the female seal. This time, rather than subtly nudging her in the toes, Mr. Pink took a more direct approach. Seeing the teasing flipper dabbling in the water, Mr. Pink grabbed it in his mouth and yanked. A visibly shocked Vasquez rolled off of the edge and into the dive hole, landing with a resounding splash that sent salt water across the entire lab.

As scientists, it was inappropriate to assign any kind of seal emotions to the scene that followed. Yet, it surely had all the makings of a lover's quarrel born of mistaken intentions. Vasquez sputtered in the water and then tore into Mr. Pink.

Admittedly an aggressive maneuver, Mr. Pink's flipper yank never drew blood—something that we knew he could have easily done. This appeared to have little bearing on the female seal's response. Mr. Pink tried to fend off Vasquez's attack by slowly backing up. Soon the two seals were below the dive hole circling so furiously that it was difficult to tell who was chasing whom. A few chirps and low-frequency thumps were passed back and forth until

Vasquez slowly took off with the stiff, "Don't mess with me" demeanor of her namesake.

Once again, for all of his efforts, Mr. Pink was left alone in his dive hole, waiting for the next female who would surely come.

With several Weddell seals diving simultaneously across McMurdo Sound carrying all of our expensive instrumentation, we had to come up with an innovative way to keep track of their whereabouts. Ice conditions were noticeably different this year, with large leads snaking across the entire Sound. New breathing holes seemed to appear out of nowhere every day, and it became obvious to the team that trying to determine the underwater paths of the seals by tracking over the sea ice with snowmobiles would be impossible given the expansive area. The seals could go anywhere, in any direction, and undoubtedly in opposite paths to one another. There were only two points that we knew for sure: where the seals started and where they ended up. What we really wanted to know was where they went for all of the days in between.

Several frustrating weeks of trying to identify and map the location of individual breathing holes and attempting to radio track seals in chilling, blowing snow finally inspired Matt.

"Why don't we just have the seals make their own maps of the ice holes in the Sound?" he asked wearily as he tried to warm up by the preway stove. He had been out for hours on a snowmobile in an icy fog following the line of cracks radiating from Weddell World.

"They're wearing cameras, aren't they? So all we need to do is mark the breathing holes somehow," he continued to think out loud while he rubbed his cold withered fingers over the heat. "Say with a colored ball or something. Then when the seal comes to the surface to breath, it will take a picture of the ball and we'll know where it has been when we get the videotapes back."

It was a brilliant, simple, low-tech solution to our nagging problem. We had originally hoped to have the seals record their own position by adding a GPS unit to the camera on the head of the seal.

Based on the same technology that allowed ships and automobiles to navigate, the instrument would have allowed us to automatically track which breathing holes the seals were using and which direction they were moving under the ice. Each time the seal popped its head up to breathe, an overhead satellite would provide a location that would be recorded in the VDAP.

Theoretically the high-tech approach should have worked, but the idea was thwarted by the natural behavior of the seals. The GPS unit needed at least ten seconds for the overhead satellite to pick up the signal. For navigating ships and automobiles, this was not a problem. For an animal that came to the water surface only to grab a breath of air before diving again, it was a severe handicap. The seals could not wait that long in the breathing holes. From the videotapes of Ally McSeal with Scarface, as well as Ms. Apnea, Godzilla, and Mayflower, we knew that Weddell seals popped into breathing holes, grabbed a quick breath, and then immediately submerged their heads to watch their trailing hind flippers. In the real world of too many seals and not enough breathing spots, it was the prudent seal that kept a wary eye on what was happening below it in the water. To do otherwise risked a vicious nip in the flippers or worse as a breath-holding seal below demanded its time in the breathing hole. As a consequence, the nervous seals bobbed in a quick repetitive cycle of breathing and dipping to look below. Only rarely could a seal relax and lounge at the water surface breathing peaceably. Ten seconds would have been a luxury; most often the animal's head was above water for less than one tenth of that time. Consequently, the GPS units and satellites never had a chance to communicate with one another unless a seal completely hauled out on top of the ice to sleep.

Matt's solution was found in several cardboard boxes filled with small, nearly indestructible fluorescent orange balls that were used as floats on fishing gear. Using black indelible pens, the team spent their evenings marking each ball with an identification symbol. Then the balls were taken by snowmobile parties and placed in breathing holes that were frequented by the seals all around the

Sound. The location of the holes containing the balls were checked with a handheld GPS unit, recorded on a map, and then identified with a labeled flag so we could find the holes again if blowing snow covered them. There was the requisite "A hole" followed by "B hole" through "Z hole," and "1 hole" though "9 hole." When we ran out of letters and numbers, the team became more creative as they marked the balls. There was "pumpkin hole," which contained an orange ball made to look like a jack-o'-lantern in honor of Halloween. There was also "eyeball hole," "cat hole," "face hole," and "basketball" and "football holes." Once marked, it was just a matter of waiting to see where the seals turned up on the videotapes.

The numbered flags on the sea ice marking the breathing holes created a golf course appearance behind Weddell World, an effect that was not lost on Matt as he pulled out two golf clubs and several neon-colored golf balls from his duffel bag. After dinner Matt headed out to the makeshift golf course followed by an enthusiastic Bill and me. The evening was cold but clear and windless, perfect Antarctic conditions for driving a few golf balls. With Mount Erebus puffing in the background, Matt wound up his swing only to drive the ball less than three feet away deep into the snow. I followed by hitting a mean slice into the side of the outhouse, and Bill managed a reasonable distance over the top of the Jamesway.

"Aren't we supposed to yell 'fore' or something?" I asked the others, hoping that it would help my aim.

Lack of golfing experience notwithstanding, it was apparent that the cold had frozen the bounce out of the balls. Hitting them was like smacking a rock with a shovel, and had as much accuracy.

While we were playing with the golf balls on top of the sea ice, Weddell seals were busy constructing their own games with the orange plastic balls in the breathing holes below. The next day when we surveyed the area we found several of the orange marker balls lying on the ice next to the breathing holes. Although it was curious, we presumed that the balls had been accidentally displaced when one of the seals made a splashing entrance or exit from the hole. We dropped the balls back into their proper holes only to find them mysteriously lying out on the ice the next day. Again we popped the balls back into the breathing holes, and again they were strewn on the ice by the next morning.

Determined to find out how the balls were being moved, Matt and I sat next to one of the breathing holes and waited. It didn't take long for the culprit to reveal himself. One of the male Weddell seals popped his head into the breathing hole and exhaled loudly. Like Mr. Pink he surveyed the hole only to find the water surface partially blocked by one of the orange balls. He nuzzled at the ball with his whiskers, and inspected it from all sides. After staring at the ball the seal quickly dove beneath it and hit the ball with his retreating flippers. The ball was thrown out of the hole along with chunks of ice in the resulting tidal wave.

We were never quite sure if what we witnessed was normal behavior for Weddell seals to keep a breathing hole clear of debris or if tossing out the marker balls was a source of entertainment for the animals. The end result was that we spent the rest of the field season playing kickball with the seals as we replaced every ball that they actively shoved out of the holes.

The efforts to mark the holes paid off. When we retrieved the VDAP from Number 25, there was eyeball hole and then pumpkin hole in clear view when she surfaced to breathe. This was just the information that Lee needed to begin constructing the three-dimensional travels of the seal as she hunted beneath the ice. Using the hole locations, compass bearings, and speed-meter readings from the VDAP as well as the current meter readings, Lee navigated via computer with Number 25 to the bottom of McMurdo Sound.

And what a journey it was. On her first dive, Number 25 had left the Jamesway under the watchful gaze of Mr. Pink and had traveled quickly to Tent Island. After spending time hauled out with the other female seals, she had slipped into the tidal crack by the island where she cruised in the sun-dappled shallows. Jellyfish streaming by in the currents were ignored as she puttered in and out of breathing holes. Finally, she went for the big dive, descending over 300 meters (984 feet) into the dark.

She passed to the south beneath Weddell World and hit the gravely floor of the Sound. After skimming among giant sponges she surveyed the area and ascended to pumpkin hole, nine miles southwest of Weddell World. From there she began a series of foraging dives. Again and again she dove into the depths to feed on Antarctic silverfish as she ascended. Each meal was the same, twenty fish gulped down and then to pumpkin hole to take a breath. When she had finally taken her fill, she hauled out onto the ice.

Over the course of nine days Number 25 had traveled more than twenty miles in a three-dimensional search for food. Pumpkin hole, a single breathing hole in the middle of McMurdo Sound, was her home base. It was where the team eventually found her lying in the sun with all of our instruments intact.

With the return of the VDAP unit from Number 25, the team prepared for Seal 29 and then Seal 30 and finally Seal 31. Over the course of the three-month expedition, we doubled our research efforts from the previous year, resulting in twenty-four different VDAP deployments on seven different seals. Mr. Pink tried his best with each female, to no avail. Every seal simply swam away from Weddell World in search of food or sleep, ignoring the lone male and his private bachelor diving hole in the Jamesway.

By mid-November, the sun shown so intensely that we abandoned our parkas for windbreakers. For the first time during the season we could work outdoors without the use of gloves. The seals also took advantage of the warmth and began to pop out of breathing holes and ice cracks. They had been stuck below the ice for nearly two weeks during a series of windstorms and blowing snow. Our four instrumented seals followed the others, hauling out as soon as the clouds broke. Suddenly the Jamesway computers were alive with e-mail messages providing satellite transmission locations from their tags.

Seal 26 had moved out into the middle of McMurdo Sound about six miles southwest of Weddell World. Vasquez had hauled out on the ice over sixteen miles north towards Cape Royds, while the two other seals had just started to lie in the sun a half-mile away at Tent Island. Although we expected all of the seals to remain on the ice surface for hours, we had to prioritize which instruments we would recover first and which we were willing to let go for a future date. The team chose the seal that had been missing the longest, Seal 26, as the first candidate for instrument retrieval followed by Vasquez.

The first snowmobile team headed out to the middle of the Sound, with Matt taking the lead with a GPS unit attached to the saddle of his snowmobile. Markus, Lee, and I followed him as he wove through the sastrugi with blind faith in the satellite coordinates he had programmed into the unit. Directly ahead was the Royal Society Mountain Range, thirty-five miles away and crystalline sharp against a deep-blue sky. The frozen ocean spread out in a vast flat plain that had no shadows or interruptions. Little attention was paid to the sea of solid white that surrounded us other than what was necessary to avoid dumping the machines. With so little surface relief the effect was like running on a treadmill. The horizon just never seemed to get any closer despite all of the driving.

The ice was exceptionally rough, with storm-hardened snow pack and wind-forced pressure ridges. Across the miles the four of us crouched down and hung onto the snowmobiles as we tried to track down Seal 26. Five miles from Weddell World we stopped short to let Markus try to pick up the radio signals from the seal's tags. Standing on top of the snowmobile, he cocked the handheld radio antenna to his right and left. Finally, we all heard it—the chirp, chirping of her radio tags softly pinging in the far distance. On the horizon there was nothing but white ice and snow, backed by the mountain range. Again we placed our trust in the instruments and headed into the emptiness in the direction where the radio signals led us.

Matt had just turned a sharp left leading us north when we saw a lone seal in the distance. She was little more than a black speck of pepper on a white tablecloth, but there was little doubt that it was Seal 26. Revving the snowmobiles we rushed up to the snoozing seal, all the while surveying the area for her breathing hole. If the seal spooked with our sudden appearance she could have easily slipped into the hole with our instruments, leaving us empty-handed on top of the ice. But Seal 26 was as mild as the rest of the Weddell seals, and merely rolled over on her back on our approach. A few minutes later we had the VDAP, the neoprene blanket, and all of the sensors, and Seal 26 humped away across the ice to find another, quieter place to resume her nap in the sun.

Back at camp, we regrouped with the rest of the team. On initial inspection, the instrumentation from Seal 26 looked in near-perfect condition despite her long absence during the storms. She had logged thirty-six hours of diving data and recorded six hours of videotape during her travels. Both the seal and the instruments had performed admirably, and the deployment was declared a success. The long trip to locate the seal also made us realize that the sea ice was deteriorating at a faster rate this year. It was time to bring in the rest of the units from the other seals and complete our project.

Finding Vasquez would take us farther north than we had ever traveled in search of a seal, towards Cape Royds, the ice edge, and the open sea. Not only was the ice breaking up along the route, but also the areas that remained frozen were heaved and fractured into a complicated maze of pressure ridges. We had no idea if the sea ice around Cape Royds was even passable by snowmobile.

Under the warmth of an early evening sun, our snowmobile party headed up to the Cape in search of the instrumented seal. For the second time in one day I faced a thirty-mile journey over rough ice. Recognizing that we would be traveling through the same pressure-ridged area that had been the scene of my previous snowmobile accident, I was especially careful.

As we traveled north, the team passed Tent and Inaccessible

Islands and several large cracks that were beginning to open up the sea ice. The most prominent crack occurred at the tip of the Barne Glacier and was cause for growing concern as we drew closer. The width of the crack in some stretches was large enough to swallow our snowmobile party. We also found that the ice in this part of the Sound was scoured into a flat, slippery surface, providing little traction for stopping. At one point Jesse spun out in front of me in a sickening twisting maneuver. Luckily he gained control of the machine before hitting snow or the looming crack, and never even lost his place in our lineup.

Along the sparsely flagged route we passed near the base of the Barne Glacier. Rising over 200 feet straight up into the sky, the majesty of the icy-blue face took me by surprise. For months I had seen the glacier from afar while standing outside Weddell World. From our camp it was little more that a thin wedge of blue pasted against the white of the sea ice. In the presence of the towering ice, I was instantly awestruck. Unlike the snow-covered, sloping edges of the Erebus Glacier Ice Tongue, the front of the Barne Glacier had been sheared off, appearing as a solid turquoise wall carved out of the side of Ross Island. Massive icefalls had created a sharp rim that cut into the sky overhead. The sight was so magnificent that the entire team stopped instinctively to stare.

My response to the glacier was purely visceral, although the search for some meaning in it was as varied as the individuals who stood in its shadow. There was unconstrained power in the face of the glacier that some would attribute to the hand of God, others to nature, and still others to the physics of cold temperatures, water, and gravity. The presence of an overwhelming force was undeniable, leaving me feeling simultaneously oppressed and uplifted. The others felt it, too, and stood quietly trying to take it all in.

I realized that the powerful, conflicting mix of emotions was part of the lure of Antarctica. It was what drove explorers South again and again.

In time the flagged route gave out altogether, leaving us in a jumble of pressured ice. With the aid of the handheld radio antenna, we could hear the chirping of Vasquez's radio tag. She was somewhere in the ragged ice, but nowhere to be seen. Tuxedoed Adelie penguins from a nearby rookery on the coast of Ross Island waddled by, hopping the smaller cracks, and gathering in confused parties by the large ridges. There were times when our team felt the watchful, beady eyes of the penguins, who appeared waiting for our decision as to how to proceed forward through the icy maze.

Moving on foot, the team climbed across several pressure ridges to find Vasquez hauled out with two other seals. She was in a difficult position for us, wedged in a bowl of blue ice surrounded by jagged ridges on all sides. We also knew that there was an open hole somewhere in the sea ice that she had climbed out of. The team stepped as lightly as feasible in the heavy bunny boots, climbing over the ice ridges and slipping down into the bowl. As the other seals looked on we carefully retrieved the VDAP and instruments piece by piece from Vasquez. By the time we had finished packing up our gear she slid into a small crack that we had not even noticed. Only the tips of her flippers were visible, and these also disappeared into the ice as she took off for the open ocean to the north.

The field season progressed much in the same way as in the previous years. Fatigue, bumps, and bruises haunted the team by the end of November as we made our final instrument retrievals and prepared to leave the ice. Each seal provided new details about the hunting strategies and the daily underwater travels of Weddells. With four VDAP units deployed simultaneously, we became so preoccupied with working with the animals that there was little time to analyze the data or view the videos. That would have to wait until after the field season.

By December, with all of the instruments from the last seals back in the lab, the team began the process of packing up the camp. The shelves were cleared and all of our scientific equipment was crated for the last time under the watchful gaze of Mr. Pink. He never abandoned his diving hole in the lab although we had stopped delivering female seals weeks before. As matchmakers we had failed him. However, nature came to his rescue at the last moment. In the second week of December, as we dismantled Weddell World, three female seals from Tent Island wandered into Mr. Pink's territory. For the first time, the females inexplicably decided to stay. Jesse kept his hydrophones and cameras running up to last minute, recording the seals' courtship behaviors, vocalizations, and group breathing sessions in the dive hole. The scene had all of the inviting trappings of a singles' hot tub experience if it had not been for the freezing water temperatures.

Jesse saw Mr. Pink make his move and sidle up to each of the females in succession. The male and female seals cruised together below the hole, circling and chirping at one another. At the same time the females sparred with each other as if trying to win over Mr. Pink.

The courtship was just beginning to heat up when the generators were cut off—our time on the ice was finished.

Jesse never got to see who finally won Mr. Pink's affections. He was never able to videotape the underwater mating maneuvers or witness copulation by any of the seals. He didn't know if one female or all three stayed with Mr. Pink in his private diving hole, or if the attraction was short-lived or for the duration of the mating season. Undoubtedly, one would gain his favor, and Jesse was confident that somewhere on the ice of McMurdo Sound there would be the arrival of a Pink, Jr., in October 2003.

CHAPTER 18

THE ANTARCTIC
EXPLORERS

DECEMBER 2002

Before we left Antarctica for the last time, there was one snow-mobile journey the team wanted to make. Beginning with the first flag in McMurdo and ending with the last flag along the route to Cape Royds, we wanted to trace the steps of the great Antarctic explorers who had come before us.

We started with Captain Robert Falcon Scott's hut situated on the tip of Hut Point just outside of McMurdo Station. Erected in 1902, the small wooden hut had withstood one hundred Antarctic winters and was stained with the fat of Weddell seal skin and blub-ber still frozen onto the veranda. The large stark building was the jumping-off point for Scott's great southern expedition to the South Pole in November 1911. It was also the focal point of activities for the search parties and dog teams that eventually discovered the frozen bodies of the explorer and his team on the Ross Ice Shelf a year later. The hut now served as an icy memorial to these men and contained a few desiccated tins of food along with a checkerboard table. With the checkers frozen in place, the game board spoke of long, anxious hours waiting for colleagues who would never return.

Driving farther north along the coastline we arrived at a second wooden hut located around the corner from Weddell World 2001. Built in 1911 at Cape Evans, the hut was the base camp of Scott's *Terra Nova* Expedition. The inside was a dark warren created from stacked wooden shelves and supply crates. Small wooden bunk beds formed a cramped "tenement" for the men, and a hidden den for Captain Scott. Their sleeping bags of hides and wool were grimy from sweat, fumes, seal fat, and volcanic dust. The only light streamed in from a paned glass window by the frozen remains of the scientific laboratory. Sunlight still shone through thick dusty test tubes and bottles filled with dark brown, yellowed, and clear liquids. Edward Wilson, chief scientist on Scott's Antarctic expedition, as well as the geologists, physicists, and zoologists on the team had worked among the glass vials and meteorological instruments in the lab before their fateful race to the Pole.

As if the living quarters were not already overcrowded, the men were literally surrounded by animals. Stalls and harnesses for Shetland ponies, chains, collars, and surprisingly tiny doghouses for huge sled dogs lay all about the grounds.

The fifty-foot-by-twenty-five-foot hut was less than half the size of the Weddell World Jamesway, and was home for three times as many expedition members. Overlooking the apparent cramped quarters, Scott wrote of the "palatial, light resplendent" and "comfort luxurious" interior space of the well-designed hut. His enthusiasm for the location may well have been inspired by the environs. For outside of the hut was the same spectacular view that had taken our breath away on our search for Vasquez in the previous weeks. From a small ridge just outside the front door of the hut, Scott and his men could simultaneously behold the blue-green face of the

Barne Glacier to the north, the smoking summit of Mount Erebus to the east, the changing watercolors of the Royal Society Mountain Range to the west, and the rising of Tent, Inaccessible, and the Razorback Islands from the frozen sea to the south. The grandeur of Antarctica was laid out at the explorers' doorstep.

The end of our journey was marked by the last fluttering red flag of the sea ice road twenty miles north of McMurdo Station. Walking over a volcanic gravel hillside, we came upon Ernest Shackleton's hut at Cape Royds. Constructed in 1908, the wooden hut was used during Shackleton's attempt to reach the South Pole. At the time, his journey was the closest that any human had come to 90 degrees south. Unfortunately, the party had turned back within one hundred miles of its destination.

Shackleton's hut was much more humble in appearance than Scott's at Cape Evans. The small, square building accommodated fifteen men, eight ponies, numerous sled dogs, and even a motorcar with garage. The furniture and inside walls were made of stacked wooden crates that had contained their supplies. After noticing that two of the expedition scientists, Murray and Priestley, had had makeshift bunks made of empty dog biscuit boxes, our team would never again complain of small cots and thin sleeping bags.

The dogs had been relegated to the outdoors. On the north side of the building, wind-scoured doghouses were filled in with snow and the desiccated bones of the occupants still chained in their collars.

Outside black-and-white penguin feathers blew through the air and the sharp, unmistakable odor of bird guano overwhelmed the team. Ignoring the powerful smells, I left the rest of team by the hut to climb an overlook by an Adelie penguin rookery. On the barren hillside, male and female penguins waddled about and trumpeted in greeting as partners traded egg-sitting duties on their nests. The term "nest" was relative here. Without plants to provide nesting materials, small scratches and pebbles were used as property outlines. The perimeters of these makeshift nests were defended vigorously by neighbors that pecked and flipper-whacked one another if they ventured too close. I noticed that there were fewer pairs of birds this year, leaving large tracts of prime nest real estate unclaimed on the rookery and resulting in fewer confrontations. This was the second year that the icebergs had disrupted the Adelie penguins as they tried to raise chicks, and I wondered how long the rookery could hold out. At the time of Shackleton's expedition, the waddling residents of this rookery had provided both amusement and sustenance to the explorers. The ancestors of the same birds were disappearing in our lifetime.

Looking north I could see the sea ice transition from solid flatness to jumbled pack ice, which would eventually lead to the open ocean. In their search for food Adelie penguins had climbed down from the rookery and onto the ice, where they were slowly making their way in an over-ice trek to the water.

As I followed the thin line of Adelie penguins navigating the cracks and pressure ridges of the pack towards the horizon, I realized that any accomplishment in the Antarctic rarely occurred in isolation. Our team was part of a long succession of Antarctic explorers that stretched over an entire century. We were standing in the footsteps of giants who had been the first to climb these gravel hillsides nearly one hundred years before our arrival. Early Antarctic expeditions had explored the continent with tools, instruments, and supplies that made the journey far more difficult than we would ever experience.

From the first days of discovery, Antarctica was a continent of human successes and challenges. Our team had experienced both during our brief time on the ice. Numerous equipment failures due to freezing, ice, and extraordinary pressures at depth had occurred, but we had succeeded in retrieving all of our instruments. Overcoming fatigue, loneliness, accidents, and storms, we had explored the underwater world of the Weddell seal. Eight team members, some new to the ice and others who were old hands to the Antarctic, had combined their talents to discover the secret of polar survival by the seals. All of the team members had been essential to the success of the study. Although each member had individual goals and limitations, all had one thing in common: a sense of adventure, fueled by a hunger for scientific knowledge. For us, one of the greatest thrills in life was exploring the unknown and discovering something that had never been imagined.

There were thirteen local members who also helped to achieve our goals—seals numbered 19 through 31. Each seal had taught the team something new about the Antarctic and the seals' underwater lives. Ally McSeal (Seal 19) had the distinction of being the first free-ranging Weddell seal in history to carry the instrumentation into the wild. She taught us that life at the breathing holes involved a lot of social skills for a Weddell seal—with a bite in the flippers sometimes being the only option for catching a fresh breath of air. Godzilla was the only male seal officially on the project, and mostly sat on the ocean bottom sleeping. He showed the team how seals used long glides to save energy during their deepest dives until he broke the camera after two hours. The other seals took us on an amazing tour though twisting caves and tunnels on the underside of the Erebus Glacier Ice Tongue, a place we thought was always beyond our reach. Mayflower and the seals of 2002 brought us to the bottom of the ocean, where giant sponges, soft-bodied sea tulips, huge starfish, and prickly spider-like animals lived. The seals had hunted giant cod, slurped down silverfish, and chirped, boomed, squeaked, and trilled their way into our lives.

In addition to the official seals, there was one more seal that never wore an instrument but at a remarkably young age was able to teach the team about life, death, and survival in the Antarctic. It was Lucky Pup. True to his name, he had made it through the summer of the B-15 iceberg with the help of his dedicated mom. He turned out to be one of the lucky ones, escaping the starvation that had killed so many young and old seals and penguins over the previous two years. The last time the team saw Lucky Pup, he had grown out of his gray fuzzy puppy fur and had a new adult spotted coat. He had finally learned how to swim and dive in spite of his initial reluctance to enter the water. Lucky Pup had also outgrown his name. He was now an independent juvenile seal off on his own, with his mother only a faded memory. As a young male, his survival would depend on how well he stayed out of the way of the larger, aggressive territorial males until he was old enough to join the mating game. In the meantime, he would grow larger and stronger as he foraged in his own world.

As the sun made one more pass over the Royal Society Mountain Range, I realized that the science had just begun for our team. Regardless of all we had learned from our research, there remained one huge unanswered question: If vision is so important for Weddell seals to hunt and navigate in the summer, how do they survive in the total darkness of the Antarctic winter?

The answer to that question will have to wait, as my time on the ice has ended. For years, from the comfort of my university office, I will continue to discover and explore the world of the Weddell seal. Like the other members of my team, I'll review the videotapes and sort through, analyze, and synthesize a mountain of data brought back by Seals 19 to 31. We'll graph the results, write scientific papers, and present technical lectures to our colleagues. In this way, the next team of scientists will be able to build upon our discoveries.

Along with the science, I also hope that in some small way we have contributed to the long history of exploration that characterizes Antarctica. Exploration of this mysterious continent began with great men and women willing to make tremendous sacrifices, both in the field and at home. Over the past one hundred years, it cost many their lives. The spirit of polar exploration lives on, spurred on by heroes who are willing to risk everything in the quest for discovery and the search of the unknown.

The future will undoubtedly bring new teams of explorers to this frozen place. Their qualifications will have little to do with innate intelligence, money, status, size, race, or gender. Instead, they will be the adventurers among us, those men and women who are willing to break from the pack and accept risks in order to experience the sweet thrill of discovery. They will be limited only by their imagination, and I have found that such an explorer lives in every one of us.

Life is an adventure—go and discover it!

SCIENTIFIC PAPERS FROM THE EXPEDITION

Davis, R. W., Fuiman, L. A., Williams, T. M., Collier, S. O., Hagey, W. P., Kanatous, S. B., Kohin, S., Horning, M. (1999) Hunting behavior of a marine mammal beneath the Antarctic fast-ice. *Science* 283: 993–996.

Fuiman, L. A., Davis, R. W., Williams, T. M. (2002) Behavior of mid-water fishes under the Antarctic sea ice: Observations by a predator. *Marine Biology* 140:815–822.

Williams, T. M., Davis, R. W., Fuiman, L., Francis, J., Le Boeuf, B. J., Horning, M., Calambokidis, J., Croll, D. A. (2000) Sink or swim: Strategies for cost-efficient diving by marine mammals. *Science* 288:133–136.

Williams, T. M. (2001) Intermittent swimming by mammals: A strategy for increasing energetic efficiency during diving. *Amer. Zool.* 41:166–176.

Williams, T. M., Haun, J., Davis, R. W., Fuiman, L. A., and Kohin, S. (2001) A killer appetite: Metabolic consequences of carnivory in marine mammals. *Comp. Biochem. Physiol.* Part A 129:785–796.

ACKNOWLEDGEMENTS

Any expedition, whether it navigates to the polar frontier or through life, is filled with people who inspire. Such is the case with this book. The inspiration for reaching beyond the halls of academia was Stephanie Mills and her creation of the Ida Benson Lynne Chair in Ocean Health. Through her and her mother, I learned that marine conservation is the responsibility of both the young and the old. Through the Chair in Ocean Health, I was given free reign to "Do something different." This book is the result, and my wish is that all scientists at some point in their career be given the same opportunity. It's an exhilarating jump into the deep end of the pool.

Perhaps most remarkable was that several hardened New Yorkers were intrigued by the antics of Weddell seals in Antarctica. Noah Lukeman, my agent, found me in a stack of proposals and hunted me down on the ice of McMurdo Sound. His persistence through e-mail made this book a reality, and for that I will be forever grateful. I only hope that his driving skills improve and that he continues to enjoy nature at its best even if it means in the middle of an L.A. tar pit. From the beginning PJ Dempsey demonstrated that she was an enthusiastic naturalist, asking all of the tough questions to satisfy her curiosity about daily seal life. Her questions inspired the heart of this book, and proved that an editor can be both a demanding boss and an amusing friend. One day I hope to show her that boy and girl seals really do look different. I am especially grateful to the many people at M. Evans and Company, Inc., for taking a risk on this neophyte writer; they helped guide me into the world of publishing with grace and insight. My only regret is that I never had the pleasure of meeting

George deKay. My thanks also to the Maui Writers Group who, from the beginning, encouraged the power of the writer within.

Dr. Gerry Kooyman at Scripps Institution of Oceanography was the inspiration to travel South for all of us. Through his tales, photographs, and excitement about Weddell seals, he made Antarctica come alive before I had even set foot on the continent. It would have been impossible not to join in, and for that I will always be thankful. Dr. Polly Penhale, program manager for Polar Programs at the National Science Foundation, has remained an encouraging force throughout my endeavors South and beyond. Her love of Antarctica and her support of women in science have made a remarkable difference on the ice and in my science. Without her, the expeditions would never have happened. Additional financial support and a sense of wonder about how marine mammals move through water were provided by Dr. Robert Gisiner at the Office of Naval Research.

As for the stories, they could not have happened without the encouragement of my teammates. Randy, Lee, Bill, Markus, Jesse, Don, and Matt are Antarctic heroes in my eyes and truly the best. Enough said—"What happens on the ice, stays on the ice." Randolph, Suzy, Rebecca, and Shane were all physiologists on ice who helped me with the science and made polar living fun; I only wish I could have shared all of your stories. There were also many, many others who traveled to the ice or assisted through NSF, ASA, and Raytheon in McMurdo, who helped on this project. Too numerous to name, you are all a part of this book in spirit.

And the seals. The many Weddell seals that I met over the years made me see the world in a new way and appreciate how nature works. It was always more elegant than I could have imagined.

Always last, it seems, is Dr. Jim Estes—husband, friend, and confidant. We shared this book from beginning to end, even when our travels took us to opposite ends of the globe. Your encouragement when my writing froze as solid as a glacier inspired me to carry on; hopefully, we can reside in one hemisphere for a while . . . and I'll feed the dogs.

All photographs were taken under National Marine Fisheries Permit Number 821-1588-01 with authorization from Dr. Randall Davis.

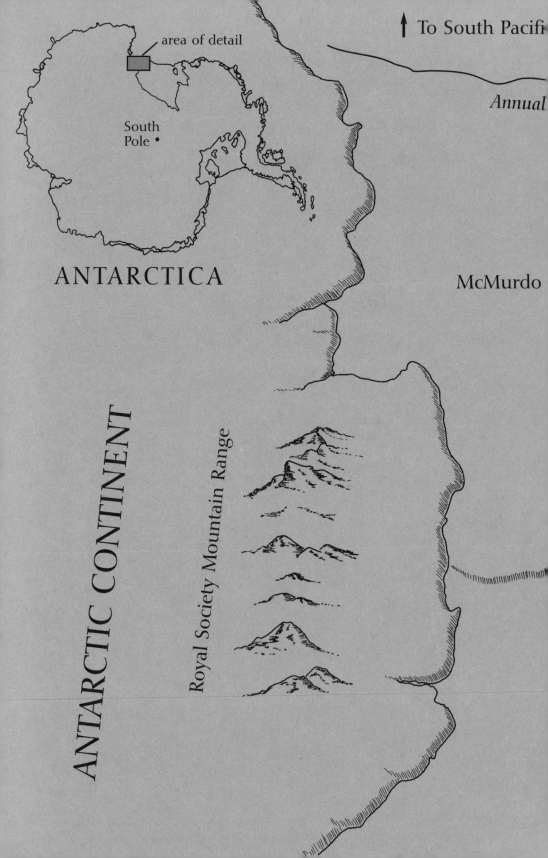